Ezra Pound & Japan

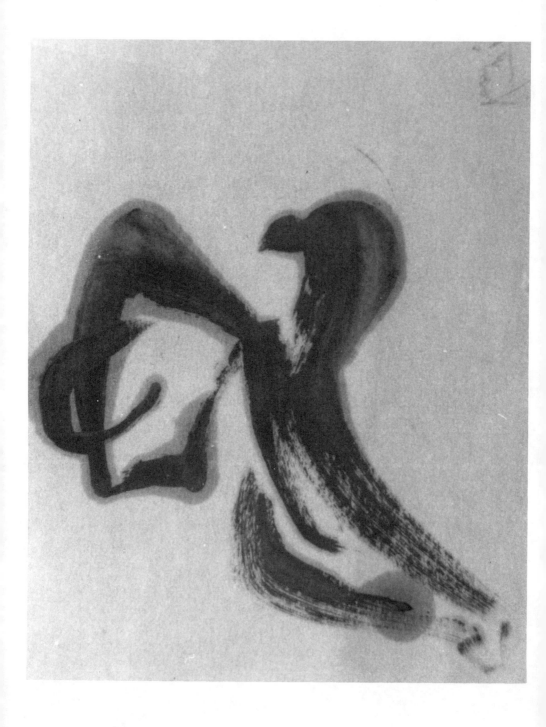

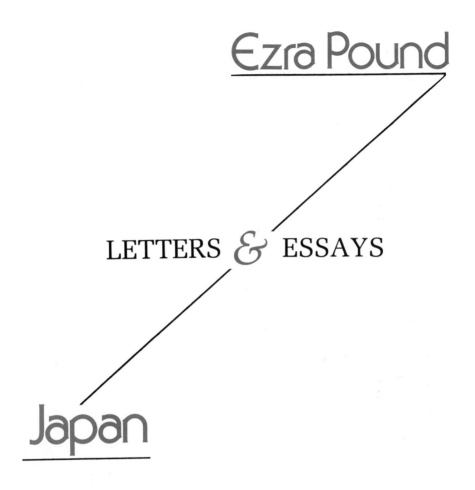

Ezra Pound

LETTERS & ESSAYS

Japan

edited by Sanehide Kodama

BLACK SWAN BOOKS

This publication has been greatly assisted by a generous
grant from
THE SUNTORY FOUNDATION.

First edition

Published by
BLACK SWAN BOOKS Ltd.
P. O. Box 327
Redding Ridge, CT 06876
U.S.A.

ISBN 0-933806-27-2

Contents

ACKNOWLEDGEMENTS

First I should like to thank Mary de Rachewiltz both for what she has done for me and for the publication of this book. The idea of collecting Ezra Pound's letters to his Japanese friends started with her. She introduced me to John Walsh in 1980 and together they provided me with much valuable material for the text and notes. They have read the expanded manuscript, and provided a preface and a postscript for the book. I am also grateful to Mrs. Sakae Hashimoto, widow of Katue Kitasono, and to Yasuo Fujitomi, poet, for their enthusiastic help in Japan.

I wish also to thank the following people for their assistance in many forms: Donald Gallup, Carroll F. Terrell, Jim Generoso, John Solt, Naoki Inagaki, and above all Megumi Nakamura for providing me with information that I needed for the notes; Kenji Arai for his arrangement with the Japan Times, Inc. for permission to reprint Ezra Pound's articles; Michiko Shimizu for typing the greater part of the text; Tōru Haga for recommending me to the Suntory Foundation; Akiko Miyake, Motoyuki Yoshida, and the librarians and staff at the Beinecke Library at Yale University for their courteous help and encouragement; and the Trustees of the Suntory Foundation, Osaka, for their generous financial assistance for this publication.

Grateful acknowledgement and thanks are given to the following for permission to include the varied Ezra Pound material: The Ezra Pound Literary Property Trust and New Directions Publishing Corp.; The Beinecke Rare Book and Manuscript Library, Yale University; Ikuko Atsumi, for a letter from *Yone Noguchi's Collected English Letters* (Tokyo: Zōkei Bijutsu Kyōkai, 1975); Kōichi Iwasaki, for letters to his father, Ryōzō Iwasaki; Yukio Satō, for a letter to the Japanese Ambassador in Rome; Tokutaro Shigehisa, for a letter to Tomoji Okada; *Townsman*, for the essay "VOU Club"; and Shirō Tsunoda, for his help and for the fragment of the letter addressed to himself. The citations for previously published material by Ezra Pound are as follows: *The Cantos* (copyright 1934, 1937, 1940, 1948, 1956, 1959, 1962, 1963, 1966, 1968 by Ezra Pound; copyright © 1972 by the Estate of Ezra Pound); *Selected Letters, 1907–1941*, ed. D. D. Paige (copyright 1950 by Ezra Pound; copyright © 1971 by New Directions Publishing Corp.); *Ezra Pound Speaking*, ed. Leonard Doob (copyright © 1978 by the Ezra Pound Literary Property Trust). Permission to reprint the articles which first appeared in the papers published by the Japan Times, Inc. has been granted by Gyō Hani, Chief Editor, The Japan Times, Inc.

Likewise grateful acknowledgement and thanks are extended to the following for permission to include the varied material by Pound's Japanese correspondents. The Beinecke Rare Book and Manuscript Library, Yale University; Lilly Library, Indiana University; Harry Ransom Humanities Research Center, the University of Texas at Austin; Kunio Itō (Koreyo Senda) for letters by his brother, Michio Itō; Kōichi Iwasaki, for letters from his father, Ryōzō Iwasaki; Masayoshi Kumé, for material of his father, Tamijūrō Kumé; Yoshinobu Mōri, for a letter by his father,

Yasotarō Mōri; Masao Noguchi, for letters of Yonijirō Noguchi; and Eiichirō Oshima, for a letter by his father, Shōtarō Oshima; *Townsman* for Katue Kitasono's "Notes" and *New Directions* for the VOU poems and "Modern Poets of Japan."

Further acknowledgement and thanks are offered to the following for various permissions: Mary de Rachewiltz, James Laughlin and Fosco Maraini, for their own material; Omar Pound, for letters by Dorothy Pound (copyright © 1987 by Omar S. Pound); and Michael Reck, for his own material, and that by Ezra Pound and Katue Kitasono included in his *Ezra Pound: A Close-Up* (NY: McGraw-Hill, 1967). Acknowledgement is also made to Basil Bunting, *Collected Poems* (Oxford: Oxford University Press, 1979, copyright © 1978 by Basil Bunting), and to Van Wyck Brooks, *Fenollosa and His Circle* (NY: E. P. Dutton, 1962).

Finally, my special thanks are due to John Walsh. I should like to express my heartfelt appreciation for the encouragement and assistance I received from him in many forms and over a period of many years.—S. K.

NOTE ON THE TEXT

In rendering the Pound material in typeset format, certain translations have been utilized: underlined words have been placed in italics; double underlined words are indicated by boldface; and triple underlining appears as italic capitals. Words originally in block letters appear in small capitals. Handwritten inserts have been placed in the text where indicated by Pound and appear in italics within angle brackets. Phrases and words in foreign languages, as well as titles, have been italicized. With few exceptions, Pound's original spelling, punctuation and spacing have been retained, and a line-for-line approximation has been attempted. In only a few cases have the letters from Japanese correspondents been corrected to aid clarification; no attempt has been made to regularize Japanese names and terms, as this forms one of the themes of the correspondence. The following manuscript abbreviations (followed by the number of pages of the original) have been used: TL = typed letter; TLS = typed letter signed; PC = postcard; AL = handwritten letter; and ALS = handwritten letter signed.

In the Notes, citations to the editions of Pound's works as listed in Donald Gallup's *Ezra Pound: A Bibliography*, 2nd ed. (Charlottesville: University of Virginia Press, 1983) have been placed within brackets.

Two additional references are to be included: Ezra Pound, *Plays Modelled on the Noh (1916)*, ed. Donald Gallup (Toledo: Friends of the University of Toledo Libraries, 1987); and Octavio Paz, Jacques Roubaud, Eduardo Sanguinetti and Charles Tomlinson, *Renga: A Chain of Poems* (NY: Braziller, 1971)—with special reference to letter 73: The modern chain poem is a descendant of the Japanese "kusari-renga" ["linked poems"] developed between the Heian (794–1183) and Muromachi (1336–1573) periods.

PREFACE

On THE WALLS of the Boston Museum of Fine Arts hangs a painting by the American painter William Paxton entitled *The New Necklace*. In the painting is depicted a young American woman, wrapped in an oriental jacket placed over her long frilled dress; she is seated by an oriental screen, set in front of the Western painting and tapestry on the wall; an encased oriental statuette is on top of the woman's lacquered writing desk-chest. The date of the painting is 1910.

The intermixing of styles in this painting reflects the extent of the current vogue of *Japonisme*, in a setting most likely proximate to one of the ports of the Yankee clipper trade which flourished between Yokohama and Salem. "Things Japanese" had most definitely entered American fashion by this time, a good fifty years after the American painters La Farge and Whistler had begun their collections of Japanese Ukiyoe [woodblock] prints. Such artistic transport, facilitated by the speed of the Yankee clipper ships, prompted Van Wyck Brooks to remark that "the Far East seemed closer to Salem than to any other American town when Ernest Fenollosa* was born there in 1853" (*Fenollosa and His Circle*).

The Museum of Fine Arts in Boston, and the nearby Peabody Museum in Salem, were the recipients of much of the art and artifacts of traditional Japanese culture that were shored up against time, thanks to a determined effort on the part of a group of Boston-based Americans who had travelled to Japan—fortuitously arriving at precisely the critical moment for their enterprise. Ernest Fenollosa and Edward Morse, followed by William Sturgis Bigelow and Percival Lowell, and later by Henry Adams, John La Farge, and then Lafcadio Hearn—all arrived in Japan within nearly a decade (1878–90), at a time when the traditional culture of Japan was on the brink of being swept away. "For twenty years," remarks Van Wyck Brooks, "the most precious works were treated as rubbish." Masterpieces were paradoxically more commonly to be found in trash-heaps than in showrooms. With a broad gesture, the Japanese had turned their backs on their past in favor of Western modernity. A year after Fenollosa had arrived in Japan, he had been able to acquire a masterpiece by the painter Ganku from a dealer who had never even heard of the master's name, and he was still able to find in 1884 a fine ceramic head of the Buddha—one of the earliest relics of Tendai sculpture—in an ash barrel where it had been discarded. Along with Fenollosa and Morse, these Americans eagerly took to the task of attempt-

ing to preserve what they feared to be the last surviving traces of a vanishing
civilization. Fenollosa took sculpture and painting as his specialty, while
Morse chose pottery. Morse also took lessons in the traditional tea ceremony, and studied Japanese singing with the Nō master, Minoru Umewaka,
under whom Fenollosa studied as well.

At a time when the Japanese feudal system was in its death-throes and
noble families found it necessary to sell their great collections to stave off
poverty, excellent examples of traditional art—swords, guards, emblems,
lacquer boxes, along with statues, paintings, scrolls and pottery—
abounded in a radically devalued market. And Fenollosa and Morse bought
discerningly and extensively, shipping off vast collections to the Museum
of Fine Arts in Boston.

Along with Okakura Kakuzo (who organized the Imperial Art School in
Tokyo), Fenollosa acted as Imperial Commissioner of Fine Art and scoured
the countryside in search of cast-off treasures. Ironically, however, most of
this treasure was being shipped to America. Morse, well aware of the
contradiction, remarked: "It is like the life-blood of Japan seeping from a
hidden wound." But this wound was soon to be staunched; in 1884, further
transport of national Japanese treasures (now recognized to be so) began to
be discussed by the Japanese government. By 1885, a rebirth of interest in
the traditional culture of Japan had begun.

Certainly, the crucial role played by this small group of American
Japanophiles had not been forgotten by the Japanese; in the words of Prof.
Yaichi Haga, "An American, Ernest Fenollosa, taught us how to admire the
unique beauty of our art." And upon preparing to return to America in
1886, Fenollosa was told by the Emperor: "You have taught my people to
know their own art; in going back to your great country, I charge you, teach
them also."

*   *   *

When Ezra Pound in London received his first letter from a Japanese
correspondent in 1911 (a year before the publication of Fenollosa's *Epochs
of Chinese and Japanese Art*), he probably was not as yet familiar with the
work of Fenollosa. Perhaps he had not yet at that time thought much
directly about Japan, even though he was certainly familiar with the art of
Whistler. Were he in London at the time, he most probably would have seen
the Japanese Exhibition held at Shepherd's Bush in 1910. Perhaps he had
even discussed Fenollosa when he met, in October 1913, the American
photographer Alvin Langdon Coburn, who had intensively studied the
collection of Chinese and Japanese art set up by Fenollosa in the Boston

Museum of Fine Arts. But when towards the end of 1913 he received from Mary Fenollosa the notebooks containing Fenollosa's notes on oriental literature, draft translations of Chinese poetry and Japanese Nō dramas, along with his essay "The Chinese Written Character as a Medium for Poetry"—with the stipulation that Fenollosa wanted the material treated as literature, not philology—a world opened. In March 1909, Pound had heard Laurence Binyon lecture on "Oriental and European Art," and in the spring of 1911, he had written his haiku-like poem on the Paris Métro (see Sanehide Kodama, *American Poetry and Japanese Culture*). He had also written in 1913, prior to the receipt of the bulk of Fenollosa material, the Chinese-inspired poems "After Ch'u Yuan," "Fan-Piece for Her Imperial Lord," and "Liu Ch'e." Most significantly, Pound's "A Few Don'ts by an Imagiste" had already appeared. But what accompanied China in the Fenollosa notebooks was the near-virgin world of Japan—territory which he set about exploring almost immediately. Pound and W. B. Yeats spent much of the winter of 1913 in Stone Cottage immersed in the study and translation of Nō drama. By January of 1914 Pound was able to send off to Harriet Monroe of *Poetry* the finished version of *Nishikigi*. And so began his lifetime enthrallment.

Ironically, Pound's discovery of Japanese drama coincided with another phase of modern Japan's turning away from its traditional culture. When the Japanese dancer Michio Ito arrived in London in 1914, he knew next to nothing about classical Japanese drama—but, most fortunately, a fellow expatriate, the painter Tami Koumé, *did*. So it was in London, not Tokyo, that Ito learned about his own cultural tradition. (Perhaps the apocryphal story of Ito's visit with Yeats to the London zoo to watch the movements of a caged hawk justifiedly merits being preserved.) From these seeds, the study of Nō drama became an enduring passion for Pound.

The importance of the Nō drama for Pound echoes throughout this correspondence. Seated in the cinema in Rapallo watching the film *Mitsouko*, Pound is filled with nostalgia, struck by the sound of the singing, and remembering a Nō performance enacted in Paris by Tami Koumé and other Japanese: "You have a treasure like nothing we have in the Occident." In a later letter of 1957, Pound most succinctly and poignantly remarks: "*Hagoromo* is a sacrament." And Pound seriously and fondly hoped that his own play, *Women of Trachis* (1954), would be translated into Japanese and be staged by a Nō troupe: "Am convinced the Noh technique is only way of doing it properly, in whatever language."

It was to preserve this induplicable treasure of the Nō that Pound went to the extreme of suggesting that the American-occupied island of Guam be negotiated with the Japanese in exchange for a set of films of classic Nō plays—along with their authentic music. "INSIST," wrote Pound to the Japanese poet Katue Kitasono, "on having 300 Noh plays done properly AND recorded on sound film so as to be able to EDUCATE such American students as are capable of being cultured."

Ironic indeed that this was being said by an American at a time when many modern Japanese were in another phase of turning away from their cultural heritage—the avant-garde poet, Katue Kitasono, most certainly included. When in 1952 Michael Reck—who made a pilgrimage to Fenollosa's grave above Lake Biwa (cf. Canto LXXXIX)—upon Pound's urging met Kitasono, he discovered that the Japanese poet evidenced no enthusiasm at all at the prospect of attending a Nō performance—to such an extent that he sent his wife in his place to accompany the young American. And after a short time, she politely excused herself and left the performance, leaving the American to discover the classical world of Japan on his own. There is a certain humor in the fact that Pound in his letters to Kitasono is continually asking questions about Japan's traditional culture—ironic in that Kitasono was not at all as interested in it as was Pound himself. For Kitasono embodied *contemporary* Japan.

What Kitasono, in turn, presented to Pound was not the past but the *new*. He introduced Pound to what the young avant-garde was doing as reflected in poems written by members of the VOU Club and published in its magazine. Pound seized upon the potential offered by this poetry—washed clean as if by acid—written in halting English translations by these young Japanese, for he saw that they approached the language with fresh eyes, without preconceptions, and used English freely, idiosyncratically and inventively. "All the moss and fuzz that for twenty years we have been trying to scrape off our language—these young men start without it." He praised this "vortex of poetic alertness" for its immense clarity and rapidity: "The Japanese eye is like those new camera shutters that catch the bullet leaving the gun. . . . They see the crystal set, the chemical laboratory and the pine tree with untrammeled clearness. . . . The Japanese poet has gone from one peak of [thought] to another faster than our slow wits permit us to follow before we have got used to his pace."

Rather than condescendingly dismissing these poems for their technical flaws, Pound positively saw in them a *new beginning* and enthusiastically recommended them to Ronald Duncan of *Townsman* and James Laughlin of New Directions for publication. While one need not necessarily agree with Pound's generous evaluation of them as "better work than any save those of E. E. Cummings," by seeing them in the manner that Pound saw them and for the qualities that he cited, lessons could be learned. Here Japan was making its contemporary contribution to the West.

This collection of letters and essays documents Pound's lifelong involvement with the art, literature and culture of Japan. Extending from 1911 to 1968, Pound's correspondence with Japanese artists and poets forms a record of a vital cultural interchange from which both East and West gained through the interaction. Included in this volume are letters from the Japanese painter Tami Koumé and the dancer Michio Ito dating from Pound's early years in London—when he was at work with W. B. Yeats on translating Japanese Nō dramas—and his years in Paris during the early 1920's; the correspondence between Pound and the Japanese modernist poet Katue Kitasono (editor of **VOU**) while Pound was residing in Rapallo (and later from St. Elizabeths); and articles written by Pound which appeared in the *Japan Times* just prior to the outbreak of World War II, promoting cross-cultural communication and insisting that "diplomacy alone could not do it." Letters from Mary Fenollosa and various other Japanese correspondents, along with the pertinent material included in the appendix, further round out the portrait.

Similar to the influence exerted by a previous generation of Americans who had travelled to Japan (Fenollosa, Bigelow, Morse, La Farge and Hearn), Ezra Pound from afar also made his contribution to the preservation of the classic Japanese tradition, drawing attention to its masterworks as an essential component of world culture and a crucial means to increase East-West understanding.

—*John Walsh*

---

*For further on Fenollosa, *see* note to letter 4 on Mary Fenollosa; *see also* Van Wyck Brooks, *Fenollosa and His Circle* (NY: E. P. Dutton, 1962).

INTRODUCTION

IN THIS BOOK are collected letters exchanged between Ezra Pound and his Japanese friends, ranging between the years 1911 to 1968. These letters are, in most cases, chronologically arranged so that the reader may have an historical overview of Pound's involvement with the art and culture of Japan. The book also includes Pound's contributions to Japanese periodicals written shortly before World War II, at a time when he had little outlet elsewhere. Supplementary letters, such as those between Ezra Pound and Mary Fenollosa, Katue Kitasono to Dorothy Pound and Mary de Rachewiltz, etc., which touch on material regarding Japan have also been included.

In the summer of 1911 Ezra Pound received a completely unexpected letter postmarked from Japan. "Dear Mr. Pound," the letter opened, "As I believe you may not know my work at all, I send you, under a separate cover, my new book of poems called *The Pilgrimage.* . . ." It was from Yonejirō Noguchi, a Japanese poet who was ten years older than Pound and had been favorably received in England and America. He had published a few books of verse and prose in English in both countries: *Seen and Unseen* (1897), *The American Diary of a Japanese Girl* (1902) and *From the Eastern Sea* (1902), and had returned to Japan after spending thirteen years abroad.

In his polite response to Noguchi Pound wrote, "of your country I know almost nothing." But he also wrote, "I had, of course, known of you." One may wonder how much knowledge Pound actually had of Japan when he said, "I know almost nothing." It can be assumed that by 1911 Pound already had some knowledge of Japanese haiku, as he had regularly been attending T. E. Hulme's meetings at the Café Tour d'Eiffel since 1909, where haiku had by then become common knowledge. Basil Hall Chamberlain's *Classical Poetry of the Japanese* (London, 1880) had long been out. One of the members of the group, Joseph Campbell, had written three-line poems such as "The Dawn Whiteness," and Edward Storer had written "Image." F. S. Flint had translated some haiku into English from Paul-Louis Couchoud's French translations, including a piece by Arakida Takeari, which Pound was later to quote. Actually Pound might already have read Couchoud's and Chamberlain's translations himself.

But haiku was not the only aspect of Japan that Pound was acquainted with by that time. He surely would have known something of Japan's political and social aspects as well: news of the unexpected victory of Japan

over Imperial Russia in 1905 and reports concerning the Baltic Fleet, the
battles at Lüshun, and the following negotiations at Portsmouth, New
Hampshire, most certainly.

Moreover, Pound's juvenescence had coincided with the period of
Japonisme. Certainly, Japan had been "opened" to the American market for
some time. Even Sears, Roebuck and Co. had listed Japanese fans with
illustrations in their catalogue of 1902. Lacquer ware, paper napkins, kimo-
no, netsuke, wood-block prints, and other *objets d'art* had been imported
through Yamanaka & Co. for domestic usage. French and American painters had been influenced for some time by Japanese art, and in his early
essays Pound had already made frequent mention of the connection between Whistler and Hokusai.

But Pound in 1911 was still looking at Japan through the back end of a
pair of opera glasses. Pound viewed Japan as a far-away, beautiful country,
inhabited by people with a delicate and subtle sensibility, by women
pretty, gentle, obedient, and loveable, and by men courageous enough to
defeat Imperial Russia. When he received a businesslike letter from Yone
Noguchi, therefore, Pound must have been surprised, but he does not seem
to have changed his basic view of Japan. The image of a dream-like Japan
had been so strongly imprinted on his young mind that it could not easily
be changed or removed.

When he wrote "The Encounter," Pound compared the graceful fingers
of a London woman to the "tissue" of a soft and lissome "Japanese paper
napkin." And when he wrote the "Metro" poem suggested by haiku, Pound
presented the image of the glimmering petals scattered upon "the wet,
black bough" as if painted on soft Japanese paper, to be "superimposed"
upon the image of the beautiful faces of women and children in Paris.

By the time Pound met Mary Fenollosa, in 1913—and soon afterwards
received the bundle of her late husband's notebooks on the Nō plays and
Japanese interpretations of Chinese classics—his knowledge of Japan had
been substantially enhanced. Yet he does not seem even then to have
changed his basic image of Japan. Rather, he became more enthusiastic
about "beautifying" Japan. While promoting the production of Yeats' *At the
Hawk's Well*, Pound met Michio Ito, Tamijūrō Kumé and Jisoichi Kayano,
and through them became acquainted with the Japanese language, Japanese
customs, the Nō plays, Zen and various other aspects of Japan. He experienced, as it were, some new phases of the realities of Japan, including
the awkward English of many Japanese. But still he rarefied and mythologized Japan by translating the Nō plays and the Chinese classics into
beautiful English poetry. Certainly Pound tried to finish the translations as

"Ernest Fenollosa would have wanted them done." But in any event the more Pound learned about Japanese realities, the more he emphasized their beauty and positive value.

The same can be said of *Canto* 49. That is, Pound read the manuscript poems in Japanese and Chinese on the lakes and hills around the River Hisaio-Hsiang in China, and he used the images to create an unworldly lyrical world of "stillness" suggestive of the *paradiso terrestre*. And again we find that aspect when he began correspondence with Kitasono in 1936. Pound read the "crystal" poems by the members of the VOU Club, and introduced them as the "vortex of poetic alertness" in the *Townsman* (see Appendix). He urged the publisher James Laughlin to introduce them also in his yearly *New Directions Anthology*. In his essay "Orientamenti" in *Broletto* (1938), Pound also introduced Japan favorably as being in a new "cycle," though he was aware of the Japanese invasion of Manchuria.

In 1939 Pound had begun to subscribe to the *Japan Times & Mail*, and was thus exposed to much more concerning the political, economic and social realities of contemporary Japan. But in 1940 he mythologized the whole history of Japan by writing that all the emperors "were of heaven descended" in *Canto* 58. (His source was most probably Heinrich Julius Klaproth's translation of *Nippon Odai Ichiran. See* Pound's letter to Kitasono. 3 March 1939.)

When we trace Pound's view of Japan, we come to realize that even though he continued to further his knowledge of Japan throughout his life, his earlier image of Japan as a far-off, dreamlike country persisted; a treasure land for the æsthete, a country entangled with pleasant memories of youth. We cannot neglect the basic fact that Pound grew up in the era of *Japonisme*, and the image of Japan registered in his mind in his early youth as a land of lotus and butterfly was not to be erased from his mind throughout his life. And we must also remember that Fenollosa's impact was so very strong on him that Fenollosa's admiration for Japanese values could only reinforce Pound's idealized image.

However, the important thing is that Pound had the intuitive critical sensibility to sift "*to kalon*" from the chaff, and he did discover authentic treasures in his study of Far Eastern cultures. Although one might wish that Pound could have written more objectively of the realities of Japan, whether approvingly or not, the fact was that Japan remained for him the distant, mythic country of Hagoromo, Aoi, and Komachi.

—*Sanehide Kodama*

I POUND'S EARLY CONTACTS WITH JAPAN: 1911–23

In this section are collected three letters of Yonejirō Noguchi to Pound, one letter of Pound to Noguchi, four letters of Mary Fenollosa to Pound, one letter by her to Dorothy Pound, three letters of Michio Ito to Pound, seventeen letters of Tamijūrō Kumé to Pound, and an invitation card to Tamijūrō Kumé's exhibition in Paris. Pound must have written back to his Japanese friends at that time, but unfortunately most of Pound's letters to them were lost in the earthquake of 1923 and during the bombing of the Second World War.

Yonejirō Noguchi (1875–1947), a Japanese poet, went to California in 1893, studied poetry under Joaquin Miller for some time, and published there his books of poems, *Seen and Unseen* (San Francisco Press, 1897), and *The Voice of the Valley* (The Doxey Press, 1897). He then went to London to publish *Eastern Sea* (1903), first at his own expense, and then by Macmillan. Because of the *Japonisme* then fashionable, the Macmillan edition went into three printings. After his return to Japan, he was invited by Oxford University to give a series of lectures, and he sailed again to England. While there (1913–14), he met, as he writes in his essay "Irish Atmosphere," W. B. Yeats and Ezra Pound. The first two letters printed in the following pages were obviously written before these meetings had occurred.

After Noguchi returned to Japan in 1914, he maintained a correspondence with Pound. The strange article, "To Criticize *Aoi no Ue* by Ezra Pound" which appeared in Japanese in *Yōkyokukai* (October, 1916) may most probably be the anonymous translation, or rather adaptation, of Pound's "Introduction" to "*Awoi no Uye*: A Play by Ujinobu" which had appeared in *Quarterly Notebook* (Kansas City, June 1916). If so, Pound must have sent to Noguchi a copy of the American journal. In the editorial note to the article Pound is thus portrayed:

> Mr. Ezra Pound is a young poet, born in the U.S.A., now living in England. He has published three or four books of poems, and has translated Li Po into English. He is a vigorous poet and is said to have been claiming himself a revolutionist of the literary world. He is a friend of Mr. Yonejirō Noguchi.

In certain ways, Noguchi and Pound did evidence a kinship. Both were interested in "certain forgotten odours": Pound in "the spirit of romance" and Noguchi in "the spirit of Japan." And both were fascinated by the Nō play. Though their sensibilities and their styles of writing were different, closer examination might reveal certain reciprocal echoes.

Michio Itō (1893–1961) was a Japanese modern dancer, who played the part of the hawk in a performance of Yeats' *At the Hawk's Well* in 1916. He had gone to Germany to study music when he was 18, but the course of his life was changed after he saw Isadora Duncan. When the war broke out, he escaped from Germany, but he was stranded when his father stopped sending him money. One day in 1914 when he did not have a penny to feed the gasometer at his flat in London, he was invited to dance at a party. At the dinner table he sat next to an elderly gentleman who admired him highly. But Itō could not understand English, and he asked him if he could speak in German. After hesitation the gentleman consented, and they talked for two hours. A few days later Itō received from that gentleman, who turned out to be Prime Minister Herbert Henry Asquith, a letter enclosing a check for £20. Pound writes of the episode in *Canto 77*:

> So Mischio sat in the dark lacking the gasometer penny
>   but then said: "Do you speak German?"
> to Asquith, 1914.

Pound had met Itō at the Café Royal where the refugee artists met. He asked him to help him with the editing of the Nō plays in the Fenollosa notebooks, and then to help Yeats with *At the Hawk's Well*. Itō had himself little knowledge of the Nō play then, but his Japanese classmates who happened to be in London were versed in it. Tamijūrō Kumé and Jisoichi Kayano (Torahiko Kōri)—especially the former—taught them about the Nō play and assisted Pound in interpreting Fenollosa's notebooks, continuing even after Itō had left for New York.

Tamijūrō Kumé (1893–1923), a Japanese painter, had begun taking lessons in Nō and Kyōgen from Minoru Umewaka when he was still in primary school. His father, Taminosuke Kumé, a successful businessman, had a Nō theatre in his large house in Yoyogi, Tokyo, where his family and guests often sang and played. Not much is recorded about his first son, Tamijūrō. But according to the family legend, he began painting while he was a student at Gakushūin Middle School. He went to Europe after graduation to study oil painting. During World War I, he met Pound in London, through his classmate, Michio Itō. Obviously he played a crucial part in Pound's rendering of the Nō plays and Dulac's production of Yeats' *At the Hawk's Well*. He performed *utai*, the vocal part of the Nō, at Pound's flat in

London. How much affection Pound had for him, especially after Pound lost Gaudier-Brzeska, may be gleaned from the following letters. But nothing much is known about the actual role he played in assisting Yeats and Pound in their research.

He returned to Japan in July 1918, vigorously worked at his "hideout" studio near Lake Yamanaka, and went to New York in January 1921 to exhibit his paintings (February 1–12). He then went to Paris in January 1922 and there again met Pound who arranged an exhibition for "Tami Koumé" in July. Though Tamijūrō Kumé had a love affair in Paris, he left there in February 1923, returning to Tokyo by boat. On September 1, 1923, he was in Yokohama, again on the verge of sailing abroad, this time to America to launch a second exhibition in New York. His wife, Kiyo, and his 5-year-old son, Masayoshi, were at their villa in Koshigoe, Kamakura, planning to join him briefly at Yokohama and then see him off at the pier. However, the great earthquake occurred, just when Tamijūrō Kumé was in the dining room in the basement of the Oriental Hotel with a friend of his. His body was pulled out from under the bricks and ashes with his watch and rings on.

1: *Yone Noguchi to Ezra Pound*
ALS-1   Kamakura, Japan. 16 July 1911

Dear Mr. Pound:

As I think you may not know my work at all, I send you, under a separate cover, my new book of poems called *The Pilgrimage*. As I [am] not yet acquainted with your work, I wish you will send your book or books which you like to have me to read. This little note may sound quite businesslike, but I can promise you that I can do better in my next letter to you.

Yours truly,
Yone Noguchi

P.S.   I am anxious to read not only your poetical work but also your criticism.

2: *Ezra Pound to Yone Noguchi*
TLS-2   c/o Elkin Mathews, Vigo St., London. Pmk: 2 September 1911

Dear Yone Noguchi:

I want to thank you very much for your lovely books & for your kindness in sending them to me.

I had, of course, known of you, but I am much occupied with my mediæval studies & had neglected to read your books altho' they lie with my own in Mathews shop & I am very familiar with the appearance of their covers.

I am reading those you sent me but I do not yet know what to say of them except that they have delighted me. Besides it is very hard to write to you until I know more about you; you are older than I am—I gather from the dates of the poems—you have been to New York. You are giving us the spirit of Japan, is it not? very much as I am trying to deliver from obscurity certain forgotten odours of Provence & Tuscany (my works on Guido Cavalcanti, & Arnaut Daniel, are, the one in press, the other ready to be printed).

I have sent you two volumes of poems. I do not know whether to send you *The Spirit of Romance* or not: It treats of mediæval poetry in southern Europe but has many flaws of workmanship.

I can not help wondering how much you know of our contemporary poets & in what things of ours you would be likely to be interested.

I mean I do not want to write you things that you already know as well or better than I do.

Of your country I know almost nothing—surely if the east & the west are ever to understand each other that understanding must come slowly & come first through the arts.

You ask about my "criticism." There is some criticism in the *Spirit of Romance* & there will be some in the prefaces to the "Guido" & the "Arnaut." But I might be more to the point if we who are artists should discuss the matters of technique & motive between ourselves. Also if you should write about these matters I would discuss your letters with Mr. Yeats & likewise my answers.

I have not answered before because your letter & your books have followed me through America, France, Italy, Germany and have reached me but lately.

Let me thank you again for sending them, and believe me

Yours Very Sincerely
Ezra Pound

3: *Yone Noguchi to Ezra Pound*
ACS-1   Kamakura, Japan. 22 October 1911

Dear Mr. Pound:

Many thanks for your kind letter [together] with *Exultations* and *Canzoni*. I was glad to be acquainted with *Exultations*, and what a difference of your work from mine! I like to follow closely after your poetry.

Sincerely yours,
Yone Noguchi

4: *Mary Fenollosa to Ezra Pound*
ALS-3   159 Church Street, Mobile, Alabama. 24 November [1913]

Dear Ezra:

Your violet ray from Stone Cottage has just penetrated. Since you announced that you are to be there "forever," I suppose I might as well begin addressing you there. It certainly sounds good enough to be a forever,—with the aigrette of the usual "day."

I am beginning with right now, to send you material. I am going to number the rolls, envelopes, packets, or whatever form they go in. So if you merely let me know that No. 1 has safely arrived—then No. 2—, and so on, it will be enough to bring me "*anshin*," which is to say "peace of the spirit." I fear it will go to you in a pretty mixed up condition, but the great fact is that it will all go.

I know you are pining for hieroglyphs and ideographs: but I must keep to our plan and send the Nō stuff first. That is a complete book in itself—I almost think that you had better spell it Nōh, as some French writers do. It looks just a little more impressive. Don't you think so? Later I will have something to say about the illustrations, but the time hasn't come, yet, for that.

If you ever see Sarojini, or write to her, wont you please say to her that if she could have sprouted a new petal every time I've thought of her, or wanted to write to her, she would be the shape and size of a chrysanthemum by this.

I used to think I was somewhat rushed in London, but it was a long hour of silent prayer by this! I've a million relatives, more or less, and they all feel hurt when I shut myself up even to write letters. By the way, don't forget to give me your mother's address. After Christmas I shall be wandering between the cauldron of Pittsburgh and "My City, my beloved, my white!" I want to meet your mother.

                                                    Mary Fenollosa

5: *Mary Fenollosa to Ezra Pound*
TLS-3   159 Church Street, Mobile, Alabama. 25 November [1913]

Dear Ezra:

Please don't get discouraged at the ragged way this manuscript is coming to you. As I said yesterday, it will all get there in time,—which is the most important thing.

For instance, chronologically, the lectures taken down by my husband, from old Umèwaka Minoru are so rough, and so many abbreviations are used, that I can't send them until I have time to make quite copious notes to help you understand. It is going to be something of a puzzle, at best.

In these notes the initials "U. M." are constantly used. Sometimes they are put "M. U.," for to this day, the Japanese are a little undecided whether to place the family name first, according to their own custom, or last. In any case, whenever you see these initials together they mean the old lecturer. He was brought up in the last Shogun's court, and comes from a long line of famous Nōh players. He had all the costumes, masks, literature and traditions. I had thought, if ever I attempted editing the book, to begin it with this personal note of old U. M. and the Professor. (Whenever I say "Professor" I mean E. F. F.). He had two beautiful young sons, still living and acting— whether real or adopted I am not sure, but that doesn't matter in Japan. The son who is adopted for reasons of fitness, talent, and capability of carrying on an artistic tradition is considered more real than a son who is merely of the flesh. All the great artists of old times adopted successors this way. These sons, also very often referred to in the notes, and in the studies of the Nōh plays, were Manzaburo Umèwaka and Takeyo Umèwaka. Both were beautiful,—the former, a tall and rather stout youth, did not look unlike a picture of a cavalier by Franz Hals, and the younger, our teacher in the singing of Nōh, was more like a soulful and very handsome East Indian poet than a Japanese. I hope I come across a photograph of him, but I haven't yet. However I have an excellent one of the old Umèwaka to send.

I shall go over these notes of his lectures, and wherever you see new ink writing you will know that I put it.

I must explain at more length the recurring term "cats." This would surely be a puzzler. At the back of the stage in many,—in fact most, of the pieces, there are always two queer old, old musicians that come in with funny little folding stools, sit facing each other for a moment, and then turn themselves and the stools so that they face the audience. They have weird little drums, and at intervals, during the performance, they utter the most astonishing sounds, suppressed wails, throaty gurgles, and muted banshee howls. These sounds are more like the noises of back-yard fence cats than anything else on earth, and the Professor and I got into the way of calling them "cats." I didn't realize that he had accepted the term seriously enough to put it all through the notes. In rare cases there are sometimes four cats, or even more; but, as I remember it, always there were two. I don't believe they were ever used in the comic interludes, or "kyogen." You will see also frequent reference to "Mr. H." This always means little Mr. Hirata, a pupil of my husband's, who always went to the Nōh performances with us, and did the translations. I don't think much of his literary style. Neither will you. I should suggest that the examples you wish to present in full should be taken only from those pieces where the Professor has written out the Japanese words too, and given the literal translation.

Please remember, from the first, that whenever I say "suggest," I mean just that thing, and nothing more stringent. What I am hoping is that you will become really interested in the material, absorb it in your own way, and then make practically new translations from the Japanese text as rendered into Romaji. It seems going ahead of myself a little, but I might as well tell you the Nōh pieces that have seemed to us most beautiful. I think that first I would place "Kinuta." Old U. M. considered it so, and also said that it took nearly a life-time, and much prayer and fasting, to learn to sing properly. Another that the Professor specially loved was "Nishi ki gi." "Yōrōboshi" was the first I heard, really to understand, and I care a lot for it. "Hagoromo" is perhaps the favorite of all, with the average Japanese Nōh lover, and is a legend strangely like the old Celtic one of the mermaid who had her magic sea-garments stolen by a mortal. "Sumidagawa" is another wonder. Most, if not all of these, are carefully translated.

This is a big enough dose for one day. When you get into it, please don't hesitate to ask me questions. I only wish I were there with you and Yeats, working on it. I am homesick for London already.

Mary Fenollosa

6: *Michio Ito to Ezra Pound*
ACS-1   82 St. John's Wood Terrace, London, N.W. Pmk: 8 May 1915

Dear Ezra Pound,

Thank you very much for your letter. I understand quite well this time. I should be very pleased [to] meet you on this Sunday night, but I have been very busy now as I have an engagement at Coliseum Theater from 10th of May. Then, if I could not call you at 7 o'clock, I should come [a] little later.

Yours truly
Michio Ito

7: *Mary Fenollosa to Ezra Pound*
ALS-3   Kobinata, Spring Hill, Alabama. 27 February 1916

My dear Ezra:

I haven't any envelopes to go with this lovely hand laid Japanese paper—am too poor to buy any more—but I'm writing on it because the address is my permanent one in America— From now on, into a vague future, I shall be living here, or else my widowed mother. Letters will surely be forwarded. We've had all sorts of bereavements and unpleasant things in our family. Finances in the South are poignantly *rotten*. Only the vile munition makers of your part of America are thriving.

Your letter was one of the very few bright spots that has come my way lately. It certainly has cheered me up. My getting to England is now so indefinite that I am going to try and get you that roll of Nōh illustrations by post. Heaven knows whether it ever will reach you! As I write these— Germans are battering the forts near Verdun. One has already fallen— What is going to happen to the world any way? I believe I'll go back to Japan— scoop out a rock, and be a hermitess.

> Devotedly yours
> Mary Fenollosa

8: *Tami Koumé to Ezra Pound*
ALS-1   3c Warwick Ave. W. 22 March 1916

My dear Mr. Pound,

I am awfully sorry to hear that you are sick in bed. I received your telegraph and was pain. How are you now? To-day I tried to go and ask after your health, but I was temptated by Itow, and staing long time at Mr. Dulac's, where we study some play. I am so anxious how are you now. I hope that you are well soon.

> I am your's great friend
> T. M. Koumé

9: *Mary Fenollosa to Ezra Pound*
ALS-3   c/o Grant-Thompson, Co., 280 Madison Avenue, New York, N.Y. 24
July 1916

You dear Ezra:

This certainly is good news—that you have succeeded in getting
McMillan to publish E. F. F. And what splendid, steadfast work you have
been doing—in spite of my seeming half-beastness.

My own involved domestic troubles still continue—there are all sorts
of entanglements—sickness, finances and all other ills—but I'm not going
to fill space with them now. The one thing I want to get "over the foot-
lights," in this letter, concerns those illustrations to Nōh. The whole roll of
them is here in the North with me— I hope to be allowed to remain
somewhere within reasonable distance of N.Y. for the rest of the year—
Haven't any definite address yet, as you will gather from the heading of
this—but, for the present c/o Grant-Thompson Co. will get me with less
delay than any other address—

If McMillan is to bring out Nōh in dignified form, I should think they
might desire illustrations.— I have them all—not only pictures of high
moments in the various plays—but some good ones of the conventional
Nōh settings—the shape of stage—the "cloud-bridge" etc.— These pictures
make quite a bulky roll—short and thick—nearly as big around as 5 lb. lard
bucket—if that conveys an idea—

Shall I—risking English censors and German sub-marines—try to get
these over to you? Or would it be a better idea for you to put me in direct
communication with the N.Y. McMillan's—and let me take the pictures
down to their office? I think you are now in possession of just about all of
E. F. F.'s Nōh material—but if there is hope—in the future, of further
volumes—I have still, stored away down at Kobinata, a priceless treasury of
mss.—Chinese poetry—translations of it giving each ideograph embedded
in various nuances of meaning—E. F. F.'s essays and studies of Chinese
poetry—also of philosophy, civilization, etc. etc.—I cannot believe that any
coming student of these things is to have E. F. F.'s peculiar advantages—
And China is the coming nation! This new agreement between Japan and
Russia makes it the more certain— Let me know at once about the Nōh
illustrations— You are an angel!

Affectionately
Mary Fenollosa

10: *Michio Ito to Ezra Pound*
ACS-1   Pmk: Times Sq. Sta., New York, N.Y. 18 August 1916

Safely arrived in New York on 13th August. New York is not so bad what I expected, but the weather is too hot for me. I couldn't tell you about New York yet as I don't know.

I will try to write you so much as I can. Will you give me answers? Kindest regard to your Mrs and mother-in-law.

Ever
from Michio

11: *Mary Fenollosa to Dorothy Pound*
ALS-6   c/o Grant-Thompson, Co., 280 Madison Avenue, New York, N.Y. 18 October 1916

My dear Dorothy Pound:

This delightful letter of yours not only puts me in possession of several opportune facts concerning the work that Ezra is doing so splendidly;—but it has accomplished—in its few pages—something even more desirable—it has given me—you! Until this letter I felt you only as the shadow of a personality—shall I confess, too, that it was an Ezra Pound shadow?!

I think the core of the real you-ness comes from the fact that twice you misspelled the word "desperate"—writing it "desparate"—which is, indubitably a better word.

Tell Ezra that I received the *Lustra* and joyed in it— Also the two copies of *Certain Noble Plays*— The excellence of Ezra's work on the Fenollosa mss. doesn't surprise me— The only regrets connected with it are from my side of effort— I have failed in getting any more friendly contributions to the endeavor— Then, too, the royalties from my own books are falling off badly—

But all this is merely by the way. I am in New York still. Miss Bisland arrived last week on the *Lafayette*— For a few days she was a physical wreck—not only because the voyage was rough and she a bad sailor—but all the night before reaching N.Y. the ship was chased by a hellish German sub-marine— The passengers went about in straight jackets of cork—and no one slept.

Miss Bisland and I must stay up here for a few weeks longer—but already we are negotiating for quarters in Southern Florida, where we plan to spend about 4 months—rushing work on a certain literary venture that promises to bring in immediate returns— Of course no one ever knows— but this, at least, is sure— In going to Florida, I shall go by way of my own house in Southern Alabama—and this means that I can go through all the Chinese stuff, and send Ezra any or all of it—so you will see—that I can follow your advice and not feel "desparate"—

I suppose you and Ezra never think of coming to America—I wish you would—and join us in this quiet out-of-the-world nook in Florida—

For the present, the address given at the head of this letter is the only one that had better be used—

Thank Ezra for the letter from Tagore— From what I am hearing about that exotic near-divinity, I am not going to be able to use it. The gossip about him really sounds too picturesque and absurd to be true. They say that a band of his countrymen are hounding him—and purpose to remove him violently from this incarnation—that he is hiding, incognito, somewhere in Southern California—

I truly hope that I have misspelled something in this letter, but I don't dare look back for it. With bushels of love to you both.

                                                        Mary Fenollosa

12: *Tami Koumé to Ezra Pound*
APCS-1   Pmk: Maida Hill W. 8 February 1917

My dear Ezra

So sorry have not written long time as I am still ill in bed it was awful, but getting better now. I think I can call upon you soon. & I would like to have your charming lunch. Kindest Regard to Mrs.

                                                        Tami

13: *Yone Noguchi to Ezra Pound*
ALS-1   Nakano, near Tokyo, Japan. 8 December 1917

Dear Ezra Pound,

Perhaps you can ask your publisher to send me a review copy of your book on poor Gaudier Brzeska; I like to write him up in the *Japan Times,* a daily in English—which I keep a regular literary column. Some months ago I recommended your Noh book to our readers; also I had written a Japanese article on the book. Your Noh book is now quite well-known in Japan.

Perhaps you had seen some specimens of my Noh translation; how did you like one I published in the *Egoist?* The *Quest* and the *Poetry Review* also published my Noh plays. I like to talk about this subject further with you.

> Yours truly
> Yone Noguchi

14: *Tami Koumé to Ezra Pound*
ALS-1   Royal Bath & East Cliff Hotel, Bournemouth. Tuesday 13 [December?] 1917

My dear Ezra,

I came here yesterday. It is a little warmer than London but not much different. Sorrow coming down with thin rain from heaven, & sparkling to my ears "So live bravely." But I am not strong enough to do work. Sorrow! Agony! I am absolutely cach by sentimentalism. Send to me nice poems? I shall be cheery then.

> good bye
> your's friend
> *Tami*

15: *Tami Koumé to Ezra Pound*

ALS-4   Royal Bath & East Cliff Hotel, Bournemouth. Friday [16 December? 1917]

My dear Ezra,

Thank you very much for your letter, poems, and kindness. I was so pleased when I received them. The poems are rather difficult to understand for me. I can see the meaning, but my poor english will not understand the important subtle part. It is great a shame. But your kindness comforts me more than your interesting poems. I feel better day by day. So I think can see you soon at your place.

Am writing play. about Fox. It might be waste of paper, but, somehow it is nice english lesson to me. So I do.

The sun shines every day here. nice & warm, but awfully vulgar here. Many uninteresting people. Skate rink cinema. Old gloomy men & women. And especially the hotel is so expensive about £10 a week. I am sure those horrid things send me back to London soon.

(I couldn't write until to-day. Sunday).

I feel to go back London, beginning of this week. To-day is Sunday, many horrid rude officers crowded in the dining room. I felt sick again when I saw one of those groups.

It was such a nice day to-day. I kissed to the sun shine as much as I want.

Now I must ask you to help me about my studio. am going to leave there end of this month. And Madam Karina advised me to stay there. There are two rooms third floor of her house. It is quite cheap 19s, a week. But I don't like her husband. So am hesitating about it.

Tell me what do you think that idea.

I am sure shall get back in one or two days. & I will join with your dinner party. Send my greeting to your dearest Mrs.

good night
Tami

16: *Tami Koumé to Ezra Pound*

ALS-2   Royal Bath & East Cliff Hotel, Bournemouth. Thursday [1917]

My dear Ezra,

I am going to home this afternoon. am waiting the taxi now. in one hour

I shall be offended by the sea. But I feel cherry when I think of the life of town. I shall change my life & start work very hard. Am just going to say good bye to the sea. & I will tell her your love too.

Well, my dear Ezra. We can see very soon, shalln't we.

I will call upon you to-morrow afternoon or Saturday morning. Am getting quite strong, but sometimes not.

How I shall be pleased when shall see you.

I hope you are quite well & waiting my visit. Remember me to Mrs Pound.

Yours Ever
Tami

17: *Tami Koumé to Ezra Pound*
ALS-1   9 & 10 Marble Arch. W. Sunday [1 January 1918?]

My dear Ezra,

First of all, we will send our greeting of New Year to both of you.

We were enjoied very much last night. I hope we did not disterve your work. We are so envious the piecefull atmosfair, which you emit around us.

We hope you would come & see us soon.

Kind Rememberence from Toshi.

Yours
Tami K.

18: *Tami Koumé to Ezra Pound*
ALS-3   Yoyogi mura, Toyotamagun, Tokyo 5 July 1918

My dear Ezra,

I have just got home. I found myself rather funy as many of my old friends has passed away.

It is not pleasant at all my Japanese life.

Though I have a good brother, who admired your photo, which Coburn kindly let me have.

I got home day before yesterday, and still very busy for visiting and received many people.

Please let me write again when shall have more spare time. Please send my love to Mrs. Pound.   with Love,

Tami

19: *Tami Koumé to Ezra Pound*
APCS-2   [Mt. Fuji, Lake Yamanaka?] 29 August 1918

My dear Ezra,

This is where I am staying now. fresh air. beautiful sun. birds singing. and the view is simply splendid. Hope you will come next week end, won't you?

Tami

20: *Tami Koumé to Ezra Pound*
ALS-5   Yoyogi, Yoyohata, Tokyo, Japan, EAST FROM YOUR SIDE. 21 December 1918

MY DEAREST FRIEND ON THE EARTH,

Thank you ever so much for your wonderful letter, received just this minute.

I am so pleased to hear from you about the London news. & very glad to know that you are working so very hard. I have painted about a dozen of the pictures since I have come back, and some of them are most wonderfull. I will send few of them to International and London group. If I will send them to you first, will you arrange for me?

I missed you and London life so much. I should love to come again. I suppose London is very glorious after this horrid war. How our London people are pleased! I am sure!

Toshi is not well ever since, staying at hospital. She is so pessimistic and broken our engagement. I am so disapointed. I lose my light, hope and enjoyment of the life.

I can not help to send away the sadness from my life.

I never go out to the town. always keep myself in the studio.

However, the life is tragedy itself. Can't be helped.

Pleas write to me often, will you? You can't imagine how much your letter would please me. I read it as if a hunger stand front of a dinner table.

By, By,
yours ever
Tami

Rememberence to Mrs. Pound.

21: *Tami Koumé to Ezra and Dorothy Pound*
APCS-1   [n. p.] 1 January 1919

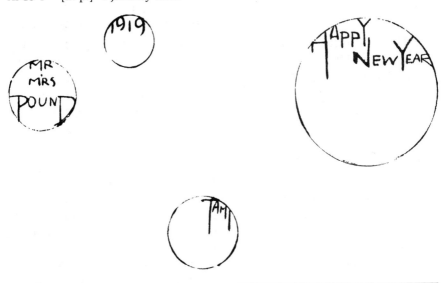

22: *Michio Ito to Ezra Pound*
TLS-3   Michio Itow's School, 121 West 83rd Street, New York City. 19 December 1920

Dear Ezra:

Forgive me, I have been neglected for many years to write to you. I hope you are quite well. I do not know, how to begin this letter, it's already four years, since I left from you, there is thousand things happened to me during these years, and I should like to tell you all about it, but, it's impossible to write.

Since I came to New York, there were many peoples who asked me to perform "Noh drama" to the American public, but I hesitated to do this, on account of my imperfect English, as I find the real value of "Noh Drama" would be lost to the western public, if performed in the Japanese language; also, I did not find any actors or musicians who has suitable training to take part in this kind of drama; for these reasons I could not perform this before. Two years ago, I started my school here in New York, with an idea to make dancer as an artist. Through study with my pupils, I find a strong possibility to carry out "the Noh drama's movement," for the Western stage, as the Universal drama.

So, last summer I took twenty-five pupils, and went in a mountain in East Stroudsburg, PA. and we worked very hard on the Noh drama. Of course, your book "NOH" I had always in my hand.

We stayed two months in the mountain, we were very pleased with our study. Beginning of October, we came back to New York, then, I picked out fifteen pupils from my school and formed a group of players, we have no name yet, because our idea in forming this group is not [to] copy or imitate the Japanese Noh drama or Greek drama, we are going to produce modern drama, on the same foundation as the Greek drama and Noh drama, our production will belong to the universe.

Our players production is not for the momentary art, we want to build up play which will last forever: so we will work on the one drama until so durable, that our production would be beyond criticism and would have to be what they assert the Japanese Noh drama to be FOR ALL TIME.

Our fifteen players are studying English diction and chanting, Dalcroze Eurhythmics for training of Rhythm and *solfège* (ear training) and dancing as material foundation, so we are all musicians, actors, chorus, we hope that in the future we will become as professional actors. First, we did not wish to perform our study before public during period of our studies, but as we need money so badly for our studies, so we are planning to give our first performance about end of January 1921. I am going to give program of three Japanese Noh drama and one Kyogen.

The program will be:

SHOJO   KAGEKIYO   HAGOROMO   BUSU

The above three Noh drama, I should like to use from your book. Will you allow us to use them? My plan is going to perform twice in a week, about four weeks. Also I am planning [to] go back to Japan with my players, next summer, and we will stay in Japan three months. And next winter I am hoping to go back [to] England.

Fortunately I received sixteen old Japanese Noh masks, from Noh actors, and also Tami Koumé is here in New York at present helping me every day. We hope you are here. Tami will tell you all about my plan. I wonder, where is Mr. Yeats, will you please tell him, that very soon Itow will be ready at his service.

Please kind regard to Mrs. Pound, Mr. & Mrs. Dulac, and Mr. & Mrs. Yeats.

Ever Yours
Michio

TULLE LINDAHL — TOSHI KOMORI

MICHIO ITOW

IN A SECOND SERIES OF RECITALS
AT THE

GREENWICH VILLAGE THEATRE
7th AVE & 4th STREET — SUNDAY NIGHTS - APRIL 7-14-21
TICKETS NOW ON SALE — TELEPHONE SPRING 6409

ENTIRE NEW PROGRAM

23: *Tami Koumé to Ezra Pound*
ALS-2   33 West 67, New York 21 January 1921

My dear Ezra,

I have expected your letter everyday. What have you been doing over there? where are you now, please tell me. I am awfully sorry I lost the chance to meet you in London. But I shall come to Paris about March. So please let me know your address. My exhibition in New York will commencing from 1st of February until 12th. And then I want exhibit at Paris for announce to public of my new art. And I need your help great deal. If possible I want you to ask arrange the best gallery for that purpose. And some articles for my art. I will send to you some critics of New York art world. But I am afraid they will hardly understand as my art come from essence of Buddism "ZEN." And its so far from such a materialistic New York people. And I want your help to explain this to Parisian. They have more quality in that way. I think my art will be talked about by next week's papers. I will send them to you. And I will send cable, as soon as I shall settle up when I leave here for London. I can stay very short in France so I want [to] arrange for my exhibition before I shall arrive at Paris. Please let me know whether you could do this or not. Itow will go to Japan for his production by Jan. And I must go with him. And if you should manage I hope you will come to Japan with us. For the travelling in peace, I think either Itow's Company or myself could do it for you. Simply I want to know if you have the idea of going to Japan or not. Please write to me soon for all these questions. will write again soon.   Love

from Tami

24: *Tami Koumé to Ezra Pound*
TLS-1   New York 10 March 1921

My dear Ezra,

POEMS

> MAN who has no shape and
> shadow
> To draw water from a well
> When the water has a ripple
> The well which has never been
> created.

> WHEN I listen to the silent
> Caws of crows in the dark night,
> Much beloved of my parents
> Beyond my existence.

> WHAT you call the soul
> Is!
> Hearing the inaudible voice
> From the picture of DORIAN GREY.

Tami Koumé

25: *Tami Koumé to Ezra Pound*
ALS-3   33 W. 67 [New York] 11 April 1921

Dearest Ezra,

Thank you so much for your letter. ZEN means nothing! & everything. without bodily experience. ZEN is nothing. How could I explain this nothing by our inperfect language!! However! I am not ZEN monk. I do not care what it would be.

I suppose it was my fault that I have written the essay of my art. There is no ratiocination nor logic in my art. However, I feel the most spiritual art in west is far [more] materialistic than most material art in Japan. I do not know about Kandinsky. . . . News Paper in New York spent quite large space for me. But I do not know how far they would understand me!

I think I will sail for my home land, as I realized. Most spiritual work of art is appreciated in *spiritual country*.

I am sorry I could not send to you, copy of paper's critic, as I have none.

I have some Japanese papers although! May call me genious but they won't interest you any bit!

Well Dear Ezra.

How it would be lovely when we should meet again, some where on this earth.

Write to me again. Best wishes to your wife.

Ever
Tami

26: *Tami Koumé to Ezra Pound*
ALS-2   [n. p.] 1 January 1922

Dear Ezra,

Presence of New Year. Towards nearer to the next existence. We have to work hard. How are you since? last when I saw you on the street? How is Mrs Pound? Please send my greeting of New Year to her.

How is M. Picabia at the hospital? I know him by his work. Promoteur of Dada, isn't he?

We are standing (*M. Picabia et moi*) absolutely other side spiritual (This distance is quite near) material yet. We are quite near.

Especially against to the old *past* art we are the same apostle. I probably like to meet him if you will kindly introduce me. Let me come and see you one morning of this week.

Love
Tami

27: *Card for exhibition of paintings by Tami Koumé*
TC-1   [1922]

Mr. **EZRA POUND** Mr. **TAMI**

KOUMÉ AND CAPT. **J. BRINKLEY**

INVITE YOU TO TEA AT Mr **POUND'S**

STUDIO.

70BIS, RUE NOTRE-DAME-DES-CHAMPS

On Tuesday July 11th From 3-6.

TO SEE SOME PAINTINGS BY.

TAMI KOUMÉ

28: *Tami Koumé to Ezra Pound*
ALS-1   [n. p.] [n. d.]

Dear Ezra,

So sorry found you out.

1. I am engaged with *Mlle.* Lazarus whom you know. 2. will exhibit pictures soon. Can I come to fetch the picture tomorrow morning?

with Love
Tami

29: *Tami Koumé to Ezra Pound*
ALS-2   Chez M. Lazarus, La Chaumière Landemer par Nacqueville Manche.
Wednesday [n. d.]

Ezra,

So sorry for my long silence, hope that you are quite fit. I am awfully sorry that I could not come the other evening. Do forgive me. I left Paris last Thursday and come here. and breathing lot of sea air. Setting very much better health now. Not having single faint but eat much meals. Here I enclose the photo of the other evening, not good, but still can you amuse, I believe. And I will enclose the photo of the picture as well, expecting your "Terrible critic"?!

I will be back to Paris on Thursday week. I will come and see you as soon as get back.

With Love
Tami

P.S. If you think this photo will be all right, I will print more.

30: Tami Koumé to Ezra Pound
ALS-5   Saigon. 24 Mars 1923

My dear Ezra,

It seems ages since I saw you last, on the evening before your departure for Italie. How did you enjoy your voyage? As for myself, I left France 23rd Feb. And now I am on way back to Nippon. After a fortnight I shall be [in] the Country of cherry blossom. I shall not stay there long. However, I will try my best and will manage my affairs. at the same time I will [talk to] some people of Gakushuin or University for to find you [a] situation. I hope I could do something for you. Anyway I will try my best.

Now, my dear old friend! I must tell you about my fiancée. Tell you the truth, I love her very much now. It seems very unnatural for me not to marry with her. So I decided to marry with her. At last, I have to marry!

Denise, she is not very pretty. However, I am sure she will help my art. She is an artist and she has a sentiment. She is very good hearted. I am sure you will like her, as you do like me, after you shall know her a little more.

I strongly hope that you will be glad for my marriage. Toshi is in Paris.

Very unfortunately we could not marry each other. We have a reason that we cannot go cn together.

Toshi and Denise know each other. They have understanding. I have nothing to keep secret with them.

I went very often to Miss Barney after you've left Paris. She is very good. I like her very much. I am going to send three hundreds of lanterns from Japan, as we are going to have Japanese party. what can I bring for you? Just write to me, in care of my secretary c/o Kawakami, 44 Matsumoto cho, Shiba Tokio.

Well, my dear old thing I have to stop now. I will let you know about Gakushuin as soon as I shall get some informations.

Please send my best wishes and hearty love to madame. I might not write often from Japan as I shall stay there only six weeks and shall be very much busy.

> with Love
> Yours Ever
> *Tami*

II   POUND / KITASONO CORRESPONDENCE: 1936–66

IN THIS SECTION are collected fifty letters of Ezra Pound to Katue Kitasono, a Japanese avant-garde poet, and thirty-four letters of Kitasono to Pound, exchanged over the period 1936–66. It also contains one letter from Kitasono's VOU Club members to Pound; one letter of Pound to the Japanese Ambassador in Italy; one letter of Pound to Yasotarō Mōri, the editor of the *Japan Times* whom Kitasono introduced to Pound; one letter of Mōri to Pound; one letter of Fosco Maraini, an Italian art historian and anthropologist in Japan, to Ezra Pound; one letter of Ezra Pound to Maraini; one letter of Dorothy Pound to Kitasono; eight letters of Kitasono to Dorothy Pound; one letter of Shōtarō Oshima to Pound; and three letters of Kitasono to Maria Pound (later Mary de Rachewiltz).

Katue Kitasono (1902–78) was one of the most important Modernist poets in Japan. He was also known as a vigorous avant-garde literary critic, versatile essayist, haiku poet, book designer and painter. About the time he began writing poetry, he was much influenced by contemporary Western schools of thought: Futurism, Cubism, Expressionism and Dadaism, and in 1924 he started as co-editor, a little magazine, **GE GJMGJGAM PRRR GJMGEM,** which continued its publication for two years. In December 1927, Kitasono, according to John Solt, wrote a note on surrealism with two other poets in Japan; published on January 1, 1928, it is considered as "the declaration of surrealism in Japan" (Yasuo Fujitomi). About this time, according to Kikyo Sasaki, he began using the pen name "Katue Kitasono," his real name being Kenkichi Hashimoto. He published his first book of poems, *White Album,* in 1929, which includes "Semiotics":

white plates	prism architecture	evening dress
flowers	white animals	evening dress
spoons	space	evening dress
3 p.m. in spring		evening dress
white	blue flag	evening dress
white	apple and lady	uninteresting
red	white scene	

In 1931 he started another poetry magazine, *White Paper,* but he changed its title to *Madame Blanche* in 1932 when he organized the "Arcueil Club" (after Erik Satie) and decided the Club should publish the magazine. In 1933 he published two books of poetry, *Ma Petite Maison* and *Conical*

Poetry. He also published a book of criticism, *Heaven's Glove*, and a book of translations (of poems by Paul Eluard), *Les Petites Justes* in the same year.

In 1935 he began working at the Library of Japan Dental University where he was to work until retirement. In the same year he organized the "VOU Club," started the widely-known avant-garde magazine **VOU** (pronounced "vow"), and continued to edit it until his death. Before he began his correspondence with Pound, Kitasono was already an established poet in Japan. He had been familiar with Imagist poetry and its traces can be found in such a poem as "Shower":

> Apollo is again running from the sea
> His harp of rain glittering—
> My friend
> Evening glow is pooled in a shell

He continued to write poetry vigorously all through his life. His poetry in later years is sometimes tenderly lyrical, sometimes extremely abstract and close to geometry, and sometimes humorously "concrete."

When he first wrote to Pound, the latter quickly responded: "Two things I should do before I die, and they are to contrive a better understanding between the U.S.A. and Japan, and between Italy and Japan." Pound introduced Kitasono and other Japanese poets to Western readers, and Kitasono reciprocated, introducing Pound to Japanese readers. When Pound's literary outlet had become limited due to the approaching war, Kitasono arranged for him to publish articles in Japanese newspapers. (See Part IV.)

Through the *Japan Times and Mail*, to which Pound subscribed, Pound was able to obtain information about Japan and the world at large. "*J.T.* my last remaining source of information re/ the U/S," Pound wrote on October 29, 1940. How this affected his thought, writing and broadcasting would be worth serious investigation. Further information on Kitasono is available in Kikyo Sasaki, *Katue Kitasono and Modernist Magazines* (Tokyo: Press Biblioman, 1981) and Yasuo Fujitomi, *Katue Kitasono: A Biographical Study* (Tokyo: Yūseido, 1983); *see also Plastic Poems: Kitasono Katue and the VOU Group* (Museum of Art, Rhode Island School of Design, 1986). [The publication of John Solt's study of Kitasono is eagerly awaited.]

31: *Katue Kitasono to Ezra Pound*
TLS-2   No. 1649, Nishi l-chome, Magomemachi, Omori-ku, Tokio. Japan. 26
April 1936

Dear Sir,

You will please excuse me that I take the liberty of writing you. For a
long time, since Imagism movement, we have always expected you as a
leader on new literature. Especially your profound appreciation in the
Chinese literature and the Japanese literature has greatly pleased us.

Last year, we established "VOU Club" and have continued our lively
strife for the newest art. Now the existence of our group has come to be
attentively watched by the younger generations of this country.

We started from Dada and passed Surrealism. And at present we are
connected with no "-ism" of Europe. Under the close influence of contemporary architecture and technology, we are making progress in our theory
on art and are forming a characteristic form of ourselves.

"VOU Club" consists of poets, artists, composers, architects and technologists. The members are now twenty one, two-third of them being poets.

I send you two copies of our review **VOU** under separate cover. I shall
be very much obliged if you will kindly make some ideas of our group by
them.

Hoping you will receive this letter as soon as possible.

I remain,
Yours truly,
Katue Kitasono

32: Ezra Pound to Katue Kitasono
TLS-2   On stationery imprinted: Anno XIV 1936, Via Marsala 12-5, Rapallo,
with Gaudier-Brzeska profile head. 24 May 1936

Dear Mr Katue

Thank you for your friendly letter of April 26.

You must not run away with the idea that I really know enough to
read Japanese, or that I can do more than spell out ideograms VERY slowly with a dictionary.

I had all Fenollosa's notes, and the results of what he had learned
from Umewaka Minoru, Dr. Mori, Dr. Ariga. But since Tami Koumé was

killed in that earth quake I have had no one to explain the obscure passages or fill up the enormous gaps of my IGNORANCE.

Had Tami lived I might have come to Tokio. It is one thing to live
on the sea coast and another to have traveling expenses.

Your magazine will, I suppose, arrive in due time. Printed matter
takes longer than letters.

Your technologists can perhaps follow what people suppose,
WRONGLY, to be no fit subject for a poet (despite Dante, Shakespear, and
various other excellent writers who have understood why a poet can not
neglect ethics, and why an ethic which is afraid of analyzing the motives
of actions is very poor sham).

I believe C. H. Douglas' writings are known in Tokio. I wonder
whether Gesell is yet known there?

Two things I should do before I die, and they are to contrive a better
understanding between the U.S.A. and Japan, and between Italy and
Japan.

And this line of action I should always be glad to discuss with
any traveling student, or any official who came through Rapallo or
whom I could meet in Rome or Venice.

Surrealism existed in Italy (though I think the young frenchmen do
not in the least know it) in ⟨a.d.⟩ 1290, and Cavalcanti was certainly surrealist.

And if ⟨some of⟩ the Noh plays are not surrealist in the best sense,
I shd. welcome a statement as to what they shd. be called.

I am sending you my *Cavalcanti*. I wonder whether my *ABC of
Reading* has yet got to Japan.

May the club, whatever the number of its members, stay 21 years young.

very truly yours
Ezra Pound

33: *Katue Kitasono to Ezra Pound*
TLS-2   [n. p.] [17 July 1936]

Dear Mr. E. Pound,

Many thanks for your kindly letter of May 24, and your wonderful work
Cavalcanti. They were brought to my Mediterranean blue desk, passing
through the garden where smell sweet the white flowers of Gardenia.

I cannot do more than spell out Italian very slowly with a dictionary as well as you cannot do more than on Japanese. But I hope you would never give up your interest and love over Japanese as I should never be desperated of Italian.

It is a great regret that I have no more knowledge of *Noh* than an ordinary Japanese. I think you have a better appreciation of it than I. Though I may not be able to become a good assistant, for you, like Tami Koumé of whom I don't know at all, I should be happy to be of service to you for your study.

I am pleased with your idea of our technologists and a poet. Our technologists follow what people suppose to be no fit subject for a poet, and our poets give up over what people suppose, wrongly, to be a fit subject for a poet.

In Japan, there are very few who know about Mr. C. H. Douglas' writings, and Mr. Gesell is not known here.

I express my respect and gratitude for your great idea to establish a better understanding between Japan and the U.S.A., and between Japan and Italy. Please let me know any proper method about it if you have.

I will tell your kindly will to any Japanese student or any official who will travel in Italy.

Cavalcanti is known very little in Japan. But through your translation and your interesting essays I could have some idea about this great poet. Your *Cavalcanti* will lead me to understand the strange and wonderful Mediævalism in Italy.

I have already read your *ABC of Reading*, and a poetess of our club is now reading it, very interested. Surely it is the best pioneer to show young poets their right course to follow.

In the end of May, Mr. Jean Cocteau passed Japan. He was not as a poet, but an ordinary tourist.

I send you my poetical work *Kon* which means an imaginary gigantic fish. I intended, in each poem, to express the classical atmosphere of Tea Ceremony and Zen, the "L'ESPRIT du JAPON." I made only one hundred copies to give them to my most intimate friends.

All the members of our club are very happy with your friendship. At present those who live in Tokio signed for you to show their gratitude.

I remain,
Yours very sincerely,
Kitasono Katue

34: *Katue Kitasono to Ezra Pound*
TLS-1   [n. p.] 17 July 1936

Dear Mr. Ezra Pound,

We greet you with our deepest thanks for your sending us your beautiful book. How glad we were when we saw your splendid work. Mr. Katue Kitasono has shown your friendly letter to all of us.

We, the Japanese younger generation, heartily wish to success in our work, staying always at the twenty-one years old, as you hoped us in your letter.

Thank you again for your present.

Yours truly,

Minoru Nakahara
Katue Kitasono
Shozo Iwamoto
Soko Yoshida   *Akiko Ema*
Shuichi Nagayasu   *Haruki Sou*
M. Yasoshima   *Takeshi Fuji*
Itiro Isida   *Chio Nakamura*

35: *Ezra Pound to Katue Kitasono*
ALS-3   Siena. 12 August 1936 [Anno XIV]

Dear Mr Katue
        And friends.

Thank you for your two letters. I have come here for the Palio, one of the last ceremonies left in Europe—a horse race with banners & memories. And not having a typewriter with me, I shall answer as briefly as possible.

I. For an understanding, the first moves toward communication could be to send any traveling friends to me.

II. Let the Japanese legation in Rome have my Rapallo address or arrange for me to call there when I next go to Rome.

III. Print a few lines of french or english in your magazine giving such news as you want a few european & american poets to get.

Last year Izzo & Camerino of Venice, Bunting then in the Canary Islands, Laughlin & Zukofsky in the U.S., Angold & a welsh scholar in

England thought they could communicate by circular letter about verse technique, all of them knowing several languages, but alas none of them either Japanese or Chinese ideogram. Bunting writes a beautiful hand in Persian.

IV. I remember that Mr. Yeats was invited to Tokyo university some years ago, but I think he declined the invitation.—

Since then several English writers have lectured there, but none of them has been a poet of first rank, so far as I remember.

This is the only town where I have ever been able to live in a palace with a painted ceiling. With a pine tree and the cornice of a renaissance church under this window.

> Cordially.
> EZRA
> Pound

36: *Ezra Pound to Katue Kitasono*
ALS-4   Siena. [13 August 1936]

Dear Mr Katue

Continuing yesterday's letter.
you will not think me unappreciative of Zen if you see my edition of Noh plays & Tami Koumé in 1922 was already dreaming of the incidence of Zen in abstract art.

But neither Zen nor Christianity can serve toward international understanding in practical action in the way the *Ta Hio* of Kung fu Tseu can.

I mean that gives us a basis of ethics & of national action, (patriotic) which does not produce international discord.

Do you know anything of a new international confucianist association? (I have not the Japanese addresses with me here in Siena.)

To save time I am asking this question (in ink, without waiting to get to a typewriter) to the **eleven** poets of Tokio. Also note the new phase of Italian fascism (not the externals).

The first fascists consecrated themselves to the regeneration of Italy.

The latest developments are

1. Bank reform. (money controlled by the nation not by financial bandits.)

2. Wheat law. (just price of wheat.)
3. This week the raise in wages for several million workers.

The reasons for Italo-Japanese understanding lie deep, (notice even the postage stamp which commemorates the 2000th anniversary of the roman poet Horace.)—(Orazio). The span to America may be longer. But Italy can serve as middle.

This I tried to indicate in my *Jefferson and/or Mussolini*. I will try to keep from writing any more until I get to Venice and a means of being more legible.

Yours
Ezra Pound

37: *Katue Kitasono to Ezra Pound*
TLS-3   1649 Nishi 1-chome, Magomemachi, Omori, Tokio, Japan. 7 November 1936

Dear Mr. E. Pound,

Excuse me for my long silence since I received your two letters from Siena. I have never forgotten you, but it was from two reasons, first that I was too busy in my business at the library of the Nippon Dental College, and secondly that I wanted to introduce you in the best way to the Japanese legation in Rome.

The other day I called Mr. Ken Yanagisawa who is a powerful official of the Department of Foreign Affairs, and he himself an intellectual good poet. He willingly promised me that he would immediately arrange to introduce you to the Japanese legation in Rome. Therefore, the letter of introduction will reach Italy almost at the same time with this letter, and I hope this will come to be an opportunity to you and us Japanese to come nearer with each other.

Has our magazine **VOU** 13 arrived at you? Following your advice I added certain lines in English, and I want to print some news in English or French hereafter.

It is our sorrow that, as you mentioned in your letter, we have not any foreign poet of first rank in Tokio, and therefore we desire eagerly to communicate with European and American poets, and if possible, to exchange magazines. Though our ideography and idiom is a great obstruction, we will try hard for their appreciating us. Will you please let us know some good magazines of poems?

Very interested, I translated your "Mediævalism," and published it in our magazine. We shall be very much pleased, if we can have your latest poetical work or some writings for our magazine.

Have you returned from your travel already? What a charm! a painted ceiling, a pine tree, and the cornice of a renaissance church.

Now it is fall in Tokio. The sky is crystalline, blue. The cold wind makes a mosaic of yellow leaves and Ford on the pavement of *Ginza*.

I am trying to write a poem of steel-like strength by combinating bombard **UNKER** no. 17 and pendant of Bopoto.

Yours sincerely,
Katue Kitasono

38: Ezra Pound to Katue Kitasono
TLS-2   On stationery imprinted: Anno XV 1936, Via Marsala 12-5, Rapallo, with Gaudier-Brzeska profile head. 24 November 1936

Dear Mr Katue

In haste//

I am asking Laughlin to send you his anthology
New Directions.

You might send him the **VOU** containing "Mediævalism"
    marking the page/
also send it to Alberto Carocci,
        La Riforma Letteraria
            via XX Settembre 28
                    Firenze, Italy
marking the PAGE in red/ and
the cover "*vide* Cavalcanti"
so that his Italian eye will be awakened to what it is about.

Could you send me a short article in English, giving a paragraph to each of the poets who signed that group letter to me. Saying plainly who they are, one by one, and whether they have common aim, or have signed any very brief manifesto, ⟨also paragraph or so about chief writers not in **VOU** group⟩

And then the individual differences.

I should also like a couple of poems from each WITH an english translation, but sending also the ideograms of the original, with a comment on
the important ones, so that I could emend or intensify the translation if I
saw a way of doing so.

I think I could print such an article and that Laughlin could probably
reprint it in his next year's collection.

We could call it Tokio 1937

but the Japanese date should be given first.

Tokio in the . . . . year of . . . .
1937.

as I give the Italian Era Fascista XV and the old style 1936 on my
stationery.

This would at least help us (over here) to get better acquainted with
VOUtai and who sings or paints.

I am asking W. C. Williams and Laughlin to sign a group greeting from
America.

Is an UNKER a JUNKER airplane? ⟨or different kind?⟩

from
Ez" Po"
⟨debased form of Rihaku⟩
Con espressioni di alta stima

39: *Ezra Pound to Japanese Ambassador in Rome*
TLS-1   Hotel Italia, via Quattro Fontane, Roma. 26 December 1936

His Excellency the Japanese Ambassador, Roma
Eccellenza

      If a letter from Mr. Ken Yanagisawa has reached Your Ex-
cellency, or one of yr/ staff I need only say that I am in Rome and at
Your service.

      If no such letter has arrived, I should, nevertheless be very
glad to meet any member of the Embassy who recollects Umewaka
Minoru or Ernest Fenollosa (whose papers and studies of the Noh, I have

done my best to edit) or anyone who is interested in improving the understanding of Japanese culture in Europe and America and arranging better methods for mutual cultural comprehension.

> con espressioni di alta stima
> Ezra Pound

I shall be in Rome at above address until Wednesday the 30th of this month.

40: Ezra Pound to Katue Kitasono
TLS-1   On stationery imprinted: 1937 Anno XV, Via Marsala 12-5, Rapallo, with quotes: "A tax is not a share" and "A nation need not and should not pay rent for its own credit," and griffon design. 1 January 1937

Dear Mr. Kitasono K/   Happy New Year

Thank you for yr/ Xmas greeting.
Please thank Mr. Yanagisawa for his letter to Rome. I came back here yesterday. In Rome I had a three hour talk with Mr. Hajime Matsumiya, Councillor of the Embassy. He has done book in English on Japanese poetry, which I shall try to have published in England.

I think we got as far as two strangers could get in one interview. Naturally we had too many things to discuss to do anything very thoroughly. I shall send him my *ABC* and perhaps he will approve of it as a text book to introduce Japanese students to western literature.

Or perhaps we shd/ work out a bilingual edition? or at least have a Japanese introduction to emphasize certain omissions.

The *ABC* takes Shakespeare for granted but anyone starting free from present Western school training might not know that I have neglected certain authors in the *ABC* because they are already over emphasized, or obscure other elements.

Will you please call Mr. Yanagisawa's attention to
> *A New American History*
> by W. E. Woodward.

pub/ Farrar and Rinehart. New York.

This is the first general history ⟨of the U.S.A.⟩ with the new historic consciousness. It wd. be a great joke if you started using it in your schools and giving a better teaching of U.S. history than is given in American schools.

The book is just out (not perfect, but contains a great deal of truth not easily available elsewhere in so short a compass).

Cordially
Ez
Pound

41: *Ezra Pound to Katue Kitasono*

TLS-1   On stationery imprinted: 1937 Anno XV, Via Marsala 12-5, Rapallo, with quotes: "A tax is not a share" and "A nation need not and should not pay rent for its own credit," and griffon design. 29 January 1937

Dear Mr. Katue

Here is the description of the first television transmission of *Suma Genji*, from my version based on Fenollosa's notes and study.

You will see that the Dancer enjoyed the play, however transmuted,

and that at any rate some of the Beauty has been brought over to the occident.

ever yours
Ezra Pound

42: Katue Kitasono to Ezra Pound

TLS-2   1649 Nishi 1-Chome, Magomemachi, Tokio, Japan. 30 January [1937]

Dear Mr. Ezra POUND,

I am very much obliged to you for your two letters of 24 Nov. 1936, 1 Jan. 1937, and sending me your brilliant four books.

By the *Active Anthology* I can know accurately about the contemporary poets of an activity and further development. I find them also writing actively in the *New Directions* which Mr. James Laughlin iv sent me by your request.

The critical essays *Make it New* promise to make me aware of the essential values of European literature.

It is delightful to us Orientals that such splendid books like *The Chinese Written Character* and *Ta Hio* were brought out to the world. I am going to write an introductory essay on these books.

A great excitement and encouragement to us that the English translation of our poems may be printed by your kindness. I don't know how far we
can succeed, but we do our best. They will be soon sent to you.

The other day I received from Mr. D. C. Fox *Das Urbild, Die Umschau*
and a pamphlet on Frobenius' *Paideuma*, the last of them, one of the
members of our club is now very interested translating to print in **VOU** no.
16.

Bopoto is the name of natives living in west Africa. I wrote it without a
deep meaning.

Please excuse the misprint of *Junker.*

I am pleasant to hear of the interview of you and Mr. Hajime Matsumiya
in Rome. I don't know Mr. H. Matsumiya at all but I wish his book will be
published in England.

Mr. Yanagisawa has gone to Belgique for his new post in the Embassy. I
hope you will meet him someday.

As soon as I find a proper person, I will introduce him [to] *A New
American History.*

I think in Japan those who read the *ABC of Reading* have already got the
outline of the Western literature, and they cannot misunderstand the omissions in the *ABC.*

I enjoyed your beautiful letter paper. The white 日本 in the white
paper.

Please send my good wishes to Mr. D. C. Fox, Mr. J. Laughlin IV, and Mr.
H. Matsumiya at your convenience.

> Yours very sincerely,
> *Katue Kitasono*

43: Katue Kitasono to Ezra Pound
TLS-2   [n. p.]   26 February 1937

Dear Mr. Ezra POUND,

Thank you for your letter and the description of *Suma Genji.* By Miss
Margaret Lenoa's detailed letter I could imagine, very well, the stage of it. I
think the elegant and mysterious atmosphere of that play was brought
about to tolerable extent, and I express my sincere respect for your eager-
ness and effort to do such a hard task as to reproduce the beauty of the
symbolical *Noh* play. It is a great regret that I cannot see the stills of that
fascinating play, Europeanized and modernized.

I am going to print Miss M. Lenoa's interesting report in **VOU** no. 17. I fear that you may need her letter, so I return it to you.

I have sent you the translation of our poems and my brief note.

We are eagerly looking forward to your views about them.

I am also sending you my first anthology. You will see my portrait about ten years ago. The velvet cap is the same as the uniform cap of *Meierhold* Theater at that time.

Yours sincerely,
Katue Kitasono

Appendix 1

MARCH 13th, 1936

In the night least expected, it sleets
Among pasonia-trees, and
As if to say "You are, prepared like primrose in
    the garden-frame,
Yearning for the green field?"
Such a gentle wind refreshing is born there.

Haruki Sou

Appendix 2

THE WILD LILY

When your awakening spakening sparkles pearly
with the morning dew for necklace,
When like a whiff of Houbigant
Smells your youthful breathing,
I can bear your speckled face.

When you open the curtains green
With the ancient pride slightly betrayed
In your lips obliquely turned, and
Look down the Century for Solomon's glory
In the shady hill-side from your window,
I could knock off your head.

Tuneo Osada

44: Ezra Pound to Katue Kitasono

TLS-2   On stationery imprinted: 1937 Anno XV, Via Marsala 12-5, Rapallo, with quotes: "A tax is not a share" and "A nation need not and should not pay rent for its own credit," and griffon design. 2 March 1937

Dear Mr. Katue

The most galling part of my ignorance at the moment is that I haven't the original text of the *Odes*.

Pauthier was a magnificent scholar, and I have his French to guide me in Kung, *Ta Hio, The Standing Fast in the Middle* and *The Analects*. I have ⟨also⟩ an excellent english crib with notes for these works. But the English version of the *Odes* is intolerable and an old latin one unsatisfactory.

Can you find me a cheap edition? I say cheap, I mean good, and clear but not fancy. If it has a translation into some European language that wd. help, and one wd. need to use the dictionary only for the interesting words.

Tami Koumé had a satisfactory edtn. of the Noh Plays. The kana I can not use/ But I do recognize more ideograms than I did.

Impossible to write ideogram with a Waterman pen. I am doing a little essay, starting my next book with a note on

正 名 and 一 以 貫 之

the first very clear, the latter interesting in its context.

Translations of the *Odes* are so bare one thinks the translator must have missed something, and very annoying not to be able to see WHAT.

With Sordello the fusion of word, sound, movement is so simple one only understands his superiority to other troubadours after having studied Provençal and half forgotten it, and come back to twenty years later.

When I did "Cathay" I had no inkling of the technique of sound which I am now convinced MUST exist or have existed in Chinese poetry.

Does **VOU** include a critique of Japanese past poetry as a whole? A position from which you look at Chinese poetry, Japanese poetry gradually freeing itself from (? or continuing) Chinese, as we continually sprout from or try to cut away from, or reabsorb, resynthesize, greek, latin?

There are here too many questions.

cordially yours
Ezra Pound

45: Ezra Pound to Katue Kitasono

TLS-4   On stationery imprinted: 1937 Anno XV, Via Marsala 12-5, Rapallo, with quotes: "A tax is not a share" and "A nation need not and should not pay rent for its own credit," and griffon design. 11 March 1937

Dear Katue KITASONO

          All right! Kitasono is your family name. We occidentals are very ignorant. You must TELL us, patiently, even these details.

          The poems are splendid, and the first clear lighting for me of what is going on in Japan.

          The NEW Japan. Surrealism without the half-baked ignorance of the French young.

          I shall try the poems on *Globe*. It is not a literary magazine. 新
They have printed me on Edward VIII's abdication, and announce that they will print my note on Roman Empire. Then they say my note on Geneva is "too serious for their readers." That may be because I mentioned George Tinkham, who kept the U.S.A. OUT of that sink of hypocrisy the League of Nations.

          "Uncle George" is crossing the Pacific next summer and I hope you will be able to meet him. He IS the America I was born in, and that may have disappeared ⟨almost⟩ entirely by now.

          My daughter was shocked at his lack of sartorial elegance, (age eleven) but she decided that *"l'uomo più educato"*

          had spent too MUCH time on his face massage etc.

*"l'uomo più educato"*is a S. American more
          or less millionaire fop.
          Excuse this diffuseness ...

I don't KNOW that the *Globe* will print poetry as poetry.

          It is made for the multitude and printed
55,000 copies.

Ronald (no relation of Isadora) Duncan is starting a literary magazine in London. If the *Globe* won't print poems, he will.

          AND the *Globe* may very well be kept OUT of England because I have not put on GLOVES either of antelope skin, emerald or any other material in writing about the swine who are afflicting that country.

SO THAT even if the *Globe* does print the poems, it may be possible and/or necessary to print them in *Townsman* also.

In any case the *Townsman* will want more news of **VOU**.
⟨*Which means plastic poetry singing, or what?*⟩

You have not sent the Ideograms of the poems. And in any case I should
not touch the translations. Though I would like to see the originals if
they are written in ideogram. Perhaps I already have them in **VOU**??

I shall correct only a few typing errors, or what seem such. IF the following errors have been wrongly corrected, will you please write direct to

     J. T. Dunn Esq.

     Globe, 157½ West Fifth St., St. Paul, Minn. U.S.A.

and say that I have asked you to do so.

Dear old Satie lived at **Arc**euil (not Alceuil)

     In Sasajima's poem.

       ?vonarates . . . is this a botanical term

or error for **vene**rates

speady?? steady or speedy

To save time I am sending the manuscript to *Globe*, and

     correcting the words to

     venerates and **ste**ady

Nakamura/ glisling?? I am correcting to glis**ten**ing

     this is pronounced glisning or glissening

     it means shining and shimmering.

KOIKE// I wonder whether he means Aiding or adding or aided.

     I am putting *Aiding* (last line Glassy hour).

Your own Second poem/ line 2. seorn = ? scorn

     Her head (the parrot's) replaced BY a leaden one??? (I don't see how
for will do here.)

     The sailors put a lead head in place of the

     parrot's own??

     or what do you mean?

English is very ambiguous, the typewriter can mean either the *machine à
écrire* or the *dactylo;* the young lady who types.

     packed, makes one think you mean the machine, BUT

     is much nicer verb if you mean the

     "female secretary and TYPIST."

I am leaving TYPEWRITER, but if you want the reader to understand that
you indicate the FEMALE, please write Dunn to change it to TYPIST. Then
the *she* in next line, makes it sure.

These are very nice poems. I am delighted with the lot of them. ⟨*At first*

reading they seem better written than anyone's except some of Cummings.⟩
I don't know whether ⟨*in your own poems*⟩ your inverting the order, verb before noun so often, indicates a difference in your English, or a stylistic difference between you and the others in Japanese.

That was why I wanted the Ideograms of the poems (if they are in ideogram, and not in kana. Kana I can do nothing with YET.) Ideogram I can puzzle out IF I have a crib, as I have Morrison's dictionary.

I sympathize with yr/ reticence in not sending the personal notes. I always hate 'em myself. I mean nothing is worse than having to write and rewrite one's own biography.
BUT as your editor, etc/etc/etc/
                              Can't you write brief notes about each other . . . ?
This is "in order to establish means of communication."

   Cocteau and I have both refused to write autobiographies, and as Jean said, "*Mais, oui*, those books ARE my autobiography."

   That is all very well for poets. But the *Globe* is interested in humanity at low and large.
There is a natural curiosity. . . . It is satisfied in some degree by the *Analects*. Should we be more aloof than Kung. I admit Kung did NOT write the *Analects*. We should wait for disciples to write our *Analects*. . . .
      After 2500 years the *Analects* still serve the *Ta Hio*.

                                                                ever   E.

46: Ezra Pound to Katue Kitasono
ALS-1   Siena. 14 August 1937 ⟨*address Rapallo*⟩

Dearest K. K.

          Duncan delighted with the poems. They will be in first issue of *Townsman* IF it ever gets published.
          I am spending 4 or 5 hours a day on Kung & can read a good deal of ideogram. (say as much as a five year old infant in Japan or China.) If you can't find a copy of the *Odes* with a translation, please let me know the price of a good (not fancy) text in the original—& I will send the money for it. (registered post to Rapallo.)

Sorry to bother but the labour is in a good cause.
Cordial greetings to **VOU** & 8.

> Yours
> *Ezra Pound*

47: Katue Kitasono to Ezra Pound

TLS-2   Magomemachi. 6 September 1937.

Dear Mr. Ezra POUND,

I wish you will be generous to oversee my long abscondence from you for six months.

I have been constantly thinking of you, but I couldn't write.

I received your letters of March 11, August 14, and two pleasant books.

I compared your KUNG FU TSEU with the original, and admired your sensible and relevant translation.

I cannot find out the *Odes* with a translation, therefore I have sent the originals in the accompanying package. They were presented to me before by my Chinese friend, a young poet and they are very excellent books made in China of to-day. I am making them a present to you.

If they aren't the books you need, please let me know the title of the book you want in Chinese ideograms. It will be more convenient to me, because we differ remarkably from the Chinese in pronouncing of the very same ideograms.

Japanese poetry to Chinese can be said just the same with English poetry to Latin or Greek. We are now far apart from Chinese poetry.

I express my sincere gratitude for that you are kindly thinking about our poems.

They send me the *Globe* every number from June. I am going to send you my poetical works *La Lettre d'été*.

I intend to publish another book *The Cactus Irland* within this year.

> Yours very sincerely
> *Katue Kitasono*

48: Ezra Pound to Katue Kitasono
TL-2   On stationery imprinted: Via Marsala 12-5, Rapallo, with
Gaudier-Brzeska profile head. 21 October 1937

K. Kit

Dear Friend at too great a distance
I have at last got back to Rapallo and find four beautiful volumes; which
don't seem to correspond to the latin version of the *Chi King* (sometimes
spelled *Shi King*)   詩 經   經

The *Shi* or *Chi King* I ⟨might⟩ read with the cribs (translations) I have.
The four books you have so kindly sent; I MAY be able to read in time, at
the rate of three lines a day.
they seem to be

MAO	(eyebrow, or kind of bamboo)
SHE	Odes
CH-HÍNG?? 郑	An ancient province as near as Morrison comes to it; with top left hand corner slightly different.
tsëen	To note or write down memoranda.

[*Crossout*: Whether this is a collection sometimes called bamboo grove;
the Lord alone knows.]
Is it a commentary on the *Odes* of CH HING which are Book VII of the
First part of the *Chi King*?
               on the other hand I see something that looks like WIND; foo //
               At any rate it is all very good for my ignorance and will keep
me occupied, and I am very grateful to you for sending it.

I thought I was asking for a book that wd/ be as easy to get in Tokio as
the bible in New York.
Kung fu Tseu refers to it in the *Ta Hio*, and it is continually mentioned
in the *Analects* and in *Mencius* as THE book of poetry.
     Confucius (Kung fu Tseu) anthology that he had selected.

At any rate I seem to discern some kind of preface, then a line of verse
in black type.

Kwan	passing the pass; (or possibly a pun)
Kwan	
Tsheu etc//	water bird or difficult
KEW, congregate	yellow river's course

49: Ezra Pound to Katue Kitasono
TLS-(fragment; probably a continuation of previous letter)

as superior man ⟨or girl⟩ loves (or good)
"right left"
Well, heaven knows MAY BE that idiot Jennings and the good old latin
bloke were working on this poem, calling it song of Chou; the south/
Tcheou Nan.
In which case their translations!!! add to MY confusion.
Nothing to do but keep at it.
I see **VOU** has Hemingway's "They all made peace"
printed at an opportune moment.
                                    I am glad that my country seems at the
moment to be having a little more sense than it had ten days ago. In any
case . . . understanding must come/ but WHEN.
I can't get to Japan unless I get a JOB presumably as professor there
        OR unless I make a great deal of money SOON; that is a great deal
more than I ever have made yet.
Butchart and Duncan keep saying they are going to print *Townsman* and
that it is in the press, and that your poems will be in it.
    PATIENCE . . .
                said to be an oriental virtue. I have used up so large a %
of my own already that I can't speak with authority. Thanks once more. I
will write again as soon as my head is clearer.

                                    yours ever   *Ezra Pound*

50: Ezra Pound to Katue Kitasono
TLS-1   Rapallo. Sometime in October [22?], 1937

Dear K/K

I seem to be finding a clue/ and I THINK the Odes you sent are the ones I wanted.
At least they seem to be arranged thus??????

Introduction:
Long sentence saying what the poem means.
ONE LINE OF POEM and then a commentary
ANOTHER LINE OF POEM then an explanation
AND SO FORTH.

at any rate something seems to fit Jennings' appalling translation. I haven't got much further than identifying a refrain or two.

Townsman announcement very tangled. Duncan trying to condense and merely attaining density.

envelope as a specimen document/ I have sent them your address AGAIN.

ever EP

51: Ezra Pound to Katue Kitasono
TLS-1   On stationery imprinted: Via Marsala 12-5, Rapallo, with Gaudier-Brzeska profile head. 23 October 1937

Dear K/Kit

Your very beautiful book has just come, and I have started TRYING to read it, though some of the type forms are not as in Morrison.

I have also subscribed to the Tokyo Times. In the hope of getting a little English and French news. I wonder if it is Brinkley's old paper? I also wonder if they wd. print my news or interpretations of Europe. Might be a first step toward getting to Tokyo. I think the paper is unlikely to be delivered "in all parts of China" for the next few w..rks, but the rest of their statements seem plausible.

//

The poems LOOK as if you were going in for some extreme form of simplification, at greatest possible remove from Chinese elaboration. NOT
that I have been able to read even a single sentence at sight.

      I take it no one has tried to make poems containing quite so
many simple radicals.

          BUT my ignorance is appalling
and my memory beneath contempt.

                          ever yours
                          E. P.

52: Ezra Pound to Katue Kitasono

TCS-1   Via Marsala 12-5. 28 October 1937

28 Oct. getting on NICELY.

nowt	(old form for nothing, but scans
red	better here.)
not	strikes me as way
fox	poetry can be very nicely written.
nowt	Now that I have found out what is
black	which, and how carefully
not	they count up all the lines in
crow	strophes/ Am going to try
	seriously to understand your book, once I have
	rushed thru the *Odes*

                              ever EP

53: Ezra Pound to Katue Kitasono

TLS-2   On stationery imprinted: Via Marsala 12-5, Rapallo, with
Gaudier-Brzeska profile head. 2 November 1937

Dear K/K

      Here is an article or letter, either ⟨for⟩ Tokio *Times* or for **VOU**.
Not necessary to translate more than the meaning. And that only if you
think there is some USE in doing it.

      I have said "an occidental language" to avoid argument at the
start, but English is indicated for all translation from ideogram

1. because it is richest in monosyllables

2. because it is least cluttered with syntax, and does not therefore put IN such a lot which isn't in ideogram

AND because a literal translation without inflection shocks us less than it wd/ french and Italians

A very skillful translator might get Japanese SOUND into an Italian translation but I know of no one capable of doing it.

The question to Japan is: instead of dumping cheap products which we already have too much of, in the occident, why not send us some cheap books which we NEED

at least a few of us need them very badly and if they were on the market more of us would wake up to the fact that we need them.

the rest of the subject is I hope clear in the enclosed notes.

ever EP

If you translate the article, change anything you feel needs improving.

⟨vide P.S. EP⟩

nowt	莫	nowt	This is my idea of how the
red	赤	black	page should appear.
not	匪	not	The ideograms in one column
fox	狐	crow	the english words to the
nowt	莫		left in next column.
black	黑		
not	匪		
crow	鳥		

The explanatory notes either to one side or, I think better, at the foot of the page.

If one put them at the left they would be confused with the Titles of the Poems.

54: Katue Kitasono to Ezra Pound
TLS-2   [n. p.] 15 November 1937

Dear Mr. Ezra POUND,

How anxiously I was waiting your letter at this too great distance, and your two kindly letters have just arrived at me. I ought to shorten the distance between us which was made by my too long silence.

The four volumes I sent (毛 詩) [*Mao Shih*] are identical with (詩 經) [*Shih ching*].

(毛) means eyebrow or hair as you wrote and (詩) means odes, but in this case (毛) was a family name of a person who lived in province (魯) [Lu] of China in old time. His full name was (毛 亭) [Mao Hêng], and it was by him that the anthology selected by Confucius, that is, (詩 經), was handed down to posterity. Therefore (詩 經) is also called (毛 詩).

It might be economy of time for you that I would translate (詩 經) in English, but I fear if I should deprive of you the pleasure of exploration.

You are not an archæologist, but a great poet, and I will remain an indifferent Japanese.

I am waiting the *Townsman's* appearance with the oriental virtue. My "patience" has not been yet worn out so badly as yours.

I don't know *Tokio Times*. I wonder if it may be a mistake for the *Japan Times* or the *Japan Advertiser*.

I always gape at my too simple letters to you. It is not because that I am "going in for some extreme form of simplification, at greatest possible remove from Chinese elaboration," but because of my poor broken English.

This must be improved as soon as possible.

Your very beautiful stamps entertain me exceedingly.

Yours very sincerely,
Katue Kitasono

55: Katue Kitasono to Ezra Pound
TLS-2   [n. p.] 11 December 1937

Dear Mr. Ezra Pound

I have received your article for *Tokio Times*. I translated it at once in

Japanese and it will soon appear in **VOU** no. 21. I was struck to know how earnestly those highly educated persons as you are wishing to make a special study of the orient. Your method of reading ideograph is very effective, I think.

I can not find out Tokio TIMES even in the largest book seller's in Tokio.

Therefore I asked of my friend Mr. Y. Onishi who is on the editorial staff of the *Japan Advertiser,* one of the leading paper in English, to negotiate with the publisher to put up your news in their paper.

He says that the kind of news is not quite clear, and so it is desirable that you will write about that and your wish for payment (because they cannot receive any copy without payment), and, if possible, some sample pages.

It is more convenient that you will send them directly to the acting publisher and editor, Mr. Wilfrid Fleisher, The Japan Advertiser, 1-chome, Uchi-Yamashita-Cho, Kohjimachi-Ku, Tokio.

And then my friend is going to negotiate well.

X-Mas is at close hand. I have sent you X-Mas Card of "Ukiyoe." This year's one is more beautiful than the last year's, I think.

I wished to send a card also to your daughter in America, but I don't know her address.

Will you please make me a present of your photograph?

> I remain
>> yours very sincerely,
>> Katue Kitasono

56: Katue Kitasono to Ezra Pound
TLS-2   [n. p.] 16 December 1937

Dear Mr. Ezra POUND,

This photo shows Fenollosa's grave, which my friend, a poet living in the neighbourhood of Miidera, took for me.

Fenollosa's grave situated on the hill in the grounds of Hohmyoin in Enjohji which belongs to the head temple Miidera.

There densely grow many old cypresses and maple-trees in the vicinity, and beautiful Lake Biwa can be looked down [on].

Fenollosa's gravestone is seen enclosed by the stone-balustrade.

There is seen, next to Fenollosa's, the grave of Mr. Bigelow who was a man of business and an intimate friend of Fenollosa.

It rather strikes me with sorrow to think of those honourable souls resting on the foreign land.

Mr. and Mrs. Fenollosa had both become believers in Buddhism in Japan.

Fenollosa's Buddhist name is 諦信 (teishin).

Greatness of faith, sadness of faith, you will see, too, both sides in this photo.

Fenollosa may be obliterated from the memories of those diplomats and artists of flurried progress, but he still lives loved and honoured in the hearts of serious Japanese artists and people living near by his grave.

They never forget to visit it occasionally.

I think Japanese culture has much of silver-plated gold.

If it is your desire to publish Fenollosa's notes you have, I will tell it to the Society for International Cultural Relations, though I am not sure that they will consent.

> very sincerely
> YOURS,
> *Katue Kitasono*

57: Ezra Pound to Katue Kitasono

TLS-1   Anno XVI, Via Marsala 12-5, Rapallo, with Gaudier-Brzeska profile
head. 13 January 1938

Dear K/K/

The younger members of the family are more decorative. My
daughter is not in America. In fact I am translating into English a little
book she has written for me in Italian. I think Japanese children might
like it, I mean they could learn what a child of 12 sees in the Tyrol.

I shall send you a copy as soon as I get it clearly typed.

and hope to have more to report in a day or so.

ever   E. P.

58: Ezra Pound to Katue Kitasono

TLS-1   Anno XVI, Via Marsala 12-5, Rapallo, with Gaudier-Brzeska profile
head. 18 January 1938

Dear Kitasono

If the day had 48 hours I might be civil
"if not polite." I was so happy to find the foto of
Fenollosa's tomb in yr/ letter.

Yesterday I saw proofs of *Broletto*
with "The Hand of Summer Writes" printed large and in the original
four ideograms, with the Italian translation of
your manifesto from *Townsman* ⟨*also yr. signature*⟩.

I hope *Townsman* has reached you. I have finished typing
my translation of Maria's booklet, and will send it to you as soon as I
can sew up the pages.

THEN you will see that the occidental hand is rather like a
Japanese FOOT. Neatness we have NOT.

Now we will have a little music ⟨*vide enclosure*⟩/ and then I suppose
I will have proofs of my *Guide*/ and then, may be, I will have time for
decent letter writing.

at any rate I will try to write again before summer autumn
or winter.

ever   EP

59: Katue Kitasono to Ezra Pound
TLS-2   [n. p.] 25 January 1938

Dear Mr. Ezra POUND,

I have just received beautiful *Townsman*. Little did I think our patience should be repayed so brilliantly.

Your very sensible introductory sentences for VOU Club saved us from our deficiency.

Words fail to express my gratitude for your kindness.

VOU no. 21 just finished, a little delayed, will be soon sent to you.

Tokio Poets Club which consists of several groups of poets living in Tokio is to hold the second recitation party on the 29th inst.

On that day some volunteers, Englishman, Frenchman, German, and American, are also to recite poems in each own's language.

Some poems composed by the members are to be sung too.

I am going to read a cheerful essay like a milk-Bottle.

I am trying to translate in English a collection of my brief poems "Cactus Irland," the Japanese one of which is to be published soon.

I shall be very happy if you will read them.

"M. Pom-Pom,"

Very lovely, like a shell-helicopter.

I am swelling like a pine-apple, dreaming the sun and plants of Africa.

very sincerely yours,
Katue Kitasono

60: Ezra Pound to Katue Kitasono
TLS-1   Anno XVI, Via Marsala 12-5, Rapallo, with Gaudier-Brzeska profile head. 7 February 1938

Dear K/K

I hope the rest of this will reach you in time, that is a WHOLE copy of *Broletto*, too busy to explain why this torn page precedes.

at least you will see from this that something is at last getting printed.

E

61: Katue Kitasono to Ezra Pound
TLS-2   [n. p.] 9 February 1938

Dear Mr. Ezra Pound,

Many thanks for your letter and the photos for which I have long been desirous.

I look at your impressive appearance, and find myself in such an atmosphere as floating about the heroes in the book of great Plutarch.

This feeling seems to come of some other reason beyond those realistic reasons that you live in Italy or I respect you.

The lovely girl on the snow makes me smile again and again.

I never imagined the snow in Tyrol should be so grey coloured.

I suppose that probably you pulled the shutter of kodak without taking off your snow-glasses.

The largest one is very picturesque. I like such an antique house and love such a natural garden.

The literary smile in the leaves is more *charmante*.

I am looking forward to your daughter's booklet.

> Very sincerely yours,
> *Katue Kitasono*

62: Ezra Pound to Katue Kitasono
TLS-2   Anno XVI, Via Marsala 12-5, Rapallo, with Gaudier-Brzeska profile head. 9 February 1938

Dear K

Am still too busy to be civil, and politeness floats as a vision/ attainable possibly in April.

Editors of *Broletto* and *Townsman* both here yesterday.
I hope *Broletto* has reached you. Peroni wants more NEWS of Japan. Yr/ photo of Fenollosa's grave came just in time for second issue and has gone to print shop.

//

IMPOSSIBLE to translate Japanese poetry into Italian.
send something in VERY SIMPLE english prose that you, the VOU club might like Italians to know.

if you can.

Townsman wants to print ONE poem each issue (that is every three
months, the best poem of the VOU club/ in the original either reproduc-
ing the original writing, as your signature in *Broletto* or in the beautiful
font of type used in "Summer's Hand Writes"). You can send translation,
but in each case we will want EACH character explained. As in the poem
in my edition of Fenollosa's Chinese written character. ⟨MOON *Rays* etc.⟩

also/ what does **VOU** stand for? telescope word?

. . .

. . . .

月　光耀

UTAI ?? or what

You can choose a Japanese poem; or have the whole club
choose the poem of the season which they think would be most *comprehensible* in the occident.

from editorial view point, it wd/ be preferable that the poem be the season's expression *of the group* of Tokio poets.

That wd/ be better for the bilingual publication/ and if we give a BRIEF
lesson in ideogram in every number of *Townsman*, perhaps a few readers will start learning to read.

English is middle ground/ impossible to translate ideogramic
thought into a language inflected as the latin languages are. I will continue this another day. Our Purcell music has had good press/ and I have
sent back 180 sheets of galley proof to Faber/

so my brevity might be excused.

ever   E

63: Katue Kitasono to Ezra Pound
TLS-2   Tokio, Japan. 16 March 1938

Dear Mr. Ezra Pound,

I have received Miss Maria's Book at last.

Firstly its simple original design by a good papa perfectly attracted me.
No Japanese papa would make such a pleasing booklet for his daughter,
even though he would buy for her an expensive camera or a pretty dress etc.
which could be found easily in any department store.

I have had no idea about Tyrol except forests and shepherds.

This very young lady writer eloquently tells me things in Tirol one by one. I hear her as attentively as she would have been very attentive when she listened to Peter's tales or observed the growth of hay.

She is, too, a very amusing teller.

Now I am translating it into Japanese that children of my country may read it. I fear lest I should fail to preserve the naivety of her literature, that you have done very well.

Broletto had arrived at me before your torn page. It is almost a surprise that I can see my "Letters of Summer" reproduced so gorgeously in that beautiful magazine.

Very grateful for you and Mr. Carlo Peroni.

Now I am writing some news for *Broletto*.

I enclose a poem for *Townsman*. I shall be glad if you will correct the translation suitably.

I don't know at all about the sonatas of Henry Purcell but I can guess the publication of his music will be of deep significance.

Did you explain about music and microphotography at the concert?

I have read "Music and Progress" by Olga Rudge in *Townsman*, and so can get some idea of your lecture.

Yesterday I received *New Directions 37*.

Mr. James Laughlin IV wrote me that he wants to have our poems for his review of 1938.

The word VOU has no meaning as the word DADA.

only a sign, One day I found myself arranging whimsically these three characters on the table of a café.

That's all.

On the 12th, March I went to see Youngmen's *Noh* Plays performed on the stage of Marquis Hosokawa. It was a demonstration of young professional *Noh* players under the support of leading *Noh* players. I enclose the program.

Please give my good wishes to Miss Maria.

Ever yours,
Katue
Kitasono

64: Katue Kitasono to Ezra Pound
TLS-6   [n. p.] 26 March 1938

Explanatory Notes on the Photographs
TACHI (long sword)

These four swords in the photographs are called Tachi, from 70cm. to 90cm. long, chiefly used for fighting.
(4) is also called Efudachi, special in shape, worn by Samurais in court.
(1), (2), (3) are for the usual wear of the general Samurais, also used for fighting, in this case Samurais of high rank hung it level on their sides by the fixings of (4).
The names of these swordsmiths as follows:
1 Ichimonji Yoshihira
2 Tairano Nagamori
3 Nakajima Rai
4 Shikibunojyo Nobukuni

AIKUCHI (short sword)

These three short swords are called Aikuchi, Tanto, and Sasuga, used for self-protection.
Samurai wore it on his side with a long sword, and woman put it in a brocade bag and held between her sashes.
There are many beautiful designs of Aikuchi.
Its length is between 25cm. and 30cm.
1 Insyu Kagenaga
2 Muramasa
3 Hojyu
    These above measurements are only of the blade part, excepting that part in a hilt. They were all made during the years 1100–1400.

Katue Kitasono

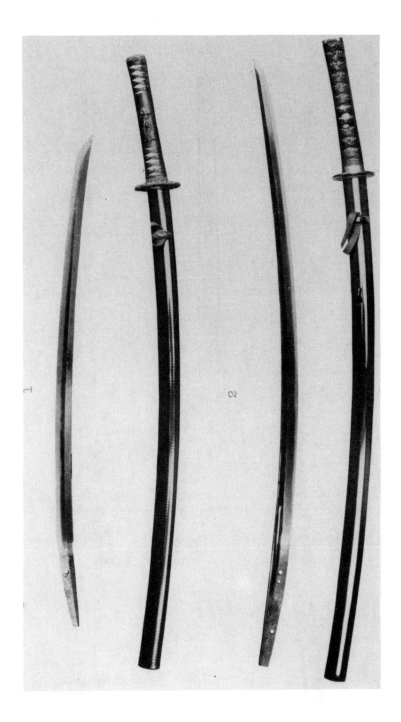

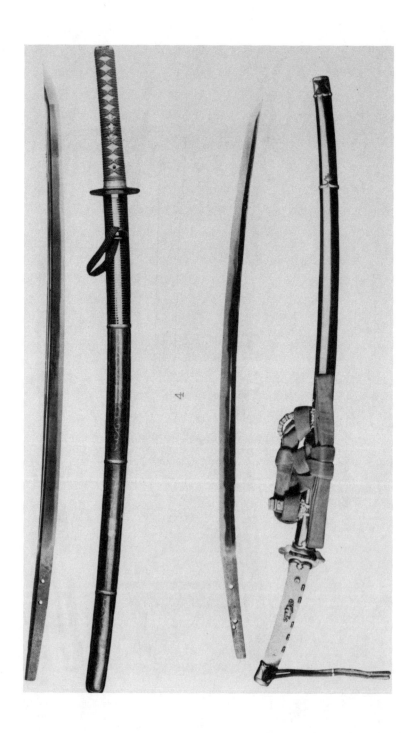

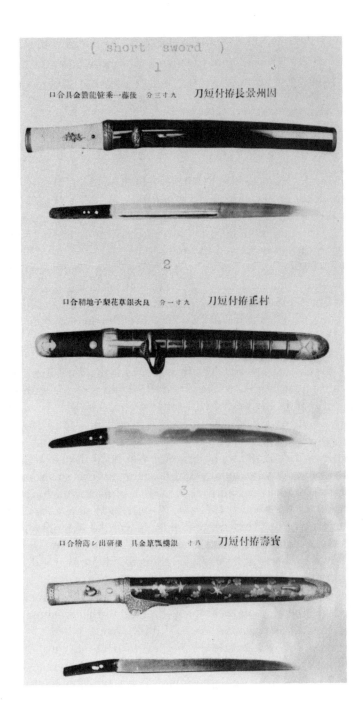

(short sword)

1

口合具金鍔龍笹乗一藤後　大三寸三分　因州景長拵付短刀

2

口合精地子梨花草銀次長　九寸一分　村正拵付短刀

3

口合輪蒔シ出研懐　具金草瓢櫻銀　八寸　賓壽拵付短刀

NIPPONTO

(Japanese Sword)

A brilliant ceremony was held to make a present of Japanese armour and sword to Premier Mussolini, on the 20th March, at Hibiya-Park, Tokio.

At this memorable event, I want to give my views about Nipponto (Japanese sword).

This is at once to tell the Japanese ideas of swords, and at the same time to make clear why we Japanese have presented Nipponto to Premier Mussolini.

At midnight, still and silent, I draw an old sword and fix my eyes on the crystalline blade in the faint light of a candle.

This is the moment I love most, and my head becomes cool and strained. It is in this moment that I feel directly the lives and morals of all the ages our ancestors passed through.

These feelings grow into a praise, adoration, and worship for our ancestors, and Japanese sword symbolizes all of them.

In old times our ancestors kept their faith with swords, which not only chastised one who broke it, but chastised even its owner when he broke it himself. The sword was the last sacred judge.

A Samurai used to say, "I will never do it in the presence of my sword," or "I will do it by my sword." The former means that he will not do such a thing because it is disgrace to his sword (the honour of a Samurai), and the latter that if he fail, his sword will settle the matter (that is, he will die).

Before 1800 the social conditions were still unsafe owing to the incomplete political system. People had to, therefore, protect themselves and their families with weapons among which were swords of excellent quality which they especially longed for. This attachment was so strong that even when to fight a duel, every one took pride in telling the antagonist the name of the maker of his sword. He said, "I will fight you with this sword, Sekinomagoroku," or "This sword, Sekinomagoroku will not forgive you."

Thus the sword was greatly respected, and excellent swords were handed down for generations as heirlooms of the family, and it was very disgraceful and undutiful to one's ancestors to lose them.

Many old Japanese tales consist of various troubles connected with a noted sword. Indeed, Japanese swords brought forth a great many legends and tragedies just as precious stones did in Europe.

It is, therefore, to express one's highest respect that he should make a present of a sword to some person.

At the Restoration of Meiji, the Samurai class was abolished and people were forbidden to wear a sword, but their attachment for swords has never become weak.

Most Japanese take Kendo (Japanese fencing) and Jyudo (Jyujitsu) lessons from primary school to university.

For three weeks in winter and in summer they have especially severe exercises early in the morning, which is the most valiant sight.

In Europe Kendo has not been so widely known as Jyudo, I think, but it is Kendo that shows the mind and the figure of Samurai rather than Jyudo.

When I hold one of the excellent swords handed down from my ancestors, I feel my eyes are not already those of moderns, but of ancients.

I feel the indomitable spirit, fearless of death, of a Spartan fighting man comes to myself.

In conclusion I wish to add that Japan will be prosperous forever as long as Japanese will not lose their faith in the sword.

March 26th, 1938
Katue Kitasono

65: Ezra Pound to Katue Kitasono

TLS-3   Anno XVI, Via Marsala 12-5, Rapallo, with Gaudier-Brzeska profile head. 14 May 1938

Dear K/K/

VOU 22 has come. I am very glad you have selected the vital points so well in the note on me. I learn to read all too slowly: And I forget the ideograms too fast. However I have now the *Li Ki/* as well as the Kung and Mang and the Odes; all with some sort of translation that helps me to practice. Ideogramic dictionary wastes too much time.

The proper way for occidental to learn ideogram is with an interpage or interlinear crib.

Will you write to

Science Service
2101 Constitution Ave
Washington D.C., U.S.A.

for information re/ microfilm reader
and their service.

That ought to accelerate the availability of the 100 best ideogramic and japanese texts IN THE ORIGINAL.

From that we cd/ get on with at least typescript translations. Price of projectors should come down. Do you know, or can you find out what Tokio University has done along these lines?

I am doing what I can to stir up the Washington people both about music study and oriental studies by means of this new system.

It will encourage them to hear from Japan, and of course collaboration between the two governments should follow. Here is a field where there can be no clash of interests, and where better understanding between the two peoples wd/ be automaticly promoted.

Kagekiyo and *Kumasaka* can NOT be boycotted like silk stockings. I hear there is a professor in the University of Formosa whose good offices we might enlist.

When dealing with government departments, it is always well to get someone whose respectability is OFFICIAL.

I believe I am now almost officially respectable because I am part of the Institute of Arts and Letters. But I am not really respectable . . . among the idiots of the more reactionary American universities . . . not yet. Although a very small Western college has at last invited me to profess in the wilderness.

//another point/ you better write to

      Harcourt, Brace and co.

      383 Madison Ave. New York

for review copy of e:e:cummings' *poems.* ⟨*Collected Poems.*⟩ Laughlin will have sent you W. C. Williams' *Life on the Passaic River.* these are the two best American books of the season. We have a couple of good historians. W. E. Woodward, *New American History/* and Claude Bowers' *Tragic Era.* Bowers is now ambassador to Spain.

The University of Tokio and yr/ government departments can certainly afford Argus microfilm reader-projectors.

I don't know what you Japs have done in the way of lense grinding. The Germans will certainly make MUCH CHEAPER projectors soon. Poets etc/ can not afford Argus de luxe microfilm readers. simpler mechanism can be made by almost any good optician, I think. At any rate Fox recommended me to have one made locally.

In any case IF your lense industry isn't developed, you cd/ get German lenses and do the rest as well or better than occidentals.

Delphian Quarterly, 307 North Michigan Ave., Chicago would probably exchange with **VOU**, if you send them current issue of **VOU** and say you wd/ like to see Olga Rudge's article on Vivaldi and my curse on American University torpor.

> there is never time enough to write
> everything in one letter.

ever
Ezra Pound

66: Ezra Pound to Katue Kitasono
TLS-2   Anno XVI, Via Marsala 12-5, Rapallo, with Gaudier-Brzeska profile head. 2 June 1938

Dear Kitasono

I don't yet know enough to deal properly with the rest of Fenollosa's notes. I have a good translation of the *Li Ki* (Bk of Ceremonies, with the original text, french and latin).
I am in the middle of de Mailla's *Histoire Générale de la Chine/* translation of *Tong Kien Kang Mou/* but only in french; not printed with the original.
Do you know of any ⟨good⟩ History of Japan, translated into any european language FROM original sources?
//
I have found mention of the "Ti-san" sort of notes left by Emperor Tai-tsong/ Tang a.d. 648, for his son.

> I am trying to think out the "100 best books" for proper
Ideogramic library/
> Possibly this ought to be one of them?
If it still exists.

> The first government note (state ticket not bank note) that I
have yet found record of is of Kao tsong 650/ but the form already developed, so I suppose Tai tsong knew the system. Sane economics. very interesting.

BUT all this is Chinese/ Whether de Mailla gets round to notice of intercourse with Japan later, I dont know. At least by 800 a.d. there ought to be Japanese records// in detail/

> What sort of Japanese history do you people get in schools?

Also Japanese poetry before the Noh? Another awful blank in my acquaintance.

Prof. Mori seems to have treated the literature (or Fenol/ has left notes showing)

> Chinese poetry/
> ///// Noh ⟨2 vols of Japanese short poems.⟩

and a lot of notes in which the chronology isn't very clear.

Mr. Matsumiya hasn't sent on his typescript/ I think he is worrying too much about getting it entirely free from small defects of english.//

> Pardon brevity/

E. P.

———

⟨Tai tsong very respectable emperor.⟩

67: Ezra Pound to Katue Kitasono
TCS-1   Via Marsala 12-5. 10 July 1938

Dear K

> Duncan (*Townsman* at 6d.)

hasn't means to publish music.

Miss R/ has played me the separate parts of Isida's. but we haven't the three instruments here to do the whole thing.

> Duncan says you want it returned so am sending it.

cordiali saluti   EP

68: Katue Kitasono to Ezra Pound
TLS-3   Tokio, Japan. 23 July 1938

Dear Mr. Ezra Pound,

Thank you for your letters of May 5 and July 2.

In Formosa the climate is not good and I cannot encourage you to become a professor there.

I think Tokio Imperial University or Kyoto Imperial University is most suitable to you.

I will watch to obtain such an opportunity, if you wish.

Reading your "Notes on Micro-Photography" in May's issue of *Globe*, I see how effectively this new system is acting on musical study.

Indeed it's a splendid idea to use it on the Oriental study, and of course we Japanese ought to willingly cooperate with you.

In Japan, so far as I know, nobody has turned his attention to the utilization of micro-photography on musical and Oriental studies.

I will speak about this on every occasion.

I don't think Japan is in financial embarrassment.

I am sorry I couldn't find out a Japanese history translated from the original. I promise you to send it, as soon as I will find a good one.

As for the "Ti-San," (飛 錢、) we have some records, but not so detailed. I suppose it may be just in the same degree as mentioned in Mailla's Chinese History.

The source of Japanese poetry was (萬葉集) Manyosyû (670–790).

An anthology of *Waka* (和 歌) or *Uta* (歌) (a form of short poem consisting of 31 letters [syllables]). This is in 20 volumes. Next we have *Kokinsyû* (古 今 集), also an anthology of *waka* (790–1190). And then we have *Sinkokinsyû* (新古今集) (1190–1603). *Noh* (能) plays were in full flourish in this period.

Chinese poetry was carried on through all the ages, sometimes overwhelming *Waka* and sometimes being subdued by *Waka*.

Of course, this is a terribly rough explanation. I will write you again about this more minutely.

Thank you very much for your *Guide to Kulchur*, a very pleasant book, which will make the world march at double-quick for half a century.

Faber & Faber wrote me to send back your essay "No, Diplomacy can not do it" for an advance copy.

But the other day I lend it to an editor of a professional literary magazine, because I wanted to let many more readers besides **VOU** read it.

Then the editor suddenly died, and I have barely taken back your copy. But the first one page has been missing, and they are very sorry that they can not find it out.

I have retranslated that part from the Japanese one in **VOU**. Will you please improve it into your own?

This is an inexcusable blunder.

I wish you will be lenient with me.

Very glad of Miss Mary's nice *dessins*, very becoming illustrations to her narratives.

Under separate cover I am sending you *A Guide to Japanese Studies,* and some pamphlets.

If there are any books you want in the catalogue of K.B.S. publications, please tell me and I will arrange them to be sent you. And also any foreign books relating to Japan published even in foreign countries, will be sent you, if you like. Any copies you and your friends may need.

Do you wish any Japanese-English dictionary?

Yours ever,
Katue Kitasono

Enclosed:

No, Diplomacy Can Not Do It

I

This title has been taken from the discourse with a Japanese diplomatist; we were talking about the mutual understanding between the Orient and the Occident.

I am convinced that the philosophy of Confucius and Mencius is the cogent convergence. Buddhism came from India and in the Occident, they have Christianity similar to Buddhism. The two doctrines do not lead to clear thinking or at least to such a calm clearness as men of different races can understand in each other.

Ernest Fenollosa who would have been respected in his lifetime in Japan, but he and his work, so far as we Occidentals know, was almost forgotten away as soon as he was buried in the sacred ground of Miidera.

It was a right permitted to me to preserve some of his work in the Occident, exerting myself in the obscurity and the unknown. If I couldn't get Japanese cooperation from Japan, it was perhaps because I didn't know the means to get it.

Fenollosa's note on Noh play has, at least, stimulated Yeats to the experiment of new drama.

Still now, the impression of poetry of Noh play is often expressed in a small theatre of England, and one of them was announced by televie.

69: Katue Kitasono to Ezra Pound

TLS-1   Tokio, Japan. 23 August 1938

Dear Ezra Pound,

I am sorry I cannot find you a book on Japanese history translated from the original. But I was told that *Japan: A Short Cultural History* by G. B. Sansom (London: The Cresset Press, 1931) is written comparatively in detail. The author had been in Japan for some twenty years. If you have not read it yet and wish to read, I will send you.

I wrote of your *Guide to Kulchur* in Sept. issue of *Mita Bungaku* which is a literary magazine published monthly by those who concern Keioh Gijiku University in Tokio.

Mr. T. Kinosita, one of the editors, will send you a copy. He sometimes writes an essay for **VOU**, though not a member.

> ever yours,
> Katue Kitasono

70: Ezra Pound to Katue Kitasono

TLS-1   Anno XVII, Via Marsala 12-5, Rapallo, with Gaudier-Brzeska profile head. 10 December 1938

Dear K/K

Thanks very much for Cactus I/ I have copied the lines on Wyndham L/ and am sending them to Duncan.

I dont yet know enough ideogram to form an opinion of the original/ and of course have no idea of its sound.

I suppose a world of perspective is inhabitable and one of approaching projectiles is not.

Have just seen W/L/ in London. ⟨his⟩ Head on duck/
he has done new portrait of me/

you can judge the two worlds when you get a photo of it/ which I will send when I get one.

the Wyndham drawing (done about 1912) that I have brought back is better than the Max Ernst that Laughlin introduced here circuitously. The Max that I had from him ⟨Max⟩ seven years ago is very fine.

In fact it goes away and the other Max approaches revolving./ If I don't send this brief note now, it will be lost in mountain of papers.

> ever EP

71: Katue Kitasono to Maria Pound
ALS-1   Tokyo, Japan. 25 December 1938

My dear Maria,

I wish you a Merry Christmas and a Happy New Year. I have translated the charming stories about Tyrol into Japanese and have contributed them to the *Reijo Kai* for current number. I am sending it to you under separate cover.

This is the most refined girl's monthly in Japan and 令 女 界 means "girl's circle."

I think Japanese girls have been attracted by your beautiful stories and touched by your tender heart for the poor.

I have subscribed for the " 令 女 界 " for a year as a reward to you, and so you will see it every month hereafter.

I wish you will write again about interesting things for Japanese girls.

> ever yours
> *Katue Kitasono*

72: Ezra Pound to Katue Kitasono
TLS-2   Anno XVII, Via Marsala 12-5, Rapallo, with Gaudier-Brzeska profile head. 14 January 1939

Dear K 2°

I trust my daughter will be properly sensible to the honour of being translated by you AND that she wont get a swelled head.

I am telling my American bank to bother you with a draft for ten bucks (i.e. dollars) for various small errands. ⟨*For which any apology, but I have no other means to hand.*⟩

I tried a year ago to get the *Tokio* or *Japan Times* but they returned my personal cheque saying they couldn't cash it. I dont think they can have tried very hard.

However *when* you do get the ⟨bank⟩ cheque will you send me 8 copies of the *Girl's Circle* containing "GAIS or the Beauties of the Tyrol." ⟨*as discipline for other members of the family.*⟩ and one month of the *Japan Times*. (and hold the rest of the ten bucks for future trials). No use in my getting a longer subscription of the *Times* ⟨now⟩ as I may be in America or at any rate not in Rapallo after March. I will start taking it again when I settle for the Autumn.

It is great fun having the child make a debut at such distance. I hope it will have a civilizing effect ⟨on her⟩. School hasn't quite quenched her intelligence. But of course impossible to tell whether she will ever be able to write anything again after having been taught Grammar etc/

Her English is now more Japanese than any japanese english from Tokio. The idea that *dont* and *cant* contain both verb and negative, just wont enter her head.

Her mother holds ME personally responsible for effect of American magazine illustrations on Japan, despite Fenollosa's efforts the other way.

Porteus has a word about **VOU** in the last *Criterion*.

Williams' *Life on the Passaic River* might interest you. In fact some of that ought to be of interest to Tokio editors.

I suppose Laughlin sends you his pubctns/

> and so forth.
> ever
> Ezra Pound

73: Katue Kitasono to Ezra Pound

TLS-1   VOU CLUB 1649 1-TIOME-NISI MAGOME-MATI, OMORIKU, TOKIO. 10 February 1939

My dear Pound,

I have just received your letter dated Jan. 14. It's pleasant that the young debutante is very satisfied. A hundred years after, Mary's idea about can't and don't will go current, I believe.

I told them to send you the *Japan Times* from Feb. 7 for a month, and I have despatched 8 copies of *Reijyokai* to you. It pleases us that Mary's mother, too, has a good will on my country.

Though we have a rise in prices in some degree in Japan, our life is little changed, we are very peaceful.

The general concern with cultural affairs has become more active than before.

Two young poets from **VOU** have gone to the front. They often write me lively. Even in the battle field, they wish to read books in high class rather than amusing books.

The other day received a letter from Charles Henri Ford inviting us to their Chain poem, and we decided to make 6 from us join in it.

with good wishes,
Katue Kitasono

74: Ezra Pound to Katue Kitasono
TLS-2   Anno XVII, Via Marsala 12-5, Rapallo, with Gaudier-Brzeska profile head. 3 March 1939

Dear K 2°

Thanks for yours of 10th Feb. *Townsman* wd/ I think like the names of the two poets at the front.

//

I have ⟨had strong⟩ nostalgia for Japan, induced by the fragment of Noh in *Mitsuco*. If you can continue such films nothing in the West can resist. We shall expect you AT LAST to deliver us from Hollywood and unbounded cheapness.

ALL the Noh plays ought to be filmed/ or at any rate ALL the music shd/ be recorded on the *sound track*.

It must be 16 years since I heard a note of Noh (Kumé [Tami] and his friends sang to me in Paris) but the instant the Noh (all too little of it in that film) sounded I knew it.

It is like no other music.

There is a mention of Japan at the edge of my chinese Cantos/ now on desk, hope to publish in Autumn

52/61 China/ 62/71 John Adams, *pater patriae* U.S.A. more than Washington or Jefferson/ though all three essential and ⟨all⟩ betrayed by the first congress.

I must go on making clean typescript of them. Now on Canto 67
I want a "Tong Kien Kang Mou"

of Japan

and a translation of the ECONOMIC volume of the Chinese encyclopedia. I think it is vol 3/

I have a
   Nipon O Dai itsi ran
but it is mere chronicle, as far as I have time to read.
   (Klaproth, translation)
⟨here's to meeting *Sometime*.⟩

Yours
Ezra Pound

75: Katue Kitasono to Ezra Pound

TLS-1   VOU CLUB 1649 1-TIOME-NISI MAGOME-MATI, OMORIKU, TOKIO. 7 March
1939

Dear Mr. Ezra Pound,

I got, all right, the cheque of 10 dollars issued by Jenkintown Bank, and cashed it Y36.60 in Japanese currency.

I paid for the *Japan Times*, as you will see in the enclosed. On that occasion I met Mr. Moori, the chief editor of the *Japan Times*, and told him of your hope of writing culture news for Tokio as you told me last year.

I ought to have met him more quickly, because he agreed to this proposal with his all heart.

If you hadn't yet given up your desire (how I hope you hadn't), I would pray you to write and send it to me.

We are expecting to it.

I received a very lonely letter in English from Mary.

Ever yours,
Katue Kitasono

76: Ezra Pound to Katue Kitasono

TLS-1   Anno XVII, Via Marsala 12-5, Rapallo, with Gaudier-Brzeska profile
head. 10 March 1939

Dear K/

I enclose review copy of my latest and shortest book. I hope the

Times (*Japan Times*) will review it. It contains the part of American history NOT taught in American Universities/ Rothschild and Sassoon wd/ spend millions to maintain their system of murder (by world wars etc.) and for 120 years the understanding of this page has been obscured.

Roosevelt's gang are unlikely to introduce this text book in American schools.

The great infamies/ Bank of England and Banque de France dare not face this one page.

Japan Times (First lot, arrived this morning.)

Yours   EP

77: Katue Kitasono to Ezra Pound
TCS-1   [Tokyo]. 20 March 1939

Dear Ezra Pound,

I fear I might have astonished the bon papa of Mary by writing in my former letter, "I received a very lonely letter from Mary."
It was, of course, a very lovely letter that she gave me.
Please disregard the mistype of my forefinger.

ever yours
Katue

78: Ezra Pound to Katue Kitasono
TLS-2   Anno XVII, Via Marsala 12-5, Rapallo, with Gaudier-Brzeska profile head. 27 March 1939

Dear K 2°

Sincere thanks for all your various disbursements of energy. I am sending two brief notes for the *Japan Times*.

Please salute Mr. Morri, AND between you let me know more exactly what you want me to do.

I mean: How often?

How long?

Whether I am to STICK to art, music and poetry or whether I am allowed to consider the arts as happening IN an ambience, expressive of states of mind coincident with different dispositions toward organized society.

I have been cited in Italian press as *"poeta economista"*
Will the *Japan Times* stand *that*?

I send *two* brief notes, rather than one long one, as the subjects do not form a unity.

　　　　　Also short notices are more convenient for a newspaper.
Cultural NEWS?
How far does Mr. Morri want me to "hold down" to notices of events, and how far am I to criticize them?

///

In all cases will he understand that my writing is subject to his editing. He can cut whatever he thinks is of no interest to his readers, and I will not take offence.

　　　　　I expect to go to America. Does he want any special reports from there? Whether on art or the state of the general mind?

　　　　　I have been out of that country for 28 years and don't know what I can effect. I should like my trip to result in better triple understanding (Japan/America/Italy). But I am not on a mission or anything save my own affairs.

in any case please answer
　　　E. Pound (to await arrival)
　　　c/o I/B. Mapel, 3301 P. Street, Washington D.C., U.S.A.

/// 　　　　　　　　　　　　　　　　　///

I trust my beloved young novelist isn't wringing your heart with sob stuff. The copies of her first OPUS have all arrived safely.

//

I should think a monthly letter wd/ be the best thing for me to do for the J/Times but do ask Mr. Morri to write me and say what *he* thinks wd/ be best. Also the EDITOR alone knows what space he has free for these features.

You spell him "Moori"/ *The Times* spells it "Morri" the address on yr/ printed stationery differs from that I have used for several years and which has worked. One of Fenollosa's friends was "Mori" with one **r**.

And what you will make of "Shinbu," "Miaco" and "Undertree's invasion of Corea" in my 62/71 Cantos, I dont know. Spelling is very mysterious. The "mandate" has shifted. Did you see my Mencius in the *Criterion* last summer? (possibly unfashionable author? how can I tell?)

ever　E. P.

79: Katue Kitasono to Ezra Pound

TLS-2   VOU CLUB 1649 1-TIOME-NISI MAGOME-MATI, OMORIKU, TOKIO. 11 April
1939

Mr. Ezra Pound,

I received your letters March 3, and March 10. I tried in vain to assign
"*Tong kien kang mou*" to ideograms. You must be patient and give me a few
explanatory words about it, or rather the ideograms themselves.

In Tokio I couldn't find the translation of Chinese Encyclopedia. But at
any rate I am making inquiry about it to Peking.

I wrote a short review of your introductory Text Book and sent it to the
Japan Times. I will send you the paper, as soon as it will be printed.

I agree with you on the *débouchement* to the West of *Noh* plays by films
and gramophone records. Some of *Noh* plays are recorded, I ask if you have
any.

Duncan has written to me to find for him some early Chinese plays, but
at present there are no adequate ones.

The Chinese incident, however, has stimulated Japan to more profound
study of China, and so we shall soon be able to get easily many Chinese
books.

I have become very imaginative about your Chinese Cantos.

I have read the echo of **VOU** in the last number of *Criterion*.

I only hope the coming of the day when we shall be compensated for the
sacrifice we are now making for superior culture in the West and in the East.

We are growing international chainpoems by the proposal of Charles
Henri Ford in America.

The scores of Igor Markewitch have recently arrived at my friend.

Ever yours,
Katue Kitasono

80: Katue Kitasono to Ezra Pound

TLS-2   VOU CLUB 1649 1-TIOME-NISI MAGOME-MATI, OMORIKU, TOKIO. 28 April
1939

Dear Ezra Pound:

Thank you for the letter March 17. The articles you kindly sent for the
Japan Times are very interesting to us.

Immediately I handed them over to Mr. Moori.

I think he will soon write to you, but at any rate I tell you. He wish you to write on anything concerned with culture. It is left to your own free will how far to hold down to notices of events and how far to criticize them.

Mr. Moori, especially wants to have your reports from America. In short Mr. Moori trusts me and I trust your sense, and so you can write everything in your own way.

The *Japan Times* would be very grateful, if you could write twice a month, within 2,000 words each time.

Mr. Moori is very sorry for that the payment for your manuscripts will prove very small owing to the bad condition of foreign exchange.

I ask if you would permit me to translate your manuscripts for *J/T* and print them in Japanese journal. A few days ago the young writer in Firenze pleaded me with a letter promising to try to write about her college life during the vacation. Hereafter I send the magazine directly to her.

Many thanks for the sending of the *Picture Post*. Mr. Lewis has made a great progress in his painting, I think. It's very funny that Royal Academy was so much afraid of his leonine head.

It seems to me, however, his *dessin* is too much stretched out like Greco or Modigliani, but it gives to his portrait a sort of nobility which I like as well as that of Greco or Modigliani.

Fenollosa's friend Dr. Mori is 森 , and Mr. Moori is 毛利 . There had been long used the Hepburn system of Romaji (writing of the spoken Japanese language in an ordinary foreign alphabet) until a new one, the Japanese Romaji was officially agreed several years ago.

I spell by Japanese system (but not faithful, sometimes change as I like), and Mr. Moori does by the old system, not being banned its use.

I expect next manuscript from you in America.

> Wishing you BON VOYAGE.
> ever yours.
> *Katue Kitasono*

The regrettable death of Yeats had instantly been reported within Japan by radio, newspapers, and magazines.

It's a great pity that *Broletto* and *Criterion* have ceased their publication; our various literary magazines have written about the latter.

81: Yasotaro Morri to Ezra Pound

TLS-1   The Japan Times, Hibiya Park. 15 May 1939

Dear Mr. Ezra Pound—

Thank you for your articles. One about the tri-lingual international means of communications is published in paper of May 14, a copy of which I'm mailing to you under separate cover. The other, concerning Yeats, we'll publish in our Book Page, on the first Sunday of June.

We shall be pleased to have you send us something of literary nature dealing with the general literary trend, or with some big giants in the literary world or something of the sort. It is quite refreshing to read articles, specially written for our paper by a person of your prominence, regarding the literary matters, when we have enough of "dopes" dealing with crises, war threats and general unrest.

The length of that tri-lingual article is just right. More later; I just dash these lines to acknowledge the receipt of your articles from Mr. Kitasono some time ago.

Trusting this will find you well,

Yours truly,

Yasotaro Morri

N.B.—Going over a copy of your letter to Mr. Kitasono, I think I should say something more. You may give us three articles a month or four. More than, we may be imposing too much on you.

Art, poetry, music—all right. So is cultural news. We know you are not on a special mission to iron out the Japan-U.S. relations, if ever there are any jagged surface, but naturally would prefer nothing which will provoke Americans in political issues. Kindly stick to literary subjects; if your criticism of current American literature is found unfavorable to Americans, for instance, it can't be helped. Have I said sufficiently to indicate what we want?

82: Ezra Pound to Katue Kitasono and Yasotaro Morri

TLS-2   Anno XVII, Via Marsala 12-5, Rapallo, with Gaudier-Brzeska profile head. 28 October 1939

Dear K/K/ and Dear Mr. Morri

(or Dear K.K. will you please pass on this letter TO Mr. Morri?)

You may have wondered where and why etc. ⟨I have been.⟩ I recd. Mr. Morri's letter while in America. No copy of the *Japan Times*, for 1st sunday in June has reached me. May have gone astray. Mr. M. said it wd. contain my note on Yeats.

As you can imagine, the war interferes with one's income. It doesn't matter how much I am paid, but I shall have to be paid something, as ZERO multiplied however many times equals always ZERO.

I shd. be willing to accept a subscription to the *Japan Times* as recompense for the first couple of articles. At any rate I want to see the paper, regularly, now that I am back at a fixed address. ⟨& I want 5 copies of issues containing my articles—distribution of which wd. be good publicity for J. Times.⟩

We are having a LOAN-Capital war. Some say a jew war against the aryan population of Europe. Mc N. Wilson sees American finance as the real enemy of England. You must know where China got her money for war. Some call it Kuhn Loeb and Co's war on Japan.

At any rate there is no understanding of the present wars without understanding of war loans/ loans by the SAME MEN to the Same men. De Wendel the banker, pays the ⟨french⟩ people's money to De Wendel the gun maker. And SO FORTH.

and all this is subject matter for literature.

My Cantos 52/71 are in the press/ Chinese dynasties and John Adams. Creator of the United States and of something not unlike a dynasty in America. The fall of which meant the END of decent civilization in the U.S. or at any rate a great and pestilent sickness in American government.

And I wd. prefer to write about history for the moment, including current history.

I will, however, during the coming week try to send you an article on the **Vivaldi** week in Siena.

I should think the *Japan Times* wd. do well to send a subscription to

Odon Por, 5 b. via Angelo Masina, Roma, Italy as exchange for some Italian publications, say *Meridiano di Roma,* and the *Rivista di Lavoro* IF any of you read Italian.

Por reads english.

I have also been meaning to report on meeting with oriental dept. ⟨of *American congressional library*⟩ and Dr. Sakanishi, in Washington re/ proposals for bilingual editions of Noh plays. Will try to get round to that shortly.

> ever yours
> *Ezra Pound*

83: Shotaro Oshima to Ezra Pound

ALS-3   c/o Fujino, 1053, 2 chome, Ikebukuro, Toshima-ku, Tokyo, Japan. 28 October 1939

Ezra Pound, Esq.
Dear Sir:

I am taking the liberty of sending you under separate cover a copy of my *Poems: Among Shapes and Shadows.* I am afraid that they are rather badly written, as I have some difficulty in expressing myself in good English. But I hope that you will find something of interest in them. And I shall be very much obliged if you kindly give me some remark upon my works, because it is the first and laborious attempt for me to write verse in English, and as to the merits of my poetry I am quite diffident. I am a Japanese and a professor of English poetry in Waseda University in Tokyo. For ten years ago, I devoted much of my time to the study of the poetry of the late Mr. W. B. Yeats. And so when I saw him in Dublin last year, he gave me a warm welcome and wrote a letter of introduction addressing to you.

I wanted eagerly to see you while I was in Europe, but owing to the Sudeten Crisis last year, I had to cut my stay in Europe short, and to my great regret, I lost the opportunity of seeing you.

I have read almost all your works with great admiration—your works of immediate intelligibility and of creative vision.

> Yours very truly
> *Mr. Shotaro Oshima*

84: Katue Kitasono to Ezra Pound
TLS-2   [n. p.] 5 December 1939

My dear POUND

"Antonio Vivaldi," *Meridiano di Roma*, the note on *Noh* play for *J.T.*, and your letter all arrived at me.

There has been such a long time that I don't know with what I should begin to write.

A few month ago, from Mr. Moori I received Y60.00 to send to you as the payment for your former two copies for *J.T.* (overwhelmingly small amount!)

I didn't know where you were, in America or Italy, and so I couldn't send it. Now I send you a money order for the sum through the post office and trust you will find it correct.

It's a pity that the copies of *J.T.* containing your articles hadn't reached you at last, which Mr. Moori said surely they had sent to America.

They will send them to you at once.

The article on *Noh* play for this time I have handed over to Mr. Moori, and your letter, too.

I asked Mr. Moori to contribute *J.T.* regularly to you hereafter, and he accepted. Of course it's an etiquette to present it to him, if any gentleman is so kind as to read such a monotonous paper. Japan has begun to suffer from paper famine.

But **VOU** no. 28 is soon to be out. Please pay attention to our *dessins*.

Our poems are progressing, I think.

I have begun to communicate with a young Chinese writer Mr. Kuan Chia Tung. When the critical condition will pass, I hope you will get from him sufficient knowledge about China which I couldn't give you.

I am going to make a *Chinese group like* the VOU Club.

It's interesting to know your opinion on modern war.

I'm sorry, but I must confess I think economics is, too, one of such uncertain sciences as medical science, psychology, etc. You can imagine how firmly I stand to this belief, as I am a barbarian who studied political economics and philosophy in university. Please excuse me, if I'm mistaken, but I guess yours is political economics. In fact it's another field to which economics should extend, but I fear which may change economics into a nasty sandwich.

For my part, I prefer to look at the vague cosmos of Marquis de Laplace, standing on my poetical philosophy of life, hanging down a ribbon from my collar, printed "I dont need such a hypothesis."

Perhaps Xmas will have passed, when this letter will reach you. Merry Xmas to you and to all the members of your family.

ever yours
Katue Kitasono

P.S. Your note on Vivaldi for *J.T.* has just arrived.

85: Ezra Pound to Katue Kitasono

TLS-2   Anno XVIII, Via Marsala 12-5, Rapallo, with Gaudier-Brzeska profile head. 13 January 1940

Dear K/K

So far I have had one packet of *Jap/ Times* containing copies of my note on NOH. Also ⟨thank you⟩ 60 yen which for some reason are payable in french francs. Thanks for the same. A plain bank cheque in either yen or dollars might be simpler if you use banks. Otherwise I shall ⟨start⟩ (in fact I have already started) move for direct exchange between Japan and Italy. France being now the less worthy country.

I am all for the triangle.

//

Am meditating a rather more serious article on elements in european thought/ etc.

//

what would ⟨to me⟩ be useful would be a REGULAR JOURNALISTS CARD. At present I am a poet. Poets have no civic status above other mere men. But JOURNALISTS can belong to the press association. Anyone can be an author. Nobody but addicts to a DAILY PAPER can get into the Press association and enjoy the privileges of being an hireling.

The *Jap Times* don't appear to have an Italian correspondent. If they wd. confer this honour upon me I will faithfully promise *not* to send them any news, or will comply with whatever other measures they like.
I could of course send news, but I shd/ have to be paid for that, as it wd. take time.

It shd/ be a distinction for the *J.T.* to have me as a regular correspondent.

It wd. cost them nothing *unless* they want a news service. In which case
they wd. have to cover expenses. But that is not the point. The point is
the formal appointment. *Globe* sent me a card, but monthly magazines
are not counted as JOURNALISM.

I believe several foreign journalists "correspond" with papers that no
longer exist or from which they have long ceased to depend.

Thanks for **VOU** with yet again my phiz. and note of my having been to
America.

// I think after I do the plea for analysis of European thought from ⟨a.d.⟩
300 to 1500 / I will send you a translation of a plan for reform of teaching U.S. history. / cd/ stand as a review of Beard/ Woodward/ Bowers/
⟨Overholser?⟩ and 25 years american historiography

> and so forth *Evviva la Poesia.*
> especial EPOS

> *Ezra Pound*

86: Ezra Pound to Katue Kitasono
TLS-1   Anno XVIII, Via Marsala 12-5, Rapallo, with Gaudier-Brzeska profile
head. 14 January 1940

Dear K/K

Tomorrow I am sending you an article which I hope will not be too
serious for the *Jap. T.*

If it is you can translate it for **VOU**. I may have been too careful. I dont
dare put in any MORE explanation for fear of its being too LONG.

The additional points wd/ be reference to the two fold influx of chinese
poetry in Japan/ i/e/ imitations of chinese poetry. And jap attempts to
write in chinese parallel to latin influence in europe and men who wrote
IN latin, down even to 1800.

> However that is not the main point. And the
question of the age at which a man begins to be interested in *politica* as
a development from *etica* wd. furnish another article. I have tried to
keep my ⟨note on⟩ "*worship to a spirit which does not belong*" inside the
J. T. limit, art, thought etc.

⟨*Besides I don't know who keeps the J.T. going.*⟩   yrs   E. P.

87: Ezra Pound to Katue Kitasono
TLS-1   Anno XVIII, Via Marsala 12-5, Rapallo, with Gaudier-Brzeska profile
head. 15 January 1940

Dear K.K   Does anyone in your group READ Italian?
Or wd/ it be better for me to send you a résumé in English of what I
publish here?

Note that London can NO longer serve as centre for contemporary
thought. Censorship forbidding us to send in printed matter save direct
from publishing offices.

Various theories of the war. One that it is really American money-
lenders against England. Naturally a desire to kill Hitler as he is aware of
the general financial infamy. You can't know why there was war between Japan and China, without going into subject of LOANS. (from Europe to China.)

Action last week printed a map showing that Russia had annexed an
area in China LARGER THAN EUROPE. Europe being unaware of it and NO
protest from England or the dirty old League of Nations.

The *British Union Quarterly* has just printed the finest historical article
that I have ever seen in ANY country or magazine whatsoever.

The *Social Creditor* has been doing valuable historical work. You shd/
read Overholser's *History of Money in the U.S.A.*

Do you see any of these papers? If you read Italian I will again tell the
editor of *Meridiano di Roma* to see that it is sent to you.

          in a d/n hurry   *EP*

88: Ezra Pound to Katue Kitasono
TLS-2   Anno XVIII, Via Marsala 12-5, Rapallo, with Gaudier-Brzeska profile
head. 22 January 1940

Dear K/K

          I have you to thank for a very elegant volume. The drawings
look as if an occidental influence had entered your life. "Decadence of
the Empire."

All I now need is a translation, as the poems are very short/ don't bother to make it literary, if I had a literal version I might possibly put it in shape. Can't tell, only a fraction of poetry will translate.

//

Did you use that bit of *Jap/ Times* on purpose ⟨*as wrapping*⟩, or is it coincidence? First thing I see is "leg conscious Japan" which reminded me of Ito's first remark to me in 1914 or 15.

"Jap'nese DANCE all time overcoat."

Then I notice the ineffable Miscio in person, but not in voice, save in the remark on the fan dance and Sally.

I believe I ⟨*could*⟩ have done a better article on Ito than the *J.T.* interviewer. Did you meet him? The paper is dated October, and says he was to return to America in Jan. so this is too late to serve as introduction, but if he is still in Tokio, give him my remembrances. I looked for him in N. York, but he was then in S. Francisco.

Mr. Masaichi Tani writes very good english, but he has missed a chance. His girls will have to be patriotic and "use Japan Knees" whatever foreign clothes they obtain.

if you do meet Miscio ask him about "Ainley's face behind that mask," or his borrowing the old lady's cat.

As to the photo in the *J.T.* I can't believe even Hollywood and facial massage has kept him 18. Not 25 years later.

Do you know whether the *J.T.* is being sent me? It doesn't get here.

yours   E. P.

⟨*Did you see the Hawk's Well—is it any use in Japanese?*⟩

89: Katue Kitasono to Ezra Pound

TLS-4   VOU CLUB 1649 1-TIOME-NISI MAGOME-MATI, OMORIKU, TOKIO. 15 March 1940

Dear Ezra Pound,

Excuse me for my long silence.

I thank you very much for your kindly letters and the copy for *J.T.* which has been just printed in the paper.

First of all I wish very much to have *Meridiano di Roma*, because I have a friend who reads Italian and will read *Meridiano di Roma* for me.

I often passed by Mitio Ito in the theatres or musical halls, but not talked to him. His hair is turning grey already, I haven't seen his dance so long. We, the VOU group, watch a young Miharu Tiba who is only unique dancer with a sense in Japan except Mitio Ito. I think Mitio Ito has not yet gone to America, and if not I will write a letter to him.

The *dessins* in my book of poems *Violet of Fire* are drawn by Seiji Togo. Really this painter is a decadent, a regrettable defect for him for which I must always blame him.

Recently Mr. Moori resigned his post, and Mr. Tamotu Iwado has become the new chief editor. He is, too, a good journalist as Mr. Moori.

J.T. is willing to designate you for an Italian correspondent.

If the enclosed certificate will be of any use to you, then BANZAI. J.T. will not restrict you in any way, but they will be glad to have your cultural news and sometimes political and economical news, if possible. Of course they will pay you for them.

I send you several poems translated from *Violet of Fire*, (p. 17–26) almost literal. At any rate, I hope these short lyrics will not take up much of your precious time.

The VOU Club plans to publish an English anthology. Will you please permit us to print your introductory note for VOU Club in the first number of *Townsman*. If you could write a poem or something for this anthology, we should be enraptured. Except the works of VOU, poems and essays of Duncan, Laughlin, Ford and other poets who have appeared in **VOU**, will be contained. The book will be about 150 pages and to be out till August.

Now and then Mary pleases me with her merry letters. She gave me a photo of her portrait painted by Mrs Frost.

I pray to Allah for your health and the meandering CANTOS.

ever yours,

Appendix: *Katue Kitasono*

HEATED MONOCLE

1

Rise from a stone
Walk to hopelessness
A red breast sings
Offended alone
The pipe's clogged
Forget even the name

2

Passing through a village of lilies
Near the down
Read a lonesome letter
Look at nothing but a shell and button
Hate severely tears and the sea

3

Eat green cakes
Go into the garden to laugh
But the parrot has a dirty tongue
The cactus is, too, filthy
Leaning sad against an oak-tree
For a long time
Listen to the poor piano

4

In pain day after day
The wind blows hard
Drink some milk and then seated
The watch's stopped
Trifling is the death of Pompey

5

With a broken beer bottle under my arm
On the rock by the seaside
To hear a horse
My hat's already broken
Pitiful forlorn
Ah
Sextus Pompeius
Your death is foolish
Said I
And yet
Your death is foolish again

6

Roaming on the path of thorns
Tread on the thorns
Oh, God may cry!
Stones are now faded
The absolute
Or genuine eyes are sad
Irritating is the warbling of a nightingale

7

Going along a small hill
Slightly slip
Death is too tardy
Wet with grief
The buttons are off
The love of Cid is even a boredom

8

Oh, friend!
But there's no friend
Solitude is stained
Going alone to a village where nightingales warble
Look at the growing potatoes
Tears trickling down
Feeling sick at the vulgar growth of fig trees

9

On the bank studded with marigolds
A flock of ducks is dazzling
On the day of fate
Lying in despair
Without glancing at the lumbers
Cries of wagtails are so noisy

10

With a black cap on
Buy the lilies
And pass through the wood
The way of summer noon is endless
The despair is so lasting
Lying in the village where tomatoes are bright
Gnawing a green cucumber
Shed tears at a peasant's love.

—*Katue Kitasono*

90: Ezra Pound to Katue Kitasono

TLS-1   Anno XVIII, Via Marsala 12-5, Rapallo, with Gaudier-Brzeska profile
head. 22 April 1940

Dear Kit Kat

Thank you ⟨very much⟩ for the translations of the poems.
Have you sent them to Duncan, or wd/ you like me to do so?

Thanks for the letter from the *Japan Times*. However, no copies of the
paper have come since the Dec. 10th lot.

I am not sure whether they want me to send only the long articles, or
occasional briefer notes. Of course no use sending news that wd. be tele-
graphed, and that they obviously get from a news agency.

I hope you find Miscio Ito.

Cantos 52/71 should have reached you. Of course if Mr. Iwado sends on
the paper regularly I can probably fit my articles to it. I mean I can get
much better Idea of whom I am writing for, and what has already been
said.

I hope to see the editor of the *Meridiano* this week, and will again ask
him to send it to you.

ever yours
E. Pound

91: Ezra Pound to Katue Kitasono

TLS-2   Anno XVIII, Via Marsala 12-5, Rapallo, with Gaudier-Brzeska profile
head and quotation "Liberty is not a right but a duty." m. 10 July 1940

Dear Kit Kat

Enclosed ⟨copy of letter to Mr. Iwado⟩ explains itself. Thanks
for the connection. I suggest that you reproduce ⟨in **VOU**⟩ the frontispage
of my TEXT BOOK and translate its contents. It is the start of the economic
history of the U.S. The pamphlet I am sending Mr. Iwado is the next
dose/ and Por has explained the matter more fully. It is probably not
your "pigeon" but still.

Has *Meridiano* begun to reach you? The J.T. is all the printed matter in
English that now arrives here. Thanks for **VOU**. Last *Meridiano* con-

tained some quotations from ⟨Cantos⟩ 52/71. Another point: *Masoliver*
has been doing some bilingual publishing in Spain. *"Poesia en la
Mano."* I dont know whether the series is going on, but you might send
him a copy of **VOU**.

> Juan Ramon Masoliver, Hotel Boston, via Lombardia
> Roma, Italy.

He has started the series with a fine translation of Dante (select pages). I
suppose french wd/ be best medium of communication ⟨*with him*⟩. He is
a cousin of Dali's.

I had about 44 other topics to write you.

I forget whether you are in touch with e. e. cummings.

> 4 Patchin Place. New York.

He is a better bet than C. H. Ford, though not a voluminous correspondent. In fact he is the best poet in America (long and ancient as is my
friendship with old Bill Bull Williams . . . can't grade poems in accord-
ance with personal relations with authors. BUT (on the other hand,) my
relations suffer like hell when a man's work declines.)

Looking over the bound vols. of *Little Review*; the amount of work done
since 1924 seems to boil down chiefly to what cummings has done, plus
what Eliot has gone on doing. ("Agon" is later.)

I wonder if a file of *The Little Review* exists in Japan? Costs like the de-
vil now. 1917/ to 19 and then quarterly issues at odd seasons till 1924.
Joyce, Lewis, Eliot and the undersigned. Last issue Max Ernst and I think
all the known surrealists. Crevel etc.

Have you had Crevel's *"Pieds dans le Plat"*? You probably have reviewed it in **VOU**, but my ideogramic knowledge moves VERY slowly and
I can't read the magazine yet. I occasionally make out what some article
is talking about. Am convinced **VOU** is livelier than anything here except Duncan's quarterly.

> ever yours
> E. Pound

92: Ezra Pound to Katue Kitasono
TLS-2   Anno XVIII, Via Marsala 12-5, Rapallo, with Gaudier-Brzeska profile
head. 17 July 1940

Dear Kit Kat

    The radio this a.m. announced "fusion of eastern and western cultures" as part of yr/ new govt. program. I dare say I have given this as much thought as anyone. You already have a few notes of mine: The important thing is to keep the BEST of both cultures and NOT CLUTTER.

    There is a whole series of my books, starting with *Spirit of Romance* (my first attempt in 1910) down to *KULCH*, aiming at telling the true story of occidental writing. Plus a few fumbles toward yours. Fenollosa's papers etc/

I don't know whether you can persuade your colleagues to save their own time by starting from where I have got to.

The moment is important, for if you start right it will save a lot of bother. I assure you that there IS a connection between the state of mind that makes good art (whether classic or romantic) and the state of mind that makes clean economics.

I dare say BOTH start with the *Ta Hio* (or however you spell it) and the definition of words (or forms). 正 名
⟨*how does one get that Ming ideogram properly drawn?*⟩   學 大

Not only for *Kulturmorphologie*, but for history, do get yr/ Kokusai *Bunka Shinkokai* to start with Brooks Adams' synthesis. *Law of Civilization and Decay, The New Empire,* and include the economists whom I have listed in my Text Book, also get ⟨them to get a⟩ copy of Butchart's *Money* (collection of opinions of last three centuries) mostly in English.

And for relations whether cultural or WHATEVER, commercial, economic try to get the essential facts of U.S. history, not the pack of evasions taught in American Universities.

I will probably try to list the ESSENTIAL facts of U.S. history for the *Jap. Times;* may send it to you to read first.

If Japan is going "fascist," might save time to start where fascism NOW is, no need to go though experimental phases. Danger in U.S. is a sham fascism with NONE of the basic merits/ German *Bauernfähig* concept; very valuable. ⟨ancient⟩ Roman empire flopped from failure to defend the purchasing power of agricultural labour.

    If these subjects bore YOU, put me in touch with your grandfather, and stick to plastic values and verbal nuances. The nuance AS definition. Nothing to despise in nuance.

Have already said in J.T. that the 　　　　君 子
intensifies racial characteristics the more he knows of these of other races.

The more 君 子
the merrier the contacts between antipodally different individuals.

If my god damned compatriots cant or WONT print decent American history, that is no reason why Tokio shouldn't.

　　　　　　　　　　　　　　　　　yours ever 　E. Pound

Notes/ Is the term JAP disliked? I mean do Japs prefer to be called Japanese? I personally prefer the monosyllable and consider it honorific.

re/ clutter. Young Laughlin thought I exaggerated when I talked of the ROT included in literary curricula, then he had to prepare for his Harvard exams in Italian literature, and was utterly amazed ⟨having read Flaubert and a few good modern authors⟩ that such twaddle as the course contained COULD be offered to ANY student.

93: Katue Kitasono to Ezra Pound

TLS-1 　VOU CLUB 1649 1-TIOME-NISI MAGOME-MATI, OMORIKU, TOKIO. 22 August 1940

My dear Ezra Pound,

　　I am very much pleased to get your letters of July 10 and July 17.

　　I am glad to print the translation of your Text Book in the next issue of **VOU** which is going to be out in September. I don't get any copy of *Meridiano*.

　　I am sending a copy of **VOU** each to Mr. Juan Ramon Masoliver and to Mr. E. E. Cummings. I have often tried to translate Cummings' poems, but never succeeded.

　　We Japanese don't like to be called Jap, because Jap has been used more often with contempt than with friendliness. There are so many examples like this in the world, I think.

　　On the 7th, August I sent you the sum of Y97.80 by Lira in the payment for your three letters for J.T. I hope you will find the enclosed receipts.

　　Cantos 52/71 has surely reached me. I wish I could translate them in

Japanese. It is a very difficult task and yet I do never give up the hope. How is Miss Mary? I haven't written her so long. I will soon send her beautiful Japanese picture books. Hoping you are doing very well over the turquoise seas.

ever yours,
Katue Kitasono

94: Ezra Pound to Katue Kitasono
TLS-3   Anno XVIII, Via Marsala 12-5, Rapallo, with Gaudier-Brzeska profile head. 25 August 1940

Dear Kit Kat

Thanks VERY much for copy *Jap Times* 21 July/ wish I had had it in Rome last week. I visited yr/ cultural relations bureau, but found it hard to convince 'em I wrote for a real daily paper. (The weekly supplement looks artistic not journalistic.)
Anyhow they said ALL you young poets were incomprehensible. I told 'em **VOU** was the liveliest magazine in existence. They finally thought that maybe they had heard of you. ⟨But *"couldn't understand one single word."*⟩ After half an hour one of 'em vaguely thought I must be some-one he had heard of; Fenollosa meant nothing to 'em. ⟨They⟩ thought I ought to get wise to MODERN Japan and not bother with (or stick to) Noh.

Well, they gave me a damn good cup of COFFEE. So I kidded 'em about disappearance of tea ceremony.

And they hoped to see me again
BUT Americans are suspect. Naturally. I do not wonder.

I enclose a bit of German publication/ might interest Mr. Iwado, if he does not already receive Hoffmann's bulletin??

If you can get Chang Kai Chek to read my Cantos 52–61 may be he wd/ make a sane peace. I see that his side kick kung/ has got his fingers burned/ and I shd/ THINK it was rightly, as he has NOT followed his great ancestor's teachings.

Mencius continues to be the most MODERN oriental author in spite im-ported sur-realism. / As far as I can make out all Chinese philosophy (*apart from* Kung and Mencius) is bunk plus opium/ but my means of knowledge are limited. Wish someone wd. get on with bilingual edition

of the INTERESTING books of the orient/ meaning Japan and China. The
bloomink hindoos and mohammeds don't ring my bloomink bell.
Oh well; THAT is a bit exaggerated/ there once was a bloke called
Avicenna.
Sorry Faber didn't print the MAP with my Cantos 52/61
it might have helped people to understand WHY Japan is in China/
and the altar of heaven etc/

Every time I meet an oriental I am told to
pronounce everything differently. God knows what the censorship here
makes of ideogram. Any how, last week I was told to pronounce it "Taa
Sheu" (which is written Ta Hio??) How do YOU say it in Giappone? Taku
Shoshi??

//

As to Mr. whatshisname at yr/ Kultur buro/ I shd/ have thought that the
J. Times with especially its advertising matter/ "GRRRReatest electric etc/"
in the WORLD/ etc. was adequate to tell the occident about how modern
(and/or American) Japan is.

Matsumiya has left Rome, so I couldn't get round to poesy/ I mean if etc/
Noh is OUT/ and the living writers incomprehensible. Anyhow they were
nice blokes. And so forth.

The article you sent is the FOURTH of mine that I have seen in print in
the J/T/
I don't know how many they have received?
If there is anything YOU, personally, want me to write about do say so.

Is there any way for me to get a copy of K. Takashi ⟨Itoh's⟩ British
Empire and People/ one YEN. 80 ⟨Seinen shobo, Kanda. Publishers.⟩ I wd/
gladly review it here if the editors will send it/ OR I will buy it if you can
extract one yen. 80 from Mr. Iwado to be deducted from my next cheque,
plus postage. And as soon as we have a sane peace with FUNK's european plan in action and proper monetary system, I will stop boring
you to death with econ/politico/geo/etc. and behave like an æsthete/
occupying myself with dramady/ poesy/ music etc. as a true inhabitant of
Miaco (or however you now spell it, after the interval).

Maybe if Mr. Takashi ⟨Itoh⟩ cd/ see my stuff in the J/T. he wd. think me
competent to review his volume/ Tell him to vary his reading of Mencius
with reading of the London Who's Who of company directors/ ⟨or vice
versa⟩ (may be he has, I can't tell from the brief notice of his book. J.T.
supplement 18th July.)

Laughlin is supposed to bring out *Cantos* in Sept. American mail comes here via Japan or by air/ when the damn brit/yitts dont swipe it in Bermudah.

IF you know of any LESS glorious period of U.S. diplomacy than the present, tell papa.

And if Willkie so kindly delivers us, I shall have to go home and TELL HIM that European history didn't STOP in 1919.

Heil! Banzai! AlaLA!!

From the pinnacle of your youth look down with at least kindliness on my elderly exuberance.

ever yours

E. Pound

95: Ezra Pound to Katue Kitasono

TLS-1   Anno XVIII, Via Marsala 12-5, Rapallo, with Gaudier-Brzeska profile head. 5 September 1940

Dear Kit Kat

The poetic life is full of pitfalls. Thanks very much for bothering about the money orders. BUT 97 yen make something like 450 lire ITALIAN / the 45 or 46 lire marked on the red slip probably meant GOLD lire.

The post office here is looking into the matter. May be they will be able to pay something like the value of the 97 yen.

This note is a howl of caution. If there ever are any more yen, watch the postal clerk and see that the lire are either clearly marked GOLD (**oro**) or that the number of Italian lire ⟨should be⟩ roughly 4 and half times the ⟨number⟩ of the yen/

Such are the horrors of war/ with no english money, and considerable delay about American money.

One of the jokers in the back page of the *Times* weekly/ made some remarks about money and humour a few months ago/ meaning it arrived here a month ago.

In the mean time let us erect shrines and/or temples to Aphrodite and Apollo. That is to say let Europe do so.

and don't import sheep-cult-ites into Tokio.

Sorry to bother you with detail in first part of this note.   E. Pound

96: Katue Kitasono to Ezra Pound

TLS-1   VOU CLUB 1649 1-TIOME-NISI MAGOME-MATI, OMORIKU, TOKIO. 26
September 1940

Dear Ezra,

I received your bright letter of August 25, which made me laugh a
pelican's laugh.

It was a good comic scene that they (K.B.S.) could do nothing but gave a
damn good cup of coffee to such a great poet and said "see you again." They
are nothing more than sparrow eggs.

Chinese pronunciation is very subtle. In Japan we pronounce Ta Hio,
"Dai Gaku." The pronounciation dictionary for middle school published in
Shanghai teaches us to pronounce 大 學 "Ta Hsio." Another Chinese text
shows to pronounce it "Ta Hsu."大 學

I think the J.T. and their readers would be very glad to know your
opinion like what is to be the cultural policy in such a country like Japan.
On the 20th of August I sent you a money order for the sum of Y34.20, as you
will find the account of J.T.

I shall be able to find the best way to get a copy of Takasi Itoh's book,
British Empire and People, and I will send it to you as soon as possible.
Before posting this letter, I inquired of the publisher.

ever yours,
Katue Kitasono

97: Ezra Pound to Katue Kitasono

TLS-2   Anno XVIII, Via Marsala 12-5, Rapallo, with Gaudier-Brzeska profile
head. 2 October 1940

Dear Kit Kat

Sorry to be a damn nuisance. The post office HERE apparent-
ly cant rectify the money order. 97 yen is over 20 dollars and 46 lire
ITALIANE makes about TWO dollars.

Might be a way of pejorating nippo-merican relations but won't convince
europe that Japan is on the way to greater asia. Also attacking America
in her most exposed part (i.e. old EZ) won't affect the wicked plots/
usurers etc.

45 lire ORO/ gold lire, would come nearer to the worth of 97 yen/

Anyhow, I am chancing the 2 bucks on the possibility you can rectify/ absorption of 90% of value in transit won't do. Wont serve the Japanese cause.

Incidentally I have never used (or heard used) the term Jap as derogative. Nihon Jin is O.K.
The -anese makes very bad sound, and movement of word very difficult to get into elegant sentence. However let manners be manners.
How do you say *Li Ki* in Japanese?   禮 記

Also I haven't had copy of Ponder's *Modern Poetry*/ which supposedly appeared in April. A comfort to see oneself in print. If you can get me a copy without wasting a weeks work, I shd/ be grateful.

Sea is looking O.K. with no brit. cruisers visible.

Am just back from Siena and trying to catch up with work. Mary after two months in Tyrol "gone native" to her mother's distress, so there is tremendous effort to make her *Salonfähig* before she goes back to La Quiete/
all after my instructions that she shd/ become *Bauernfähig* to keep up with the times. At any rate her tennis is improving. I shall try that picture ⟨on her⟩ of Japanese girls *en masse* with swords, to see if it will stimulate "union of cultures."

I don't know whether *Times* wants me to insist that "Four Scarlatti wont make a Vivaldi." ⟨*Sienese music week.*⟩

They seem to be standing my economic frightfulness pretty well.
On the other hand WILL they believe me an economist if they can make me believe in the post office *idea of relation* of **yen** to ITALIAN lire?

That seems a subject for Cub Reporter (with my compliments). You can give him these notes if he is a friend.

My venerable father delighted with the Servant of the People article. My New York agent beseeching me to write literary *Reminiscence* (he wd/ probably faint if he saw a copy of *J.T.* for Aug. 22). Of course I dont know that YOU (K. K.) approve of my crawling DOWN the slopes of Parnassus. You have maintained tactful silence.

And confound it WHY does paper ruck on this machine. ⟨*I will again exhort* Meridiano *office to send you the paper.*⟩   Yours
                                                    Ezra Pound

⟨*P.S. post office is sending back the* Vaglia *money order to your p.o.*⟩

98: Fosco Maraini to Ezra Pound

ALS-1   Kita 11, Nishi 3, Sapporo, Hokkaido, Japan. 14 October 1940

Dear Sir,

I've been reading your articles in the *Meridiano*, not constantly as mails are rare up here, but with great intellectual pleasure. I must now write these two words to tell you how I agree with you about the Chinese classics. It is simply monstrous how stuffy our western outlook is still in this very year 1940, a long time after Matteo Ricci's words ought to have had some effect. We must soon soar to the level of the WORLD: Then Kungu fu Tsu 孔 夫 子 Men-tsu etc, will have their places next to the usual heroes of our school days.

It is good that somebody like you should say such things. Some one from beyond the sea has always a wonderful effect: such is the nature of man. Thank you!

Yours sincerely
Fosco Maraini

99: Ezra Pound to Katue Kitasono

TLS-3   Anno XIX, Via Marsala 12-5, Rapallo, with Gaudier-Brzeska profile head. 29 October 1940

Dear Kit Kat

                Happy New Year, and for Kristzache GET an idea of the relative value of YEN and LIRE.

I have cashed yr/ last postal order for 156 lire/ DAMN.

That is about six dollars. The regular exchange of the dollar being at 19 lire to the dollar. BUT as resident foreigner I can get a 20% bonus/ bringing it to nearly 24.

Unless the YEN has bust, it was worth about 40 cents/ so that 34 wd/ have been worth 13 dollars plus.

I dont mind putting up six or seven bucks to get the Sassoons out of Shanghai, or damaging the opium revenue in Singapore ⟨48% *due to hop*⟩, but I shd/ hate to have it used to scrag me rough-necked brothers from Iowa.

As I cant cash american cheques, save at risk to the Brits stealing 'em off the clipper in the Bahamas/ and as nothing ⟨now⟩ comes from English publications, this thin line of supplies from the J/T is, or WOULD be, useful if allowed to flow in with proper, i.e. as at the source, dimensions.

If you can't get sense out of the postal system, for gord'z sake try a BANK/ must be some Italian bank with an office in Tokio??? Or the American express co/ must exist, and continue bizniz at least until or unless hostilities bust out, which I hope they won't.

///

Cultural notes; possibly for **VOU**. Appearance of P. Tyler in J.T. reminds me that:
NO editor **in** America, save Margaret Anderson, EVER felt the need of, or responsibility for, getting the BEST writers concentrated i.e. brought together in an American periodical. She started in Chicago, went to S. Francisco, then N. York and ended by pub/ing *The Little Review* in Paris. Evidently the *aim* was ALIEN to American sensibilities.

The Dial might fool the casual observer; but its policy was NOT to get the best work or best writers. It got some. But Thayer aimed at names, wanted european CELEBRITIES, and spent vast sums getting their left overs. You wd/ see the same thing in American picture galleries. AFTER a painter is celebrated (and the Europeans have his best stuff) dealers can sell it to American "connoisseurs."

European proportions, a.d. 1940. Germans rise at 6 a.m. to GOOD music on the radio/ french radio music soppy, English music and jokes putrid. Incredible vulgarity, and jazz WORSE than the human mind had hitherto conceived possible.

There still remains a tiny minority of careful players of old music in England/ but even in that field much is weakly and sloppily played.

As to the J.T. sop about Eddie and Wallie/: you might in JAPANESE context quote the strictly ANONYMOUS
England's EMBOOzador
Getting back to Baltimore.
I don't want it in an English context as I dont want to hurt anyone's feelings. Eddie sure is for the old Baltimore boarding house.

You know (?) Max Beerbohm did a caricature ages ago when Ed. was young: It showed Ed at 40 marrying his landlady's daughter.

When I say GOOD music, in Germany, you might note that it is played in TIME; french, eng/ and Ital music most usually is NOT.

I don't say it NEVER is played in time, but the good old land of Dürer and Bach just dont LIKE slop in musical measure. In fact there IS a Germanic component of civilization, though you will find it hard to mention the subject in american jewish papers.

If you manage to read my J.T. articles at all, I wish you wd/ comment FREELY. I want guidance. I wish you folks cd/ make a peace in China. Best possible kick in the jaw for the nastiest kikes and pseudo-kikes in America. If you can manage it we might get on and have a little civilization once again.

Oh, well, Italy has just had a philosophic congress/ i.e. pow wow of blokes who write about philosophy/

Meant to write about the Scarlatti week/ but too much else needing divulgation/ "Four Scarlats don't make a Vivaldi," not by no means but Guarnieri had got the opera into shape/ orchestra etc/ playing properly, which it wasn't last year.

J.T. my last remaining source of information re/ the U/S. I don't even know whether Jas/ has got out the Am/ edtn/ 52/71 Cantos.

Itoh's book ⟨*Brit. Emp. & Peop.*⟩ OUGHT to be pubd/ *at once* in some european language. Possibly serialized in J.T. or at least summarized. After all in the Ban Gumi the pacification of the country precedes the lofty reflection, or plays of pussy-cology.

Great excitements last month/ thought of going to U.S. to annoy 'em but Clipper won't take anything except mails until Dec 15, so am back here at the old stand/ Thank god I didn't get as far as Portugal and get STUCK there.

Pious reflections on my having spent 12 years in London/ 4 in Paris and now 16 or 17 in Italy/ Which you can take as estimate etc/etc/ ⟨*of national values.*⟩ I dunno what my 23 ⟨*infantile years*⟩ in America signify/ I left as soon as motion was autarchic; I mean MY motion. Curious letch of Americans to TRY to start a civilization there/ or rather to REstart it: because there seems to have been some up till 1863/. ⟨*I shd **still** like to.*⟩

Have you ever had the gargantuan appetite necessary for comparing the J.T. with AMERICAN daily or Sunday wypers??? Or to consider what Japan does NOT import in the way of news print?? Oh well; DON'T. Let it alone, and get out another issue of **VOU**.

Any news of living authors wd/ be welcome. Gornoze whats become of Possum and Duncan and Angold, or the pacific Bunting.

Cultural Policy of Japan?? Vide Ez' *Guide to Kulchur*, facilitated by Ez system of Economics, now the program of Ministers Funk and Riccardi, tho I dont spose they know it was mine.

yours   E. P.

(re The U.S. *vide* my *Make it New*, Remy de Gourmont's letter: "Conquérir l'Amérique n'est pas sans doute votre seul but.") Funny trick of memory, I thought he had written "civilizer l'Amérique." That must have been in my note to him.

100: Ezra Pound to Fosco Maraini
TL-2   [n. p.] 11 November 1940

Dear Sig. Maraini

. . . Do you also see my notes in the *Japan Times* March 3, June 13, July 21, Aug. 22, Sept. 12?

You could assist the ⟨inboosting⟩ Confucian revival if you wd/ write both to the editors of the *Jap Times* AND to Di Marzio backing up what I say. The *Meridiano* needs MORE news of oriental books.

Do meet Kitasono Katue, VOU club (unless it is through him that you know of me). Nisi 1 tiome 1649, Magome Mati, Omori, Tokyo. He runs the liveliest magazine in the world.

Am trying to jazz up the *Meridiano* to the level of **VOU**. BUT it is heavy going and damn'd hard to get collaboration. Italians do NOT spontaneously cooperate until they have a Duce to jam 'em together. A damn furriner can't do it. Then as soon as a man is any good he gets a JOB in an office and has no time save for his job.

Do for god's sake take up some point in my articles and write on THAT, with reference TO it. If three or four of us start NOTICING each other's writings, we can get something done.

At present all Italian ⟨writers⟩ either IGNORE each other or spend their time in irrelevant chatter. EXCEPT re/ economics. Current issue of *Gerarchia* has THREE articles worth noticing. *Meridiano* never has more than two in one issue. And no two contributors ever hit the same bullseye, or rather Di Marzio and I DID cohere ONCE but quite by accident; or rather without collusion. Not by accident but accidentally as to timing.

Would be most useful if you cd/ do article saying DAMN Lao-Tsze. Attack idea of studying "chinese philosophy" as if ALL Chinese philosophy had merit/ whereas some is no better than the shitten old testament/ which is crap, immoral, barbarous/ poison injected into Europe. Xtianity, the sane part of it is a european construction/ stoic morals and cosmogony. *Deus est Amor.* That is O.K. Believe Ovid knew that, or at least *Amor Deus est.* Mencius volume is the most MODERN book in the world. Take that as FROM ME, and do an article on it for Di Marzio.

Also ⟨*my econ. book*⟩ gives a fairly full list of all the possible varieties of human imbecility. Have you, by the way, any idea what has become of a group of neo-Confucians gathered round a chink named Tuan Szetsun who used to print pamphlets in Shanghai back in 1934? 862 Boone Rd. Shanghai. World prayer, etc.

cordially yours

I think Kitasono has a number of my books, which you may not know. Give you better idea of what I have done re/ [*illegible*]. Cant get any real news from America.

⟨*What about translating Itoh?*⟩

⟨*vide enclosure*⟩

101: Ezra Pound to Katue Kitasono

TLS-2   Anno XIX, Via Marsala 12-5, Rapallo, with Gaudier-Brzeska profile head. 15 November 1940

⟨JAPERICAN??⟩

Dear K/K°

Two articles, one by Mr. Setsuo Uenoda, and one by Dr. Tatsuo Tsukui in the *J.T. Weekly* for Oct. 17th ought to start discussion in the VOU club, if you are still lucky enough to corral eleven poets in one place.

The Kana syllabic writing is clumsy and cumbersome; I mean that the latin alphabet with 26 or even 24 signs will do all the WORK of the syllable signs and is immeasurably easier to remember.

I suggest that in each issue of **VOU** you print at least one poem, prefer-

ably the best poem WITH a transliteration into roman alphabet. Stick to
the Italian significance of the vowels. Japanese sounds very much like
italian. English and french spelling does not represent the sound of the
words as logically as Italian spelling, and is not constant in indicating
what sound it implies.

IDEOGRAM is essential to ⟨the exposition of⟩ certain kinds of
thought. Greek philosophy was mostly a mere splitting, an impoverish-
ment of understanding, though it ultimately led to development of particular sciences. Socrates a distinguished gas-bag in comparison with
Confucius and Mencius.

At any rate I NEED ideogram. I mean I need it in and for my own
job, BUT I also need sound and phonetics. Several half-wits in a state of
half education have sniffed at my going on with Fenollosa's use of the
Japanese sounds for reading ideogram. I propose to continue. As sheer
sound "Dai Gaku" is better than "Ta Tsü." When it comes to the question of transmitting from the East to the West, a great part of the chinese
sound is no use at all. We don't hear parts of it, ⟨much of⟩ the rest is a
hiss, or a mumble. Fenollosa wrote, I think justly, that Japan had kept
the old sounds for the Odes long after the various invasions from the
north had ruined them in China. Tones can not be learnt at three
thousand miles distance any how, or at any rate, never have been.

The national defence of Basho and Chikamatsu can be maintained by use
of the latin alphabet. If any young Tanakas want to set out for world
conquest, on the lines Ubicumque lingua Romana ibi Roma (wherever
the latin tongue, there Rome) you will invade much better by giving us
the sound of yr/ verse in these latin signs that are understood from the
Volga to the West coast of Canada, in Australia, and from Finland to the
Capes of Good Hope and Horn.

English had conquered vast territories by absorbing other tongues,
that is to say it has pouched most latin roots and has variants on them
handy for use where french and even Italian have shown less flexibility;
it has taken in lashin's of greek, swallowed mediæval french, while
keeping its solid anglo-saxon basis. It then petrified in the tight little island, but American seems to be getting into Tokyo. Question of whether
want to "preserve" japanese in test tubes or swallow the American
vocabulary is for you to decide.

I still think, as I wrote last year, that with Italian, Ideogram and
English (American brand) you can have a tri-lingual system for world
use. But spurred on by T. T. and S. U. I wd/ amend my suggestion of using the kana writing with the ideograms and say use the latin letters.

One wd/ learn Japanese more quickly if with each chunk of conversation dictionary offered by the J. T. we could have something worth
reading printed bilingually.

Throughout all history and despite all academies, living language
has been inclusive and not exclusive.

⟨JAPERICAN⟩ Japerican may well replace pidgin even in our time but
Japanese will never become *lingua franca* until its sound is printed in
the simplest possible manner.

yours   E. Pound

102: Ezra Pound to Katue Kitasono
TCS-1   Via Marsala 12-5. 22 November Anno XIX [1940]

Dear Kit Kat

Next time I have a bit of money from J. T. please take out for
me a six months subscription to the DAILY edition. I don't get enough
news from the Weekly. However dull you may think the paper, it is a
dn/ sight more lively than the usual dailies. Have you had any news of
Duncan, or Eliot or anyone? Bloke named Maraini seems to see *Meridiano* now and then. I wonder if your copies have come? They promised
to send them.

yours
Ezra Pound

⟨I have told him to see you, but forget what town he is in; may be half
way up Fuji.⟩

103: Ezra Pound to Katue Kitasono
TLS-1   Anno XIX, Via Marsala 12-5, Rapallo, with Gaudier-Brzeska profile
head. 5 December 1940 ⟨Giovedi⟩

Dear KitKat

You will be pleased/ relieved/ honour'd/ bored OR whatever
to hear that the money order allegedly 451/ rearrove today with a supplementary order for 405/ also Polite letter in english to local postmaster

from idem in Tokyo/ saying the clerk had err'd. ⟨*The one from last August or September*⟩

      You will observe from the enclosed that it needed a "magical aspect" of two major orbs/ etc.

> **L'OROSCOPO DEL 5.**—Questo giovedi privo di configurazioni lunari, passera sotto il dominio di un magico aspetto tra il Sole e Giove che faciliterà la conclusione di buoni affari ma per contro dovremo frenare le spese, particolarmente se causate dal bel sesso.
>
> MARIO SEGATO.

Do the Jap papers include horror/scopes? Two Italian journals print 'em/ and in London several million ephemerides of the stars (Zadkiel and Old Moore) used to be sold. Yeats potty on the subject.

Not easily perceiving that men ⟨*differ one from another*⟩/ he needed some explanation or stimulus to note that some LIKE boiled ham for dinner, whereas others ⟨*genteel irish*⟩ think it vulgar. Have known him insulted by its appearance ⟨*at eventide*⟩. Acc/ him and his *Li Ki*/ it shd/ be eaten cold for breakfast ONLY, and so forth.

How long it takes for men of different even if contiguous nations etc//

Chinese diplomat said to me lately/ two peoples ought to be brothers/ they read the same books/ believe he was a Chiang K/Cheker at that.

                      salve/ banzai/ wan soui/ alala;

                             und so weiter.
                             yours
                             Ezra Pound

104: Ezra Pound to Katue Kitasono

TLS-2   Anno XIX, Via Marsala 12-5, Rapallo, with Gaudier-Brzeska profile head. 30 December 1940

Dear Kit Kat

      HAPPY NEW YEAR. And thanks for Lahiri's book. How much does he KNOW? How seriously am I to take the book? Several dozen questions. re/ Roppeita Kita. This ⟨school⟩ opposed to Umewaka Minoru's? Or not, as I note the son is called Minoru.

What is the point of the curls? Or are they only used for the red lion's mane?

/

I note that Ito is back/ pp/ in *Jap Times* a bit queer. May be O.K. Miscio's strong point was never moral fervour, and he may have a *sane* desire to popularize. ⟨or not?⟩ HOWEVER Tami Kumé who HAD studied *Noh*, though he hadn't in 1915 Ito's inventiveness etc/ had by training something that Miscio hadn't (quite naturally had NOT at age of 23) got by improvisation.

Do you see these old buzzards who are "in spite of the weight of 55 winters" etc. still amazing yr/ hindoo by being alive? I mean does Mushakoji or Kita etc/ know what you are up to? Or are the ages kept in separate compartments?

Antidote for Xtianity? I mean take it early before it poisons Japan with its semitic elements.

Any useful action to be taken, or does yr/ generation merely ignore it? Obviously almost ANY religion can be taken up by an artist who will select only its better part and ignore its evils.

Subject not simple. Am wondering whether any good can be done by starting an article in Italian: "Christianity will come out of this war like a plucked chicken. . . ." following or preceding the remark with allusions to collaboration of anglican bishops and the papal gang with usury and jews.

I suppose Y. Yashiro is bloke whose book on Botticelli I saw at Yeats' ten years or more ago?

What I dont make out is whether one cd/ talk with Mushakoji/ whether he is SET on Beethoven, or whether that list of three names is due to his unfamiliarity with what I think is better. I mean does he like 'em for their real merits/ or because they are different from Jap work/ or what?

Am all for boom in Confucius/ but hear there is some very poor neo-Confucianism on the Chinese market. Weak generalities/

Mencius is the most modern author. I mean STILL, today, the most modern/ 1940 whereas Aragon is 1920. Or was.

Put it: do japs of my age live where my elders were when they (jap contemporaries) were in Europe?

Neue Sachlichkeit sounds O.K.; naturally Italy hasn't yet heard of it.

Frobenius was contemporary. Dare say I have touched on these points before. Shd/ like pointers re/ *Jap Times*/ whether I am being too UNchristian for 'em/ or whether they are getting bored (nowt printed for some time) or whether my economics are too orthodox. Colliers wouldn't like 'em. But Senator Frazier has caught the boat/ which Volpi has NOT.

Another line of enquiry: do YOU, Ito, Mushakoji and Kita agree on ANYTHING? And if so what?

Or do you set round and NEVER meet (as in England different sects)

Sometimes damn foreigner can introduce proper people across clique frontiers. As activist, shd/ like to know if useful collaboration possible between me and any of 'em/ either to get FULL sound film of Noh/ or more lively Confucian comprehension.

Anyhow, Happy New Year/ damn Churchill and lets hope that Frankie Roosevelt will lie down now he has a third term to play with.

yours
Ezra Pound

⟨*Why am I not translated? Any one outside VOU club ever read a book by E. P.?*⟩

⟨*Don't send compliments—I am interested in knowing why.*⟩

105: Ezra Pound to Katue Kitasono
TLS-3   Anno XIX, Via Marsala 12-5, Rapallo, with Gaudier-Brzeska profile head. 31 December 1940

Dear Kit Kat

FOR **VOU**

Lahiri's book gives the impression, possibly a wrong one, that Y. Noguchi & Mushakoji may be living in what was in England and America the era of 1890 or even of 1888.

I wish I could convince VOU club that economics, and in particular the preoccupation with the nature of money and the effects of usury are not a bee in my sole and personal bonnet.

The surrealists, Max Ernst and the lot of 'em (Crevel being their best writer, and not quite of them) were all represented in *The Little Review* in 1923.

A surrealist treatment of money would be contemporary, today, 1940 or still better ANNO XIX del Era fascista.

This awareness is not a mere idiosyncrasy of mine. The most vital poets in the West, Bunting, cummings, Angold are all awake to it. So is W. C. Williams, so is Ron Duncan, editor of *Townsman*, who preceded Laughlin in printing VOU poems, so is and has been T. S. Eliot from the day he wrote Bleistein: "The jew is underneath the lot."

It is proper that up to the age of crucifixion (32) the poet be lyric. After that he withers, I think, if he does not feel some curiosity as to the LOCUS of his own perceptions and passions. By LOCUS I mean their movement in relation to the humanity about him.

E. P.

Dear K/

The preceding page is to print if **VOU** has space. This page is private, repeating possibly points from yesterday's letter.

You would help me considerably if you can find time to say why my *books* are NOT translated into Japanese. **VOU** has done all it can, and is doing all it can, as a magazine. But couldn't Japan print a series of books in English and/or other languages at a reasonable price? A Jap publisher could even sell copies in EUROPE ⟨*Continent where Eng. & Am. public haven't contracted by rights.*⟩ if he wd. go to it and print the GOOD books that that bloody swine Tauchnitz and Albatross ⟨united⟩ (a jew named Reese, amusing card but evil.) does NOT and never will print.

Naturally I wd/ be only too glad to tell the publisher what is, and has for the past 50 years been worth reading.

Half dozen of dozen H. James/ W. H. Hudson, a little of F. M. Ford. My anthology *Profile*, my *Kulch*. More Thos. Hardy. Possibly some Frobenius/ Crevel's *Pieds dans le Plat*.

Is there in Japan an available edtn/ of *Madame Bovary/ Educ Sentimentale*, or of Corbière, Laforgue, Rimbaud? Or of Gautier's *Emaux et Camées*?

Or my *Jefferson and/or Mussolini* (as simple chronicle)?

All could be done for two yen a vol/ with percentage of 10% to authors. I mean print 'em in original language. *J.T.* readers numerous enough to cover the cost of printing. You might indeed be a pubr/ instead of a *bibliotecario/* No, probably too risky. A fixed job is the basis of sanity.

But you must know a printer. I wd. cheerfully take a few shares in any company you told me was properly organized. Not as capitalist, but just to show by a few bucks, that I thought the thing good business.

Hell! Tauchnitz has made money enough.

Eliot's poems/ etc. It wd. be useful to you and **VOU** to have all the best foreign books available in Tokyo at a low price. Paper covers for preference.

/ by the way/ WHEN did Bernie Pshaw ever see a Noh play and why did he think he knew what it was driving at?

Wonder if Kita/ no he cant have/ if that was first photo/ anyhow, wonder who did the damn good performance that I saw from film in Washington?

Kita OUGHT to be smoked up to get ALL his performances onto a permanent record of that sort. BOTH the movements and the sound.

What the hell he is doing in a Louis XIV wig beats me, unless it is the blinkin old lion, Ki lin or wott t' hell?

Henya hair is red and straight/ I dare say the "coils" iz the flossie dawg.

ever yrs
E. Pound

106: Ezra Pound to Katue Kitasono
TLS-1   Anno XIX, Via Marsala 12-5, Rapallo, with Gaudier-Brzeska profile head. 2 February 1941

Dear Kit Kat

The metamorphosis of the *Jap Times* is from this distance an interesting study and very sad.

I take it the departure of Mr. Iwado coincides. I note that the village idiot has a column on Lahiri's book etc.

I should very much like to hear the whole story if you have patience to tell it. I had already indulged in conjectures during the month previous to disappearance of Mr. Iwado and the Cub Reporter. I spose boys will be boys and youth youth. Anyhow I wd/ like it if not as history at least as romance and the development of the short story in the far east. Maupassant, to Caldwell or As you like it.

In fact I wondered whether my Confucianism, or my economics, or my nationality /etc/etc/

> benedictions.
> yours
> *Ezra Pound*

107: Ezra Pound to Katue Kitasono
TL-1   [n. p.]. 16 February 1941

Kat

I lived today a *hokku,* or at least it seems more suited to a Japanese context than to my heavier hand, so I offer it to the VOU club.

With the war there are this year no concerts by the Amici del Tigullio, the foreign subscribers are gone, but that wd/ not prevent us, there is no Gerhart Münch, no pianist/ no public or perhaps there might be a public, but at any rate, I am the public.

Stage, a room on the hill among the olive trees
the violinist playing the air of Mozart's 16th violin sonata/

then a finch or some bird that escapes my ornithology tried to counterpoint. ⟨*all through in key*⟩

I suppose the subject is: War time.

> yours

⟨*Storm. high seas.*⟩
I think you have post cards of the cliffs here, and this is the season when the olives fall, partly with wind or rain/ hail for a few minutes today/
The impatient peasant rattles a bamboo in the olive twigs to get the olives down, but this is now against the regulations as they, the olives, are supposed to give more oil if they fall by themselves.

108: Ezra Pound to Katue Kitasono
TLS-2   Anno XIX, Via Marsala 12-5, Rapallo, with Gaudier-Brzeska profile
head. 12 March 1941

Dear Kit Kat

Have I asked, and have you answered: whether you have
olive trees in Japan? and whether the peasants shake off the olives with
bamboo poles?

The Janequin "*Canzone degli Uccelli,*" Münch's version for violin,
was printed in *Townsman.* I think I mention it also in *ABC of Reading.*
J. born end of *Quattrocento*/ about 1475, if I remember rightly. Otherwise
these lines from a new Canto/ or rather for a new Canto, can go to the
VOU club without explanation.

///Lines to go into Canto 72 or somewhere///

Now sun rises in Ram sign.
With clack of bamboos against olive stock
We have heard the birds praising Janequin
And the black cat's tail is exalted.
The sexton of San Pantaleo plays "*è mobile*" on his carillon
"*un' e duo . . . che la donna è mobile*"
In the hill tower (videt et urbes)
And a black head under white cherry boughs
Precedes us down the *salità.*
⟨*Italian for stone path in hills.*⟩
The water-bug's mittens show on the bright rock below him.
⟨*If I were 30 years younger I wd/ call 'em his boxing gloves.*⟩

. . . .

I wonder if it is clear that I mean the shadow of the "mittens" and can
you ideograph it . . . very like petals of blossom.

All of which shows that I am not wholly absorbed in saving Europe by
economics.

Though if yr/ minister is coming to Berlin/ Rome, the *Jap Times* OUGHT to
go on with my articles, unless the seceding editor has taken 'em with
him to enliven some other publication.

I get more and more orthodox every day by not moving from positions taken ten or 20 years ago.

Have just finished clean copy of my translation of Por's *Politica Economico-Sociale in Italia.*/ magnificently constructed as a book/ but HELL as sentence construction/ or rather hell if you don't knock EVERY sentence to bits and remake it in English. My TEMPER for past 3 weeks unfit for a self-respecting leopard cage in ANY zoo.

Do try to get some news from cummings/ etc.

benedictions/   *Ezra Pound*

Oh yes, I have spoken ⟨to U.S.A. & England⟩ on the radio several times from Rome. But I suppose the transmissions short wave for Tokio are only in Japanese??

109: Ezra Pound to Katue Kitasono
TLS-2   Anno XIX, Via Marsala 12-5, Rapallo, with Gaudier-Brzeska profile head. 25 March 1941

Dear Kit Kat

Had no sooner writ you ⟨*my last*⟩ than came "Diogenes" with yr/ mention of "olive tree"/ but no proof it was Jap olive.

///

I am still interested in *Jap Times*/ as last artcl/ of mine to appear was my whoop of joy for Matsuoka's taking on his present job. I shd/ have thought paper cd/ stand that//

Note for you and VOU club/ that I sent yesterday to United Press a statement of plan for Pacific Peace//

We shd/ give you Guam but INSIST on getting *Kumasaka* and *Kagekiyo* in return.

i.e. INSIST on having 300 Noh plays done properly AND recorded on sound film so as to be available to EDUCATE such amerikn stewdents as are capable of being cultur'd.

(parenthesis Henry Adams to Geo Santayana 45 years ago: "Ahhh, so you wish to teach at Harvard. Ah, it *can* **not** be done!")

Of course I dont know that the U. P. will print the proposal. If they don't and if I am asked to broadcast again, I shall probably put it on the air.

//

Last J. T. Weekly mentioned Hoshu Saito and Gado Ono. I don't know whether there is record in Fenollosa's notes of name of "master of ideograph" who did the ideograms that I now have. I think I merely heard the name from Mrs. Fenollosa. After 25 years one is a bit vague. I think it was Saito. I wonder if there is any way of discovering whether Saito knew Fenollosa, or of identifying the "rays" ideogram ⟨by its style⟩ which I have reproduced at start of my "Cantos 52/71."

I have merely given it as "from the Fenollosa collection"

I don't know whether you have the Nott edtn/ of the *Written Character*. All the ideograms there are, I believe, by the same hand/ at any rate all in same ink on same size sheets of rice paper; very black as to ink, very suave as to paper surface, almost a glaze.

// Mediterranean March

Black cat on the quince branch
    mousing   blossoms

Message to the ex-governor who writes hokku/
    For bigger and better glaring ⟨in the Tokyo zoo⟩
Let out the tiger
    And put in the sassoon.

                                                        Ezra Pound

110: Ezra Pound to Katue Kitasono
TLS-1   Anno XIX, Via Marsala 12-5, Rapallo, with Gaudier-Brzeska profile head. 12 April 1941

Dear Kit Kat

        "*Buona Pasqua*," Thanks for "highbrow," I can make out what the subject matter is, I don't suppose I shall ever be able to read it without a crib.
        Wouldn't Laughlin publish a translation either of the book as it stands, or of a selection of yr/ essays?
I have asked so many questions in my last six or ten letters that I don't

know what more to ask. Fine season for airmen and suspended one for the arts in Europe. Meaning, no news save what you get from the news agencies.

cordially yours   Ez. Pound

In fact the only "literary gossip" is from an old copy of *Time* I think it was, Mr. Eliot converting the Archbish. of York to a mixture of christianity, communism and economics. In about that order.

111: Katue Kitasono to Ezra Pound

TLS-1   VOU CLUB 1649 1-TIOME-NISI MAGOME-MATI, OMORIKU, TOKIO. 28 May 1941

Dear Mr. Ezra Pound,

Thank you for your letter of April 12. I am very sorry I haven't written answers for your letters so long that your questions have run out.

As you know **VOU** is changed its name to SINGIJYUTU.

My latest book of poems, *Hard Egg*, has reached you by now, hasn't it? I translated your Hokku "Mediterranean March" and wrote it in my poor hand. You will know what a great master Gado Ono is, as compared with mine.

As well as you we get very little news in Tokio.

Charles Ford has published his book of poems, *Overturned Lake*, is the only latest news?

How is Duncan?

Townsman reaches me no longer.

Your original plan for Pacific peace was quickly printed in *J. T.* May it be realized like a miracle of 20th century!

Do you receive *J.T.* regularly?

It's a matter of great regret that your works have not been translated in Japanese, and still it will need some more years for your being translated. You are difficult to most of the Japanese readers, and most of literary men in Japan are rather sentimental as they may be the same in Europe.

But you must be known in Japan more widely.

I'll do my best for it as I have been doing.

I am not sure whether there are olive trees in Japan, or not.

Yours ever,
Katue Kitasono

112: Katue Kitasono to Ezra Pound

TPC-1   1649 1-tiome nisi, Magome, Ota, Tokio. 22 [April 1947?]

Dear Ezra,

I have been very anxious about your illness which I learned in *News-week* and *Time*. I've been unable, however, to know your address, until I received a letter from James Laughlin.

How are your family? Where are they? I hope you will regain your health very soon.

I revived my magazine **VOU** last December. Japan is in severe inflation.

Ever Yours,
Katue Kitasono

113: Dorothy Pound to Katue Kitasono

TL-1   3211 10th Place, S.E., Washington, D.C. 4 May 1947

Dear Mr. Kitasono:

Ezra's wife writing. I have just been with E. P. He asks me to write you the following notes, and send on the Confucius, *Studio Integrale*.

He wants an estimate of what it would cost to print the Confucian Anthology ("as you sent me—TEXT, not Mao's comment").

Characters about as large as enclosed. NOT MORE than 6 columns of 8 [characters] per page. Or 7 if needed to complete a strophe, with 7th column for title. Each poem of the 305 to start on NEW page, no strophe to be broken—if 2 strophes (say 34 characters) won't go entirely on page, then start new page. Verse form to be indicated clearly, by disposition of characters.

Cost for 2000 copies, leaving bottom ½ page blank for translation & notes. Characters of same verse a little closer. Then break between verses as here between the characters. 8 chs. to fill height here taken by seven.

Sorry this isn't a copy of S. *Int.* on the better paper. He wants sample of font of type & of paper.

. . . so the shape of the strophe can be seen by american eye.

. . . if verse is 6 characters, the next verse starts on new column.

. . . no verse to be broken at column end, cf. my *Cavalcanti*.

. . . page size as *Integrale*, or a little larger. Pages to run occidental fashion.

Our family news—Mary is in Tyrol, married, has just had a son.

I have been over here nearly a year. Answer to me perhaps easier. Though his in-going mail is not censored, all out-going mail goes through hands of psychiatrists.

So glad to hear **VOU** has begun again.

Please write to E. P. again. A few words from outside world gives him so much pleasure, even if only a postcard.

> Greetings,
> believe me
> yours most sincerely
> *Dorothy Pound*

114: Katue Kitasono to Ezra Pound

TPC-1   [1649 1-CHOME NISHI, MAGOMEMACHI, OTAKU], TOKYO. 15 May 1947

My dear Ezra,

Very much pleased with your letter of March 15th, and glad to know you have recovered so much.

Frontiers of poetry do not lose their hope as long as you are well.

The serious inflation in this country makes it more and more difficult to bring out books.

I earnestly desire such a delightful condition will come back here as soon as possible that the very interesting plan of you about 老毛 [Lao, Mao] can be carried out as you wish.

> Ever yours,
> *Katue Kitasono*

Je mange, donc je suis.

115: Katue Kitasono to Dorothy Pound

TLS-2   VOU CLUB 1649 1-tiome-nisi, Magome-mati, Ota, Tokio. 24 September 1947

Dear Mrs. Pound,

Very sorry I have delayed so long to send you an answer for your letter.

In Japan, price of paper is very high and printing ink is not good. So I wrote to a Chinese friend of mine inquiring if Mr. E. P.'s *Confucian Anthology* could be printed in Shanghai. I have not yet got his answer, and so any way I tell you what it will cost to print it in Tokio.

Supposing 302 pages a copy, 2000 copies to be printed, it will cost Y2,000,000 for paper, and Y640,000 for printing. (Rate of conversion: Y200 for a dollar). This is an estimate on Sept. 20 at the present. The price will go up much more after two weeks or so in this inflation speed. Moreover it is difficult or almost impossible to send you sample of type and paper because of restrictions of communication by G.H.Q. I was not allowed to receive the copy of *Studio Integrale* that you wrote enclosed.

There is no means to receive the manuscripts, to send you back the copies, and to get money even if you send.

I think we must wait at least until peace treaty is concluded.

Congratulate Mary's marriage and the new birth of her son.

The other day Mr. D. D. Paige of Wellesley College wrote to me of publishing E. P. letters. I could meet his desire miraculously. A miracle would take place for the *Confucian Anthology!* Please tell Mr. E. P. not to be disappointed.

VOU is going to change its title for *Cendre*. You think it is just becoming to a poetry magazine in the defeated country, don't you?

> Ever yours,
> Katue Kitasono

116: Katue Kitasono to Ezra Pound

TLS-2   VOU CLUB 1649 1-tiome-nisi, Magome-mati, Omoriku, Tokio. 18 December 1947

Dear Ezra,

Christmas is close by, and I hope you are very much improved in health.

The magazine **VOU** is to be put out in January, 1948 under the new name *Cendre*.

The VOU Club members have changed from 1940, and almost all the most excellent poets in Japan have joined the VOU.

The young VOU poets in the twenties mostly read T. S. Eliot, T. E. Hulme, F. Kafka and P. Valéry. By touching such authors, they seem to try to reform themselves distorted in the military life.

About three weeks ago Ronald Duncan sent me his poems and his new book, *The Rape of Lucretia*. He wrote he was translating in English Cocteau's *La Belle et le Bête*. This picture will be released in Tokio, next January, and I am going to make a beautiful pamphlet about 8 pages for this film.

The translation of Cocteau's poem "Crucifixion" about 375 lines appeared in literary magazine *Europe* and I was little impressed with it.

Recently I read Paul Putnam's *Paris Was Our Mistress*. I think the fault of this book is that Putnam believes he knows artist's temperament.

A new experiment now I am trying is to bring a forceful and intellectual thrill into poetry. Such a poem like "The Raven" smelling of death and gunpowder.

D. D. Paige in Wellesley College asked me to send him E. P. letters which he is going to publish next year, and I sent them to him.

He said in his letter that the Pisan Cantos are among your finest work. Much to my regret I can't get and read them.

> Ever Yours,
> *Katue Kitasono*

117: Katue Kitasono to Ezra Pound
TPC-1   [n. p.] [January, 1948?]

DEAR E. POUND—

I send you a copy of the *Cendre* which is the rebirth of the **VOU**.

I hope a charming duck will be born out of these ashes.

I shall be so much pleased, if you will write me your impression about the *Cendre*.

> Ever yours,
> *Kit Kat*

118: Katue Kitasono to Dorothy Pound

TLS-1   VOU CLUB 1649 1-tiome-nisi Magome-mati, Ota, Tokio. 12 August 1948

Mrs. Dorothy POUND,

I thank you very much for your letter of June 30th and the extract from *Times-Herald*.

I'm so glad you read my poem in the *Four Pages*.

The other day I received "Pisan Cantos," which maybe Mr. D. D. Paige arranged for sending to me. I am going to introduce Pisan Cantos in the *Cendre* no. 5.

Sokolsky's opinion was very meaningful for me.

The Japanese is a great nation, or an uncanny robot. She is not great, even when considered in the most favourable light, then. . . .

The only way to save the Japanese in the present is anger. A man who has nothing to be angry about is no better than a Jelly-fish. PISAN CANTOS moves me with its great anger. Anger is just live God, live love. Yesterday, a small lovely book of poems arrived at me from Marcos Fingerit in la Plata.

Please give my best regards to E. P.

Ever yours,
Katue Kitasono

119: Katue Kitasono to Ezra Pound

TLS-1   VOU CLUB, 1649 1-Tiome-nisi, Magome-mati, Omoriku, Tokio. 28 September 1948

Dear Ezra Pound,

Much pleased to get your air mail of Sept. 19. I bought and read Kumasaka (recently published), which I send you under separate cover.

Did *Cendre* no. 4 reach you? Kenneth Rexroth, the Californian poet, sent me his translations in English of a hundred Manyo and Kokin Wakas.

They are done pretty well, I think.

Tokio is now in the depth of Autumn and crickets are singing away.

Ever yours,
Kitasono Katue

燕子樓中霜月夜
秋來唯為一人長
　　　　白樂天

晚膳時
把碟子排得像樹葉似的
菜花裏
尚荊
鷄兒腸等
每天
空虛
而又快樂了
碟子聲
遙入心坎
僅在哀愫裏沉重地震撼

它
穿過一斤草葉
穿過雲
充滿在陶工的
颯颯底思考裏
　　　　北園克衛

120: Katue Kitasono to Dorothy Pound

TLS-1   VOU CLUB 1649 1-nisi, Magome, Ota, Tokio. 15 December 1948

Mme. Pound,

I am so sorry I have delayed so long in answering to you about Mao Shih.

I found out a nice edition of Mao which I send you under separate cover. I fear this is not the exact one E. P. wants. As I don't know what is sealed character, I sent a letter to the librarian of Chung Shan University, asking if there is such an edition in China. I haven't got an answer yet from him. Please write me again and send the sample of the letters E. P. likes.

I will do my best in finding it.

Kit. Kat.

121: Katue Kitasono to Ezra Pound

TLS-1   VOU CLUB. 1649 1-nisi, Magome, Ota, Tokyo. 14 May 1949

Dear Ezra Pound,

I congratulate you on your winning the Bollingen Prize of 1948 for the *Pisan Cantos*. The news appeared in many newspapers and magazines in Japan. Can you imagine the deepest impression of those who love and respect you in this country?

I wish you to be in good health.

Ever yours,
Katue Kitasono

122: Katue Kitasono to Dorothy Pound

TLS-1   [Tokyo]. 20 September 1949

Dear Mrs. Dorothy Pound:

How is Mr. Pound?

As you may know, Mr. Thomas Cole accepted to write for the **VOU** the interview with Mr. Pound.

As I wish to publish it with Mr. Pound's photograph, if you have any, please be so kind as to send me one. I will return it back to you as soon as it is over.

Cendre changes its title for **VOU** again.

Ever yours,
Kitasono Katue

123: Katue Kitasono to Dorothy Pound
TLS-1   1-nishi, Magome, Ota, Tokyo. 7 December 1949

Dear Mrs. Dorothy Pound:

I have just sent out to you a photo of Fenollosa and stills of Umewaka Minoru under the separate cover. Most of these materials were burnt down or went astray during the war, but my stamina for searching them out at last caught a chance to have some of them. A few days ago I got the most splendid photo of Fenollosa from a Prof. Hisatomi Mitsugi, a student of Fenollosa. It was photoed at Yokohama in May 1939. As Prof. Hisatomi wanted to write a letter to Ez about Fenollosa, I told him your address. Please do him a favour.

One of the Umewaka Minoru stills is of *Kayoikomachi*, and the other, of *Kocho*, which were acted by Umewaka Minoru Junior. The tragical spirit of the Noh is perfectly presented in them, I think. I am sure Ez will be satisfied with them.

They will reach you about X'mas.

Mr. Thomas Cole's "Conversation with Pound" is going to appear in the **VOU** no. 35 issue.

Please remember me to Ez.
With best wishes,
Kitasono Katue

124: Katue Kitasono to Mary de Rachewiltz
TLS-2   Vou Club, 1649 1-nisi, Magome, Ota, Tokio. 8 May 1950

Dear Mary,

The air letter April 22 from you reached me in the morning on May 7.

How glad I was to hear from you again after so many years of pains of War! During the war it was a consolation for me to remember the friendship of you and your father to me. I still keep safely all your letters, photos and manuscript about Tirol that you wrote to me 10 years ago.

I knew, a few years ago, that you had married and been blessed with a baby. I should wish you joy at once, but in Japan at that time it was almost impossible to write to foreign friends.

Now I congratulate on your marriage and the births of Mr. Siegfried and Miss Patrizia. How splendid names they are!

Your father often sends me a telegram-like letter from Washington, and I, too, write him a telegram-like answer. But that's O.K. enough.

I earnestly wish the day may come swiftly when your father comes back to your Tyrolese castle with a Roman tower. You wait, I wait, and all the poets in the world over wait.

Please give my best regards to your family.

Ever Yours,
Katue Kitasono

125: Katue Kitasono to Dorothy Pound

TLS-2   VOU CLUB 1649 1-nisi, Magome, Ota, Tokio. 12 May 1950

Dear Mrs. Pound,

Excuse me for my long silence. Last Sunday I got the first letter of Mrs. Mary de Rachewiltz since the War. It was my greatest Joy to know that she was very happy in Italy.

I am reminded that I haven't yet written an answer to Mr. Ezra's letter asking how I do think about the article by Mr. Yasutaka Fumoto, "Influence of Confucius still vastly felt today," which had been published in the *Nippon Times*. Yasutaka is a moderate Sinologist, and this essay is not unique opinion of his own, but only a skillful arrangement of the issues by many Sinologists in Japan. Prof. Goto Sueo is said to be the best scholar in Sinology. He is the author of " 東西之文化流通 ." [*Cultural Currents Between East and West*] In China in 1934 朱謙之 [Chu Chïen-chih] wrote a book, " 中國思想之對歐州的影響 ." [*Influence of Chinese Ideas on Europe*]

Please tell this answer to Mr. Ezra.   With best wishes,
                                                   Kitasono Katue

126: Katue Kitasono to Dorothy Pound

TLS-1   [1649 1-nishi, Magome, Ota, Tokyo]. 24 May 1951

Dear Mrs. Pound,

I am very sorry that I have kept such a long silence, and hope you are all very well.

I have been waiting every moment for the news of Mr. Ezra's return. What a patience we must have!

Now after a year's reticence, the magazine **VOU** is ready to start again, expected to appear in the end of June, and I am anxious to translate and publish in it those exquisitely charming poems of Mr. E. P. as following:

"The Garret"

"Alba"

"In a Station of the Metro"

"The Encounter"

"Coitus"

"IMEIRΩ"

From the *Selected Poems* (N. D.)

Could I be allowed? If I could, would you be so kind as to send me a permission for my translation and publication of them?

I am eagerly looking forward to your kindest arrangement and answer. Please give my best wishes to Mr. Ez. when you meet him.

Very sincerely yours,
Kitasono Katue

127: Katue Kitasono to Ezra Pound

TLS-1   1649 1-nisi, Magome, Ota, Tokio. 4 November 1952

Dear Ezra Pound,

My friend Ueda Tamotsu who is a poet, surrealist, and now a professor of English literature in Keio University in Tokio wishes to translate and publish your *How to Read*. He has asked me to request you for him that you would kindly give him permission.

I believe that he will make the most excellent translation of it, and this will become a start for your many other important books to appear in Japanese hereafter.

I am sorry I must tell you that they cannot pay you for it, because the book will be of limited edition in a very small number.

I should be very much grateful, if you would be good enough to agree to it.

Very sincerely yours,
Kitasono Katue

128: Katue Kitasono to Ezra Pound & Dorothy Pound

Printed PC-1   1649 1-chome-nishi, Magomemachi, Otaku, Tokyo. 1 January 1953. (Two cards postmarked: 21 December 1952 and 1 January 1953, to Ezra Pound and Dorothy Pound] 謹賀新年

[A Happy New Year]

VOU CLUB
Katue Kitasono

129: Katue Kitasono to Ezra Pound

TLS-1   Tokio. 17 November 1953

Dear Ezra POUND,

I am very sorry that I haven't written to you such a long time.

The other day Michael Reck visited me (I hadn't seen him since February, and I was surprised to see him speak Japanese so fluently) and I showed him the typescript of the TRAXINIAI. He consented to take it to Mr. Ito Michio. He will soon come and tell me about it.

It was my greatest impression that I could catch the aspect of *Noh* in so vivid words and lively expression of you in *The Translations of E. P.*

Now I am reading Lewis' *Rotting Hill.*

Ever yours,
Kitasono Katue

130: Ezra Pound to Katue Kitasono
TLS-1   [n. p.] 30 January 1959

Dear and respected Kit-Kat, after many ages, and perfidies etc.

There seems at last a chance of getting DECENT edition of the *Odes*, with both seal character AND the reproduction of the magnificent text you sent me years ago. Have you any idea WHAT edition it is? I can send photo to refresh your memory. Beautiful characters, and the *Odes* without the notes, as they are in Mao etc.

I dare say Vanni sends you his printed matter?
Both the german and italian versions of TRAXINIAI are in process of production (stage) as well as print. BUT it will need the Minoru or japanese technique to get any result near to what I or Sophokles could get much pleasure from.

I recall, as ever Lady Gregory, when a north english company had mur-dered *The King's Threshold*: "An oi tell him whoi doesn't he wroite comedies, an den he would have a few pleasant moments whoile he's in deh teeYayter!"

I tell him why doesn't he write comedies and then he would have a few pleasant moments while he is in the theatre.

Projected edition of the *Odes* will have two texts in chinese, my american and Scarfoglio's italian, and the indication of the sound (which of course wont indicate MUCH, but at least the number of syllables in the original, and the tone variation).

Ever yours
Ezra Pound

131: Ezra Pound to Katue Kitasono
TLS-1   Hotel Italia, Rapallo, Italy. 12 June 1959

Dear Kit Kat

I am, as you can see from post mark, back in Rapallo where I rec'd your first letter, and where there is still a file of *Broletto*.
TRAXINIAI is being done in Berlin, heaven knows how, but some-one has said it will take them 50 years to see what has been done. I still believe that only a *Noh* company can do it properly.

I haven't learned kana YET. Pages of the magnificent text of the *Odes* that you sent have been photographed in the not extinguished hope of a decent edition, seal, that square character, my english and Scarfoglio's italian. BUT. . . .

It might help if some critic not in terror of the american "cultural" (bless your heart) "foundations," should animadvert on the delays in transmission and the spirit of Harvard and other universities. Beauson Tseng has approved the translation, if you know who he is, or if there is any survival of Tcheu's lament: they ought to be like brothers, they read the same books.

Kripalani has just sent me his translation of Tagore's novels, and some Gandhi.

Books are kept in the Warsaw cellarage. More editors might follow your method of printing a few words in the language of the books they mention, which would at least tell the ignorant alien what they consider worth notice.

I have enough superfluous bone (calcination) in my neck to supply a giraffe, and it has been slowing me down.

I don't imagine the *Japan Times* has been returned to the people who had it before my untimely note on Matsuoka? Or that other than æsthetic ideas have much more outlet in Tokyo than anywhere else? I suspect you have forgotten your english during the past 20 years. At the same time one might manage more lively exchange of correspondence. Young Reck must know enough japanese to help at it.

I don't think you have ever mentioned Junzaburo, or Iwasaki. After success of TRAXINIAI in the german translation (Eva Hesse) there are requests for *Noh*, for performance in Germany.

The charming member of your other profession, who had 200 varieties of roses in his Rapallo (quite small) garden has passed into whatever non-Bhudist realm of non- or not-non existence. There is a spate of building, in I suspect, very unstable material, and less beach open to the unorganized public. The gulf still contains water and the mountains not greatly altered by bombing raids *d'antan*.

Very interesting fotos in one **VOU** that I have passed on to the Oberti, who will, I think, send you *Ana etc.*, they and their friend Carrega will take note of anything your friends send them. Does anyone want a copy of Boris' bilingual *Book of the Dead*? No use my sending Scheiwiller notices if he has already done so. Mary's *Kagekiyo* has gone into another large edition. What does Japan do with TV?

Italian phrase heard recently: memories are the white hairs of the heart. From wife of old tennis pal of mine now invalid.

benedictions,
Ez. P.

132: Katue Kitasono to Mary de Rachewiltz
TLS-1   1-26, 5 chome, Akasaka, Minatoku, Tokyo, Japan. 28 November 1966

Dear Mary de Rachewiltz,

Your book of poems, *Di Riflesso*, reached me safely passing through many hands from my former address. I cannot read your poems, because I don't know Italian language, but visually I can see that these poems are very nice and beautiful. Many thanks.

I lost many of my books I loved during the war, among which the text of your story is included. Very, very sorry!

with best wishes,
Kitasono Katue

P.S. I also thank you for the copy of your fine work of translation, *Il Teatro Giapponese No.*

III POUND'S POST-WORLD WAR II CONTACTS WITH JAPAN: 1956–68

In THIS SECTION are collected five letters of Ryōzō Iwasaki to Ezra Pound, seven letters of Pound to Iwasaki, one letter of Shirō Tsunoda to Pound, a fragment of Pound's letter to Tsunoda, one letter of Pound to Tomoji Okada, and one letter of Pound to the Librarian, University of Virginia.

The first book-length collection of Pound's poems in Japanese appeared in 1956, the culmination of years of dedicated effort of Ryōzō Iwasaki (1908–76), then Professor of English Literature at Keio University. A scholar working in classical Greek and Latin literature, Iwasaki provided an amply annotated translation which immediately won very favorable notice.

In his letter to Pound, Iwasaki enclosed a poem by his colleague, Junzaburō Nishiwaki, who had written the "Preface" to Iwasaki's translation. On reading the poem, Pound suggested to Iwasaki that Nishiwaki be recommended to the Swedish Academy as a Nobel Prize candidate. This note from Pound, though brief, created a tremendous impact on the Japanese literary world.

Since his undergraduate days, Iwasaki had been associated with various literary circles, and had written a number of critical essays. In 1927, a year after he entered Keio University, he joined four other young people to start the magazine, *Butai Shinsei* (*New Voices on Theatre*). And in 1931, with other members of the University, he launched another magazine, *Shin Mita-ha* (*New Mita Group*).

His interest in Pound goes back to his early years. In 1934 he wrote "Poetics of Mr. Pound" for the *Shihō* (*Poetics*) edited by Shirō Murano and Azuma Kondō. He also contributed essays on modern poets including Pound to the poetry journal, *Shinryōdo* (*New Territory*), around 1937.

During World War II his main concern was directed toward classical Roman literature. He published *A History of Roman Literature* in 1940 and *Selected Works of Cicero* in 1943. But after the war, his interest in American literature was revived. He wrote "Ezra Loomis Pound" for *Seminars on Contemporary Poetry* (Sōgensha) in 1950. He then published the translation, *Ezra Pound: Selected Poems* (Arechi Shuppan, 1956). In October, 1965, Iwasaki spoke over the radio (NHK) on Ezra Pound in celebration of his 80th birthday, broadcasting also selected recordings of Pound's own readings. For the poetry magazine, *Mugen* (*Infinity*), he wrote three articles:

"The Structure of the *Cantos*" (August, 1960), "Cock and Snail: Pound and Eliot" (October, 1965), and "Ezra Pound and Cummings" (November, 1967). [As for his other works on Pound, see Donald Gallup, *A Bibliography of Ezra Pound*.] When Iwasaki traveled through Italy on his way to England in 1961, Pound's illness regrettably made it impossible for him to meet the aged poet.

While still in Washington, D.C., Pound received a letter from another Japanese scholar, Shirō Tsunoda (1922–   ), now professor at Obirin University. Though Pound was busy at that time, with various people outside the hospital trying to have the court dismiss the indictment against him, he replied providing several answers to Tsunoda's questions on his poetry. It is a pity that, except for one fragment which is printed in the following section, the remainder of the letter was lost.

Tomoji Okada, a retired businessman, wrote Pound offering a correction of a misleading passage in Pound's Introduction to his Nō translation. Pound had written that, after Fenollosa's sudden death in London, the Japanese government had "sent a warship for his body." But Okada claimed to know that Fenollosa's ashes had been brought to Japan via the Siberian Railroad. In fact, Okada had asked his friend Yasotarō Katō, who was returning to Japan via Siberia, to carry Fenollosa's ashes to Japan with him. Pound's letter to Okada may reflect his attitude toward history: "I certainly did not invent it." One may wonder if indeed the ashes were brought back to Japan on a Japanese warship over the Japan Sea. But Tokutarō Shigehisa, who later investigated the matter, suggests that the ashes probably arrived at Tsuruga from Vladivostok on September 19, 1909 on the Hōzanmaru of the Osaka Shipping Co. (Tokutarō Shigehisa, "Fenollosa's Ashes and Japan," *Comparative Literature*, vol. 2, 1959, pp. 83–4.)

In 1968 when the present editor visited with Pound in Paris, the poet wrote a note to the librarian at the University of Virginia granting permission for access to a microfilm copy of the Fenollosa notebooks. All the notebooks of Fenollosa sent to Pound by Mary Fenollosa were at that time under lock and key, and it would have been impossible otherwise for me to have read them. At the time, Hugh Kenner's microfilm of part of the notebooks had been stored at the library of the University of Virginia.

133: Ryozo Iwasaki to Ezra Pound

TLS-4   1-34, Mita, Minatoku, Tokyo, Japan. 30 November 1956

Dear Mr. Pound,

I am sending you the Japanese translation of your poems to-day. It has meant a great deal to me. I have no words to apologize to you for publishing your poems without permission. *The Waste Land* has been translated by several hands in our country, but "Hugh Selwyn Mauberley" has never been put into Japanese, and some favourable comments to my translation have appeared in Japanese newspapers. But I must confess it was a very difficult task. I wonder what it will seem to you. I want you to tell me what effect it has on you.

I had a very pleasant journey to Kobe the other day, and found that Ernest Fenollosa's lock of hair had been buried at Homyoin, Enjoji Temple in Otsu, near Kyoto. I enclose photographs of the grave, which was built by Mr. Laurence Binyon and other foreigners. The weather was most over-whelmingly lovely. He sleeps among the cedar grove and beautiful ferns by the Lake Biwa (i.e. lute). *Vale! Vale!*

Yours very sincerely,
Ryozo Iwasaki

Appendix 1

Contents of *Selected Poems of Ezra Pound* (Japanese Translation)

Appendix 2   By Junzaburo Nishiwaki

January in Kyoto

Janus, old man,
Your name is damp and grey and too prolonged
A ring to rattle in my verse;
You double-faced, diluted churl of churls,
You corn-dull, poppy-wilted, beaver-brown,

You snow-eater, a parasite on roots and berries,
Iconoclast of gins and perries,
You're really one of the pariah dogs
Yelping, thrash-worth, at the belated gods.
I know the deities would rather inflate
And flow in pipes than in metric odes, but now
You suddenly brought us shy myth,
When we, disguised as Zeus and Hermes, went
Looking for orchids that will hang oblong and dim
At cuckoo-crow at the hell lady's door,
In the Hiei foot-hills by pebbly-purring streams.

We went into a peasant's cottage to see
How one cleans and adorns one's range
With a sprig of rue and a tangle of hips
To honour the bluff god of the kitchen fire.
The old baucis-and-philemon tree rustled its top:
"Reverend sirs, you are early. Well now."
My friend, a Ben Jonson scholar at the university,
And a complete parr angler, could speak
The Yase doric: "Look what we've got,
Such lovely slender buds; may we leave
These things with you by this mercury bush,
As we're going to see Emau Convent up there?"
Again we went out into loam land, dreaming
Of Angels and pottery crystal-beaming:
This time as tinkers we wandered . . .
Post-orchid journey it will be named.
A redolent trek, there was a smell
Of yellow plum blossom in the turnip fields.
"Who is it walking with you, strangers?"
"It is a woman."
She is in holy visibility:
That was an old woman with the help of a stick
On her way from Shu-gaku-in to Iwakura
To draw out money, the account book on her head,
Nicely done up in a peony-patterned cloth
Probably to ransom her helen out of peonage.
She had a leer like a boar
And had a stutter like Darley;

But it might be thunder if she chose to parley.
Excited by our indignation on the boar ravages,
With fury and frothing she made a Delphic utterance:
"It only took them a night to devour
A middlesex acre (as Macaulay says) of your yams;
Last year they shot a huge one, but nobody
Could bear him away, so there you are . . ."
So saying she glowered at us and passed by.
Now I come to the second nonnes tale:
We greeted the ancress in a most elegant way;
Unrobed, aproned, head tonsured as azure as
The kingfisher's wings, sweeping up fallen leaves
Among the landscape stones green with moss,
Herself indistinguishable from the blue.
"Good morning, Madame Eglantine, may I
See your garden? Wonderful!
And do you happen to know my relation
Who is a prioress living near Kitano-Tenjin?"
"I wouldn't know, sir. But how odd, when I've been
Of the same tribe nearly all my life.
Bo tree, that. Very, very rare."
"Perhaps you could let me have a twig in the spring;
I'd like to graft it on a stock . . . mulberry it is."
Enlightenment . . . an entwining of rose and bay.
"By all means. Secretum secretorum!"
When we returned full circle to the roots
Of our orchids, we maundered to sanctify
Fertility . . . magic jabber . . . over cups of tea.
The wife decanted golden mead to immortalize
Our chats and our pseudo-godliness, but we tried
Hard to hide our mortality . . .

Biographical Note: J. Nishiwaki was born in 1896. He graduated at Keio
University but later studied English literature at Oxford University. He is
the author of a number of books on English and European languages and
literature and has translated Eliot's *The Waste Land* into Japanese. He has
published several books of poems and although his output has been small,
he is one of the most influential of modern poets in Japan to-day. He is at
present Professor of English literature at Keio University.

134: Ezra Pound to Ryozo Iwasaki
TLS-2   [Pmk: WASHINGTON D.C.] 28 December 1956

Dear Ryozo Iwasaki

It has been a most delightful Xmas, and I have you to thank for two of the pleasant surprises. Your elegantly printed "Mauberley" ⟨& other poems⟩, and J. N.'s Janus Poem, the latter MOST opportune, as Stock has started a magazine which badly needs it. *Edge,* edited by Noel Stock

436 Nepean Rd., East Brighton S. 6, Melbourne, Australia
Started with the highest aims of any review since Ford's *English Review* in 1908. To whom I trust you and Junzaburo will contribute *at once.* He has printed a few translations of mine and the long-needed Zielinski *Sibylle/* but there was the LACK of vortex; of concentration of creative talents such as made *The Little Review* with Lewis, Joyce, and Eliot.

Don't credit me with a knowledge of Japanese, let alone the ability to judge the style of your translation or its nearness to the original. I am delighted with the look of the edition, happy to see the W. L. portrait on the jacket (portrait now on show in N. York), and having only partially unwrapped the volume, had the second and delayed pleasure and surprise of finding D. P.'s cover design for *Ripostes* on the reverse. Looking much better enlarged to that size and with the nippon script cohering much better with the design than the heavy english lettering of the original. In short a pleasant yesterday. And the 40 year after surge of coincidence. W. L.'s preface for HIS show at the Tate and my note on La Martinelli having been done without collusion . . . in a way that would have pleased Yeats' astrological yearnings.

Junzaburo has a more vital english than any I have seen for some time. AND if you choose such good company I can well believe you have made a good job of the "Mauberley," and trust if you also write in english or translate your own poems you will send copies both to Stock and myself.
I have enjoyed that Janus poem more than anything I have come on for some time.

I recall Ford on one occasion re/ lack of literary comprehension in London: "That is why one feels so DAMN lonely." And at the opposite extreme, it is heartening to find that another good poet exists.

One or two questions, as yr/ oxfordian friend has a vocabulary which includes "ancress"/ may be he has a dictionary which includes "perries."

I have no english dictionary here/ only greek and chinese, so I can't hunt for it, and IF it is a typing slip, he might correct it before sending the ms/ to Stock (which, as above, I hope he will do). I shall tell Stock I have asked him to.

It cant be misprint for berries, which occurs as rhyme in line preceding. Probably IS oxonian, and not yankee.

Thrash-worth, or thrash-worthy

/ If he wants thrash-worth, let it stand.

It is stronger/ but one wants to be on guard when writing a foreign language. You improve it, and it is set down to ignorance. Stock must know it is intentional.

⟨These are very fussy comments on matters of small importance, but I don't want to lose time with Stock.⟩ Again parr, or par.?

Don't imagine that I ever knew how to spell in ANY language, and have certainly forgotten a good deal that I knew temporarily. I hear an Athenian taxi driver was lamenting that he couldn't help me to correct the greek in *Cantos/* which IS, at least partly, due to american printer OMITTING corrections AFTER they had been properly set up. Besides whatever state the typescript is in, Melbourne will probably ADD a few errors. Does the helen want a capital (Helen)? peri, for periwinkle? in l. 7?? A joke that I shd/ be asking for footnotes. Darley?

At the boar's ⟨is **not** necessary⟩ ravages.

so there you are

⟨*"Stetson" is used with emphasis, no implication that reader already knows of him.*⟩

(These two might be typing slips?)

Other Xmas items at this end. Amaral's *Cantares Pisanos* AT last issued by Univ. of Mexico. Eva's *Pisaner Gesänge* and popular edtn. pocket book *Dichtung und Prosa.* No. 2. *Edge* with the Zielinski. And AT last the TRAXINIAI in London with some addenda. I will send *Academia Bulletins* slow post. Thanks for the Fenollosa fotos. And give my regards to the Minoru. It was his grandfather's foto on my mantelpiece that lowered the bamboo curtain with Ito and Kumé in London, 40 years ago. And the present Minoru in Kagekiyo mask is on cover of my daughter's Italian translation of the Fenollosa-E. P. impression of that play. ⟨*They met at Venice festival.*⟩ The TRAXINIAI translation was due to rereading the Noh translations for collected translations, and to make *Verkehr* with Lorenzatos greek edition of *Cathay* . . . a current toward intercommunications.

I will ask Vanni Scheiwiller to send you some of his editions, or, as he runs on enthusiasm, perhaps the Keio Univ. will want some for their library. The stone tablet text of *Pivot* is neater in the Italian bilingual than in the larger New Directions edtn/ and the outrage of delays and sabotage in connection with Harvard press, which should have done the *Odes* with seal character and sound-graph, one more infamy on the neck of this unfortunate continent.

At any rate, do send me more news as the incarcerated live on their post-bag.

cordiali saluti to both of you.
Ezra Pound

135: Ryozo Iwasaki to Ezra Pound
TLS-1   [n. p.] 8 April 1957

Dear Mr. Pound:

I have accused myself for not writing to you. Many thanks for your cordial letter and *Academia Bulletins*. I felt as if I actually met you and listened to your witty *causerie*. I have just read through Mr. Denis Goacher's "Pictures of E. P." in the *Nimbus*, and I have been keenly feeling that the world is incompatible with the wisdom of a genuine poet. Yet I believe an artist should be allowed his own vision.

My heart was filled with intense sorrow when I heard the news of Wyndham Lewis's death. I can well understand your feelings, though *omnes eodem cogimur*.

Junzaburo Nishiwaki won the Yomiuri prize for poetry the other day for his *The Third Myth*, which contains Janus poem in Japanese version. He expresses his gratitude and delight for your helpful and inspiring criticism. I hear George Darley (1795–1846), an Irish poet, was a stutterer. He says he will send you some other poems before long.

The London edition of *Traxiniai* came to my hand this morning. I read your version in the *Hudson Review* a few years ago. I will press Kitasono to translate it into Japanese as soon as possible. (I hear he has been depressed by a love affair.) In recent years No plays written by the modern authors are on at the various theatres in Tokyo, and some of them are successful.

I think Italy must be a very pleasant country to live in. My brother-in-law is the Japanese Ambassador at Rome. I hope I shall be able to travel in

Italy—where every footstep is fraught with memories—during his tenure of office.

There is a story that when, after the last war, Norman Douglas applied to the Italian Government for permission to return to Capri, he was told that no foreigner was allowed to settle in Italy. "I do not wish to live in Italy," he replied, "I wish to die there." His request was granted.

May I ask you some questions?

1. *Or through dawn-mist*
    The grey and rose
    Of the juridical
    Flamingoes: "Mauberley" IV
    What is the meaning of the juridical in this context?

2. Who is Headlam? ("Mauberley")

    John Espey says that Headlam is the Rev. Stewart Headlam, though Friar and Brinnin say that he is the R. Rev. Arthur C. Headlam, the Bishop of Gloucester.

    Please forgive me for the trouble I am causing you.

In exchange for your kindness, I am sending you *Japanese No Plays, Confucian Analects* by Dr. Legge, and *T'ao Yüan-ming* in Chinese characters, which I am sure you will like.

Sincerely Yours,
Ryozo Iwasaki

136: Ezra Pound to Ryozo Iwasaki
TLS-1   St. Elizabeths. 11 April 1957

Dear Ryozo Iwasaki

I wonder if what Ito would have called your "brother in row" is the Ambassador my daughter met when the Minoru took the *Noh* to Venice?

I hope Junzaburo will continue to "*dérocher*," but wish you would both get in touch with Noel Stock, NOW. (Occidental vulgarity, we live in eternity, but magazines do not, and the better a periodical the more precarious its existence, and the greater the need to get the best available matter printed before the editor goes bust.)

I dont think Kit Kat knows enough english to translate TRAX-INIAI.

BUT am convinced the Noh technique is only way of doing it properly, in whatever language.

No poet shd/ be depressed by a love affair/ if accepted he can enjoy it/ if given the "heave-ho" it shd/ improve his prosody and versification. And Kit Kat must be several years younger than I am.

When you get to Italy you must spend a few days with my descendents at Schloss Brunnenburg—Tirolo, Merano.

"juridical"/ gravity of the bird, the general legal attitude/ etc.

I shd/ say the lizard is professorial/ at least one memorable occasion of main body of said animal, utterly impassive, returning to inspect the excited movements of its own tail knocked off by a cat. Of course situation much more serious for tail (irrevocable), whereas lizard cd/ replace same with patience.

Headlam, Stuart (or Stewart), member of rhymers club, I dont think he attained prebebde.

Do you know Dr. Kojiro Yoshikawa? He has sent his East-flow West-flow to Sheri, my copy hasn't come.

If you can persuade yr/ publisher to extend his operation by sending review copies of your "Mauberley" to h. de campos, r. dr. franco da rocha 232, s. paulo, Brasil
AND to Stock, and to Eva Hesse O'Donnell, Franzjosef str/ 7. vi, München 13, Germany
I think they wd/ spread the glad tidings.
Also to García Terrés, Universidad de Mexico, Mexico City, Mexico. The Ministry of Education in Brazil, and Mex. University are publishing the Spanish Pisans, and portuguese 17 Cantos.

The venerable Chiang encourages me with the jail sentence of King Wen and Confucio and other respectable chinamen.

In just what sense do you use word "stutterer" re/ Darley? I take it [it] is J. N. who is sending poems. Quicker to send 'em to Stock, and he will print 'em and send on more copies.

Jo Bard lecturing in the Canary Isles, rhymes with yr/ use of the very Possum in the preterite.

And I shall be grateful for the To Emmei.

cordiali saluti
Ez P

137: Ryozo Iwasaki to Ezra Pound

TLS-2   Keio University, Mita, Minatoku, Tokyo, Japan. 24 June 1957

Dear Mr. Ezra Pound:

I've received a parcel containing Italian *Kagekiyo, Confucio, Cantos, Iconografia* and *Lavoro ed Usura*, etc. the other day. Many many thanks for your kindness and all those wonderful books Mrs. Mary de Rachewiltz sent me. In particular *Iconografia* and *Confucio* are so beautiful that they fairly take my breath away. In exchange for her kindness I sent her my "Mauberley" and *Japanese Masks*, which I'm sure she will like. And also I sent you *Japanese Masks* and *Taiga*. Ikeno Taiga (1723–76) is one of the Southern School Artists. He had a true enthusiasm for Chinese culture, and was earnest in Chinalizing the Japanese landscape, as the Augustan poets in England used to Latinizing the English world.

J. N.'s Janus poem will be published in *Edge* no. 5. He's deeply grateful to you. I sent my "Mauberley" to Mr. Stock, h. de campos, Eva Hesse O'Donnell, and García Terrés last month.

Commemorating the fiftieth anniversary of Fenollosa's death, a biography was published in Tokyo. I'm writing now an essay on Mr. Pound and Fenollosa. Donald Davie, a young critic and Fellow of Trinity College, paid a great homage to *The Chinese Written Character* in his *Articulate Energy*. How and when did you happen to be acting as literary executor of Fenollosa? (Fenollosa's name first appeared in your letter, To William C. Williams, 19 Dec., 1913.) Please tell me the circumstances.

One of my students is writing a doctor thesis on Yeats's plays. She had been in England for three years, and brought back some photographs of Yeats's MSS. May I ask you some questions?

1. Do you know the date when Yeats started *At the Hawk's Well?*

2. Did Yeats actually write the first draft at *Coole Park*, being quite independent from your assistance?

3. To what extent did you help Yeats in the progress of writing *At the Hawk's Well*, or other plays, if any?

4. Can you give us a statement in which you testify Yeats's zeal for the Far Eastern art, etc? (including the *Noh*, of course.)

May I publish your letters in the Japanese magazine, omitting too personal passages (e.g. Kit Kat's knowledge in English) and adding some foot-notes?

Etiam atque-etiam vale,

P.S. Minoru started for Paris several days ago.   *Ryozo Iwasaki*

138: Ezra Pound to Ryozo Iwasaki
TLS-1   St. Elizabeths, D.C. 21 August 1957

Dear Ryozo Iwasaki

No literary prize or jury award can alter the weight of a consonant or change the length of a vowel, but on the practical side, if you have some sort of Japanese Academy or authoritative body, it could do no harm to bring Junzaburo Nishiwaki's work to the attention of the Swedish Academy; I do not recall their having yet honoured Nippon.

ever yours
E Pound

139: Ryozo Iwasaki to Ezra Pound
TLS-1   [n. p.] 3 September 1957

Dear Mr. Ezra Pound:

Thank you for your nice letter of the 21st; I enjoyed every word. We can conscientiously recommend Mr. J. N. most heartily. We are now looking into the proper procedure, and I believe we must get a letter of recommendation from you. He'll write you a letter asking a favour. I'll send you some materials one of these days.

The opening ceremonies of the xxix International PEN Congress was held in Tokyo yesterday. The congress will spend four days in Tokyo before moving to Kyoto for the final two days and the closing session. Its highlight will be a symposium on the theme of the current meeting: "The Reciprocal Influence of Eastern and Western Literature on Writers of the Present Day and of the Future, both in Relation to æsthetic Values and to Ways of Life."

We can find the following names in the list of Congress members: Mr. Karl Shapiro, Mrs. John G. Fletcher, John Dos Passos, John Steinbeck, Elmer Rice, Alberto Moravia, Stephen Spender etc.

We shall enjoy viewing of Noh play tomorrow afternoon.

Sincerely yours,
Ryozo Iwasaki

140: Ezra Pound to Ryozo Iwasaki
TLS-1   [n. p.] 6 September 1957

Dear Ryozo

It would be most improper for me as a private citizen to recommend J. N. formally.

I can express an opinion to you as a friend, but believe nominations can come only from organized official bodies belonging to the writer's own country or from authors who have already received the Nobel Award.

Also, not being able to read Japanese, I have only a hunch and one of his poems in English to go on.

I should be delighted if I am right in my guess, and if he gets the Award.

AS to the pollution of the orient by introduction of tainted minds from the occident and Mesopotamia

God help you. There is a popular english ditty "Heaven will PROTECT the working girl."

Let us pray that some of the real criteria/ wasn't it Mat Arnold: "The best that has been known and thought."

For gods sake get hold of the real occidental classics and consult people who are faithful to them.

AND make a start by attacking the great lie that the jews gave the world religion.

The whole of India and China and Greece OUGHT to oppose this. The history of mediæval europe is that of a conflict between maniacs and savages, with a dash of malevolence, greed of conquest, pollution.

There may be no righteous wars in the "Spring and Autumn" but I have never heard of either Bhudists or Taoists using religion as a pretext for slaughter. Nor is it Confucian.

I wonder if Elmer Rice is an innocuous centenarian or at least a contemporary whom I had thought extinct ⟨that must have been Cole Rice⟩.

I hope NO influence brought by that set of Pens will get into Tokyo. But give my *cordial greetings* to Rice, if it is the old relique, and to Fletcher's widow, neither of whom will be carrying "influence."

I dare say this will arrive after the conflict, but you can store it for next time.

Hagoromo is a sacrament. And a glory. Tami Kumé danced the tennin part before the Emperor at the age of six. And remembered it in London, where he showed us the movements in 1917 or about then. Later a Tokugawa and some daimyo gave bits of *Noh* and *Kiogen* privately in his studio in Paris. These are things to remember.

ever yours
Ezra Pound

141: Ryozo Iwasaki to Ezra Pound
TLS-1   Keio University, Mita, Minatoku, Tokyo, Japan. 9 September 1957

Dear Mr. Pound:

At your kind suggestion we have officially made an application to the Swedish Academy for Dr. Junzaburo Nishiwaki as a Nobel prize candidate, and we should be grateful if you could send us a word of recommendation for his work, which we might use as an important reference to be filed in among the necessary documents.

Yours sincerely
Ryozo Iwasaki

142: Ezra Pound to Ryozo Iwasaki
TLS-1   St. Elizabeths, D.C., 11 October 1957

Dear Ryozo Iwasaki

I am very glad to hear of your committee's decision.

It would be presumptuous of me to express an opinion on the qualities of a man's writing in a language which I am, unfortunately, unable to read, or to have views as to his status among other writers whose work is *wholly* unknown to me.

From what I have seen [of] Dr. Junzaburo Nishiwaki's work in English there is no possible doubt of his sensibility and the range and quality of his culture.

I should be delighted to have my guess confirmed by those competent, as seems to be indicated by your letter. And I should participate in the pleasure of any honour that may be done him.

cordially yours
Ezra Pound

143: Shiro Tsunoda to Ezra Pound

TLS-1   1156 Karasuyama-cho, Setagaya-ku, Tokyo. 13 January 1958

Dear Mr. Pound:

Excuse me for my rudeness in writing you a letter without anyone who introduces me to you. While I was studying modern poetry in the University of Miami, Florida, as a Fulbright Exchange teacher under the sponsorship of U.S. Office of Education, I was much interested in and deeply appreciated your poetry and study of Noh. Now teaching English and American literature in a senior high school, I am going to publish my thesis on "The Influence of Chinese Poetry and Japanese Tanka and Noh on Mr. Pound's Poetry." But I have come to several points on which I would like to ask you questions. You went to London in 1909 but did you study Noh from Mr. Fenollosa's manuscripts before that? You put the title *Personae* to the collection of your poems published in London in 1909. How did you think of the title *Personae* (etymologically *Per* = through, *Sona* = sound) meaning the mask or the role as was shown in Greek play. Did you not think of highly artistic mask of Noh plays, though you perhaps got a hint from Browning's *Dramatis Personae*? While you were absorbed by painting and sculpture, were you interested in any of Japanese or Chinese paintings?

As for your poem, "The Tree," whose first five lines run as follows:

> *I stood still and was a tree amid the wood,*
> *Knowing the truth of things unseen before;*
> *Of Daphne and the laurel bow*
> *And that god-feasting couple old*
> *That grew elm-oak amid the wold.*

Did not you think of an old man and woman symbolized by pine-trees in *Takasago*, one of the best and most illuminating Noh plays, when you wrote "that god-feasting couple old"?

And as for "The Encounter," what is meant by the last two lines which run:

> *Her fingers were like the tissue*
> *Of a Japanese paper napkin.*

If you kindly answer these questions, it will be a great help to a study of the East and West flow of literature and I am much obliged to you.

If you are still interested in Noh plays, I will gladly send you the photos of the performances of Nohs recently presented by such schools as Umewaka, Kanze, Hohsho, Kongo, etc. Some of the Americans in Tokyo such as Dr. Ulmann, Fulbright professor, are very eager to study Noh.

I will translate into English any of the plays which you want and send it to you.

Hoping that I receive your answer, I remain,

Sincerely yours,
Shiro Tsunoda

144: Ezra Pound to Shiro Tsunoda

TLS-1 (fragment)   St. Elizabeths Hospital. 18 January 1958

. . . I can't switch back to work on Noh this moment, but am having difficulty in making some people understand that only the Minoru or some other Noh company with which I am unacquainted, but not Broadway, would be able to do *Traxiniai* as I want it done. . . .

Ezra Pound

145: Ezra Pound to Ryozo Iwasaki

TLS-1   [Schloss Brunnenburg] 18 November 1958

Dear Ryozo Iwasaki

I have at last got back to ⟨my⟩ archives
and yesterday opened Fenollosa's notes on Prof. Mori's lectures on the History of Chinese Poetry.

The damned sinologues who are trying to suppress all classical intelligence will be out with the trench tools to sabotage any revival of interest.

This is the first time I have been able to look at the Fenollosa heritage since learning a bit about the ideograms.

I am still fairly defenceless re/ equivalence of Jap and Chinese names.

The work seems to be very lively. Would it incommode you to go thru my text a few pages at a time, as I dig it out from the pencil scribble, and try to get it into clear sentences?

Best wishes to Junzaburo   yours cordially
                                                            Ezra Pound

146: Ezra Pound to Ryozo Iwasaki

TLS-1   [Schloss Brunnenburg] 6 December 1958

Dear Ryozo Iwasaki

The grandson of Leo Frobenius, whom I consider was the best mind in Europe for about 40 years, wants to get to Japan, aim to continue Fenollosa's work.

It would give chance for correlation of the better thought of Europe with the japanese heritage.

I don't know what chance of exchange could be developed with the Forschungs Institut founded by his grandfather in Frankfurt, but in any case I hope he will call on you when (and/or if) he gets to Japan.

My daughter works on Junzaburo's poems, but with me on the premises and increased family, need to attend to house and farm, she cannot give all her time to literary studies. I hope our distinguished confrère will have patience, and also understand the harassments of publishers (Scheiwiller in particular) at the present time.

She has been so intent on my work that she has, for a decade, neglected to mention the importance of that of her husband. If there are any egyptologists in Japan, they might be interested in his latest publication.

I have only within the past weeks realized the amount of work he has done, and the importance of what is still unpublished, particularly in regard to agriculture and the work of Del Pelo Pardi (re/ plowing etc.)

cordially yrs.
Ezra Pound

147: Ezra Pound to Tomoji Okada
TCS-1   Brunnenburg, Tirolo di Merano. 22 [January or August] 1959

Dear Mr. Okada

To best of my memory, Mrs. Fenollosa was under impression that the Government wished to honour E. F. in manner stated. I shall of course insert your information if book is ever reprinted, though it rather detracts from government prestige. Thanking you for your letter. I wonder if the erroneous statement also occurs in the Heineman vol/ on Art? Battling against the cumulative falsification of history ancient and contemporary, I cannot keep up with all details. After nearly half a century I can't be sure Mary Fenollosa made the statement, but I certainly did not invent it.

⟨Is it possible that the Government OFFERED to provide transport?⟩

Cordially yours,
Ezra Pound

148: Ezra Pound to Sanehide Kodama
ALS-1   1 rue Grande Chaumière, Paris. 9 September 1968

Librarian, University of Virginia

Please permit Professor Kodama to consult microfilms of Fenollosa manuscripts from my collection.

Ezra Pound

IV   POUND'S CONTRIBUTIONS TO JAPANESE PERIODICALS: 1939–40

DURING THE YEARS 1939 and 1940, Pound enthusiastically wrote articles from Italy to Japanese newspapers on the European cultural, political, and economic events of the time. In 1940, he had become the Italian Correspondent of the *Japan Times*.

The *Japan Times* was founded in 1897 as the first and oldest English newspaper edited by Japanese in Japan. It wished, as the first editor, Motosada Zumoto, put it, to "endeavor to explain things and smooth the way between foreigners and Japanese." Its "slogan" has been "All the News Without Fear or Favor." In 1918 it merged with the *Japan Mail and Times* (originally started as the *Japan Mail* in 1870 but changed its name at the merger with the short-lived *Japan Times* which had been established in 1878). [For further reference *see The Japan Times: A History from 1861 to the Present*, ed. Shinichi Hasegawa (Tokyo, 1966).]

At the time Pound was contributing his articles to the newspaper, its official name was *The Japan Times and Mail*. Its chief editor, Yasotarō Mōri, was a friend of Katue Kitasono.

Pound's articles, however, are *his* observations and *his* analyses of Europe in the pre-war and early war years. Some parts are somewhat biased, but scattered throughout are some quite illuminating passages. Collected here (under somewhat regularized revised headings) are:

1 Tri-lingual System Proposed for World Communications (15 May 1939)
2 Death of Yeats: End of Irish Literary Revival (5 June 1939)
3 Study of Noh Continues in West (10 December 1939)
4 An Ezra Pound Letter from Rapallo (8 January 1940)
5 From Rapallo: An Ezra Pound Letter (4 March 1940)
6 From Rapallo: An Ezra Pound Letter (18 April 1940)
7 From Rapallo: An Ezra Pound Letter (13 June 1940)
8 Letter from Rapallo: In War Appear Responsibilities (22 July 1940)
9 From Rapallo: An Ezra Pound Letter (12 August 1940)
10 From Rapallo: An Ezra Pound Letter (26 August 1940)
11 From Rapallo: An Ezra Pound Letter (2 September 1940)
12 From Rapallo: An Ezra Pound Letter (29 September 1940)

The original title for article 1 was in Pound's typescript "Communications, or Cultural Front," and for article 2, "Cultural News: State of the Occident in April, anno XVII Era Fascisti (a.d. 1939)." Article 4 bore the sub-heading "Annual Music Week," and article 5, "Ezra Pound Asks Scholars Here to Solve Issues." Articles 6 and 7 appeared in the *Japan Times Weekly* (published also by the *Japan Times and Mail*), and articles 9, 10, 11 and 12 were reprinted in it, respectively, on 22 August, 5 September, 12 September, and 10 October (1940).

I am indebted to the work done by Shirō Tsunoda on articles 1, 2, and 3 which appeared in "A Study of Some Articles Contributed by Ezra Pound to *The Japan Times and Mail*," *Obirin University Studies of English and American Literature*, nos. 23, 24, 25 (1983, 1984, 1985).

1   Tri-Lingual System Proposed for World Communications

Noted Scholar of Noh Suggests Bilingual or Trilingual Edition of Hundred Best Books on Japanese Literature

Note: The writer of the following article, Ezra Loomis Pound, although not well-known in Japan, is one of the few foreigners who made enthusiastic introduction abroad of Japanese "Noh" plays and stands shoulder to shoulder with Ernest Fenollosa as a scholar devoted to the study of Japanese culture. Mr. Pound has a brilliant literary record and is at present visiting the United States.—Editor, The Japan Times

I AM READING *The Japan Times* with pleasure in the hope of getting some European or American news that hasn't been doctored to suit one interest or another. The difficulty in writing to a new public is to know what they have already heard. One doesn't want to bore the reader by telling him what his aunt Jemima has told him or what he has read in the week before last's picture supplement.

Perhaps I had better begin with what has not yet happened. The Italian papers are full of news of the cultural pact with Japan. I have three proposals for the Kokusai Bunka Shinkokai. First: I respectfully ask consideration for a bilingual or trilingual edition of the hundred best books of Japanese and ideogramic literature.

The Leica grainless film and microphotographic processes now make such an edition commercial. It can be produced at the same price as the Loeb library of Greek and Latin texts (which has an English translation on the opposite page). With microphotography there is no reason for not using ideogramic pages taken direct from works of master calligraphers. We in the West now have only a few such pages, notably a few from ideograms written for Ernest Fenollosa by one of the Court masters.

Wanted: Noh Film

Secondly: The whole of the Noh could be filmed, or at any rate the best Noh music could be registered on sound-track. Your film *Mitsuko* filled me with nostalgia. It is 15 years since Tami Koumé's friends sang me fragments of Noh in Paris but the instant I heard that all-too-brief reproduction here in Rapallo (in a simple village cinema) I knew whence it came. You have there a treasure like nothing we have in the Occident. We have our masterwork: Mozart, Purcell, Janequin, Dowland, but it is a different masterwork and one is not a substitute for the other.

Thirdly: I propose a tri-lingual system for world communications. None of the schemes for esperanto or other universal languages is at all satisfactory. Ogden's proposals for basic English could be developed. He has not the necessary tact or humanity to apply them. The greatest practical, that is possible, simplification would be a triple system: Ideogram, with the Japanese sound (syllabic) comment, Italian and English.

Culture in retrospect needs more languages, and no one wants to constrict it. Greek, Latin and as much else as you like: all very enjoyable.

Current culture could conceivably receive great aid from this triple basis. I am not proposing this with any intention of slighting French and German. The present political alliance would suggest German, Italian and Japanese. I sacrifice one party on either side of the immediate division of forces. I do this on strictly practical and linguistic grounds.

French contains a great treasure but, as language, it is tricky. The foreigner cannot learn it. Its sounds are difficult and its letters are not uniform in connotation. You say: neither are the English. True! but English has attained a syntactical plainness that is nowhere exceeded save in ideogram.

There is also the question of actual present diffusion.

A great many Germans speak English. English is common to the U.S.A. and the British Empire. It is already a common tongue for dozens of Indians who speak different languages in India. Ideogram as a written communication touches all Japan and China. Italian is the simplest of the Latin tongues. Its spelling is the clearest. (Both Spanish and French are full of tricks of speech that are not clearly printed on the page.)

Language Simple

None of the proposed artificial languages can be more quickly learned by other Latin groups. A Spaniard understands Italian almost at once. Any one who has studied Latin can learn Italian in a few weeks. And whatever may be said of the fancy Italian styles that have pullulated since the sixteenth century, Duce Mussolini signified among other things a great drive for direct utterance, for clear and simple speaking.

I can argue my reasons for picking these three media. I could fill most of today's paper doing it, but I think the reader will save his own time by thinking about them, and weighing up the gains against the sacrifices. The quantity of cultural heritage should be set against the sacrifices. Latin contains the matter of a great deal of Greek. I mean it has been translated into Latin. There are great claims for German. I don't think Russian has much claim. The Latin treasure is fairly accessible to anyone who knows

Italian. Italy is a rising nation. South Americans speak a good deal of Italian as well as Spanish.

I will answer serious objections if anyone has the same set after a week's reflection that they have on first reading this note.

2   Death of Yeats: End of Irish Literary Revival

THE DEATH OF Leo Frobenius last Summer is the severest shock to European cultural studies that we have had in a decade. Returning members of the Forschungsinstitut Australian expedition passed through Rapallo a few weeks ago with news of their discoveries. Mr. Fox had even found a drawing rather like the magnificent "Runner."

The death of William Butler Yeats closes the great era of the Irish literary revival. That death will doubtless have been duly recorded in Japan. Someone in Tokyo may also know of Yeats' Japanese interlude or flirtation. He, at one time, thought he would be called to a Japanese professorship and did, I think, receive some sort of invitation. You have a "link" with Dublin in those plays of Yeats which were directly stimulated by Fenollosa's reports and translations of Noh. Having worked with Yeats during the three or four years of his intensest interest in the Noh, I know how much it meant to him.

Form Searched

"The form I have been searching for all my life" was one of his comments. (That would have been about 1917.)

A determination for a new poetic drama in Europe, not merely a Celtic twilight or a side show, but a poetic drama that will enter the main stream of our life is manifested both by Jean Cocteau (recent play *Parents Terribles*) and by T. S. Eliot (*Family Reunion*).

The present chronicler is Confucian and totalitarian. To him both these plays seem to be ends of a movement. So far as I am concerned they belong to the age of Ibsen wherein people's inner wobblings and fusses were very important. I believe in, and I believe that there exists, a growing consciousness of the individual in the state. "The divine science of politics" (thought as to how people can live together in an organized or organic social system), interests me more than all the Freuds that ever existed. I consider this both a catholic (in the non-sectarian sense) and a classic *Anschauung*.

At any rate I think the great novelists and dramatists must henceforth sort out the problems dependent on economic pressure from those which remain after this pressure is removed.

A few years ago P. Bottome wrote a novel about an insane asylum. On analysis one found a common denominator, nowhere stated by the authoress and not I think present in her consciousness. All the patients were there because of economic pressure. All the doctors and nurses were moved by monetary pressures.

Of the poets included in my *Active Anthology*, the best are all aware of monetary pressure, as something more clear and incisive than the vague "social" urges to be found in last century's literature. This is not to say that Trollope and, in his last years, Henry James hadn't come to such perception. They were above and beyond their time. The keenest minds today can be grouped. They can be grouped along this axis. The best writers are aware of problems that have lain unobserved in Dante and Shakespeare, problems of usury, of the just price, of the nature of money and its mode of issue.

It may interest you to know that the clarity of some paragraphs in *The Japan Times* on these subjects is, outside Italy, rather restricted to weekly papers and papers of special movements in England and America and in the rest of the occident.

Lucid and incisive remarks of Hitler, Schacht and Funk do not get the wide and immediate publicity they deserve. They are however understood by writers of such divergent temperament as Wyndham Lewis and General J. F. C. Fuller.

Picture Post

As job lot items and notes on books worth reading: A current *Picture Post* acknowledges Wyndham Lewis to be the greatest portraitist of our time (even quotes Sickert as saying, "and of any time"—which is the generous exaggeration of an older painter for a younger one who has been too long denied his just place in contemporary art).

The best news from America is the edition of E. E. Cummings' collected poems, plus the publication of W. C. Williams' *Passaic River* (prose sketches).

Both the *Criterion* and *Broletto* have ceased publication, leaving my personal interest in current periodicals narrowed to *The British Union Quarterly*, for discussions of state organization, and to *Townsman* for very brief notices of books and the arts. *The Examiner*, published in Bethlehem, Connecticut, U.S.A., contains some very well written and carefully thought articles.

There are valuable notes in several dozens of sectarian or group week-

lies and quarterlies in which publications, however, the dross and one-
sidedness often out-weighs the sound matter, at least to such a degree that
one cannot recommend them to Orientals wanting a clear view of the west.

3   Study of Noh Continues in West
Pound Outlines New Approach to Drama
Using New Media

THE WORK INITIATED by Ernest Fenollosa for better comprehension of East
and West is by no means ended. Whatever Fenollosa may have done in the
way of awakening his Japanese friends to the need of more active preservation of Japanese values must be set against the spark lit here by his unedited
manuscripts.

W. B. Yeats was at once enkindled by the imperfect versions of Noh
which I was able to make from Fenollosa's notes. He started writing plays in
Noh form for his Irish theatre and for performances where no western stage
was available.

We in the West want an adequate edition of all the Noh in two or more
languages. A few of us have the sense to want an edition with the ideogramic text on one page large enough to convey the calligraphic beauty and the
essentially untranslatable values of ideograms themselves.

I don't mean to say that you can't in time translate an ideogram, even
the most beautiful, but you will never get into any one phonetically spelled
word all the associative forces of the more interesting picture-words.

正名 is contained or summed up in 誠
The whole of a philosophy is almost contained in the three characters: the
clear definition of terms as necessary to all real thought, and to sincerity,
and the knowing of one's own mind and one's own meaning.

Two Media Available

It may be argued that the actual seeing of the ideograms is more necessary in
the study of philosophy and the classics than in reading the romantic Noh,
but one can not do without it in the latter. Two media are at our disposal
which were not at Fenollosa's disposal, namely the sound film and micro-
photography.

Fenollosa could not, as I did by the kindness of Dr. Shio Sakanishi,
head of the Japanese Department of the Congressional Library in Washington, see and hear *Awoi no Uye* on the screen with the sound of the singing

and the crescendo of excitement as the hero rubs his rosary with ever faster rattling of beads against beads.

Every western university should have the COMPLETE SET of Noh plays on sound-film for study in its dramatic and literary courses.

That will come and will have to come for a dozen reasons as the old half-witted system of Western teaching wakes up (30 or 40 years after modern science has made photographic conveniences a daily accessory to our industries and to our commercial filing systems).

Microphotographic methods are still very little understood in Europe. The place to study them is in the Washington Congressional Library. Anything in that library can be reproduced and carried away on a reel of film in one's pocket a couple of days after one has requested it and paid the modest charge of 2 cents per page for whatever hitherto priceless and, in many cases, unduplicated and unduplicable matter one wanted.

With proper apparatus we or you could photograph all the most beautiful calligraphic editions and reproduce them as cheaply as we print our worst books.

In the case of most of the Noh plays even this is not necessary as you have a very excellent calligraphic edition which could be supplied for a few cents per play to an American firm and interleaved with the American text. These editions would allow our students to study the text before and after seeing the cinema-representation of your plays.

And this, I need not say, would get over a good deal of the difficulty that now exists for the simple-minded student. For 1200 years Japan has meant more than commerce and business wrangles. In fact irritations over trade concessions between our countries are only a man's life old and need not and (permit me the strong phrase) damn well should not and shall not be regarded as a permanent and everlasting barrier between the best minds of your country and my country and between your country and the best minds in a dozen European nations.

I don't in the least wish to detract from the merit of the *Funa-Benkei* edition sent me by Katue Kitasono but it does not satisfy the requirements: the ideogramic type is too small. The ideograms ought to be big enough to convey their *intrinsic* beauty whether in grass writing or block type, and they ought to be big enough to permit, say 7 point, gloze and explanations on the English page facing them, page per page.

When we come to the matter of WHAT English or European texts should be used, we are up against a much thornier proposition. There must of course be a plain literal version somewhere available, with explanations and notes, however tiresome and unpoetic. There *should* also be the best available translation of the poetic values, in whatever European language this may have been attained. There are now American, English, French, German and Italian versions of Noh. And there is at least one Spanish text that is quite charming in the less vital parts of the play I read but falls down when it comes to the more intense passages.

Dr. Sakanishi caused me a good deal of anguish by insisting that something I had found in Fenollosa did not exist in the original. I am puzzled as to how it got into my text. Did it spring from Umewaka Minoru, or from Professors Mori and Ariga or did Fenollosa or I catch it out of thin air?

Fenollosa wrote that the Noh was in secret language; it was, for centuries, reserved for the Samurai and Nobles. You can not translate poetry merely by translating words. Some freedom (but not too much) must be left the poet who finds a new verbal manifestation for the original thought. He or she must in some way convey the feel and the aroma of the original play and of the inter-relation of characters.

Tami Koumé had danced the *Hagoromo* before the Emperor, taking the tennin part when he was, as I remember, six years old. At twenty he still remembered the part and movements of the tennin's wings, which as she returns to the upper heaven, are the most beautiful movements I have seen on or off any stage. Tami knew something of Noh that no mere philologist can find out from a text book.

BUT when it came to the metaphysics he could not answer questions which seemed to me essential to the meaning. Very probably the original author had left those meanings in the vague. There may not have been ten men in Europe who would have asked those particular questions, but it so happened that Yeats, in my company, had spent several winters trying to correlate Lady Gregory's Irish folk-lore with the known traditions of various myths, psychologies and religions.

Two or three centuries ago Catholic missionaries bothered the Chinese court with analogous questions, such as "Did the spirit of Confucius enter his cartouche," etc.

My own ignorance is very dense, but I have no wish to maintain it. I merely want to put other students on their guard against the *needless* sacrifice of poetic values.

By all means let us have a prose translation, but where Umewaka Minoru or his friends have left a haze over the almond blossoms or the reflection of the moon in two buckets, let us be very much on our guard against any rumor that such and such a meaning is not in, or associated with, or associable with the Noh text.

Background Necessary

When I quote Æschylus, even if only to say "Thus was it" or "These are the facts," I do something more than state that certain things had occurred. It is that continual assertion of one set of acts *in relation to* a whole other set of acts, a whole series of backgrounds and memories, that enriches the Noh. The poetic translator must break his back to attain an English version that will keep at least part of this air and color. He must be allowed adequate, but not boundless, freedom toward this end, and only the finest critics and judges will be able to say when he reached it or how nearly he attains, or when he has sinned against the spirit of his original.

At any rate the news value of this article may lie in my stating that Dr. Arthur Hummel, head of the Oriental Department; Dr. Sakanishi, head of the Japanese division of the Congressional Library (Washington); the head of Arrow Editions, New York; R. Duncan, editor of *Townsman*; Margaret Leona who has tried Noh effects, on a Noh basis for the London television; Edmond Dulac, who made masks for Yeats' Irish Noh experiments; and a few dozen or hundred more of us are interested in any and every attempt toward further diffusion of the plays, and that I personally will do all that I can to correlate the fine work done by the Kokusai Bunka Shinkokai with whatever Western nuclei that exist or can be brought into being. The start had already been made in their (K. B. S.) *Funa-Benkei* program and edition for Shigefusa Hosho's performance of August 6, 1937.

I am merely asking that more plays be printed in two or more languages, and hoping that so able a translator as Michitarô Shidehara will insist on the use of larger ideograms above or facing his English version. The interlinear printing, first the Japanese spelled out phonetically in the Latin alphabet, then the ideogram and then the English, is preferable to the interleaving when the publisher has the means at his disposal, for by it the musical value of Japanese text is also conveyed to the stumbling foreign student. Nevertheless both transliteration of sound and the European version could be printed on a page facing a calligraphic text.

4   An Ezra Pound Letter from Rapallo

Annual Music Week Proposed to Introduce Each Year
Insufficiently Known Composer

AT THE BEGINNING of the war in Ethiopia, as we could not expect a concert
audience, the Rapallo group resolved itself into a study circle with the
immediate intention of hearing as many of the 310 concerti of Vivaldi as
were available in printed editions and executable by one or two violinists
and a piano. Having done that, two Americans, Olga Rudge and David
Nixon, gave a concert in Venice, made up entirely from Vivaldi's *Estro
Armonico* (Op. 3) and an abortive Vivaldi society was started in his own
city. Miss Rudge then made the first thematic catalog of the unpublished
Vivaldi lying in the Turin Library (309 concerti) and other works—which
catalog has now been printed by Count Chigi of Siena in the *Note e
Documenti* for the full-dress Vivaldi Week given there.

That festival marks a definite advance in the Italian official method in
treating their music. We have for some time been insisting that the whole of
an evening's program should have a form in itself, which need not be
inferior in structure to that of, say, a fugue or any other art form. And we
have insisted that the auditor can not get a clear or adequate conception of a
great composer's meaning unless he hear a lot of that composer's work all at
once.

Methods Suggested

We also, as Katue Kitasono noted some time ago in **VOU**, suggested various
methods of contrast between musical compositions, intended to test their
real value and to demonstrate what modern compositions could stand
comparison with past master-work.

Yeats long ago pointed out that minor poets often show up very well in
anthologies, but that the difference between them and the greater poets is
quickly apparent if you contrast whole books of their work.

The Sienese Week was admirable in various ways. Their first program
was a model of construction (due I think to Alfredo Casella). And as Mr.
Kitasono has cited some Rapallo examples, I shall perhaps be permitted to
cite the Siena evening in detail, though the reader will have to verify what I
say of it by future experiment on his own part. The program contained six
items, five by Vivaldi and one transcribed from Vivaldi by his better known
contemporary, J. S. Bach. Given in this order:

1. *Sinfonia in Do. magg.*
2. *Concerto in Sol. min.*

3. *Concerto in Si min.*
4. Aria, from *La Fida Ninfa*
5. Bach's transcription from the *Concerto in Si. min.* reworked, that is, by Bach for four harpsichords, and in the key of *La min.*
6. *Concerto Alla Rustica.*

The Week's music was ably varied: there were instrumental works, a revival of the opera *Olimpiade* (probably the first performance since Vivaldi's death in 1741), and choral works given in the Church of S. Francesco with full orchestra.

The Week amply testified to Vivaldi's being a major composer, not simply "another" Italian composer of his period to be remembered by the often reprinted "Cucco" movement from one of his violin concerti, or by the single aria, *"Un Certo non so che,"* which had been the only bit of his vocal music available in a modern edition.

All this being in accord with the beliefs printed by the violinist Rudge and by Cobbett, who had said a few years ago that Vivaldi was a composer with a future. Of course this doesn't mean that one has "discovered" Vivaldi. His name has long been in every encyclopedia or dictionary of music, but it does mean that musical history is undergoing a revision in its estimate of him. A number of general questions rise and or have been raised.

Timeliness Pointed Out

There is a timeliness in all resurrections in art; whether it be in painting, literature or in music. In Miss Rudge's own rendering of the concerto I have found a close kinship with the line of the surrealist Dali. I don't know whether this comes from the manuscript or from the executant. I have long blamed or at least teased the surrealists for their naïve belief that they had invented something which had already been present in Guido Cavalcanti's poetry when Dante was 16 years old. There is plenty of surrealism in mediæval poetry. The human spirit has recurring needs of expression.

Even before one knew the detail of Vivaldi's life, one could hear certain qualities in his music, and possibly one exaggerates one's own perceptivity when one learns the personal and human background from which the Venetian master produced his music. He was priest, professor of music to a girl's convent school, and then in later life ran an opera company, presenting his own operas and traveling from Mantua to Vienna in company with a barber's daughter, whom he had taught to sing with great success, and with assistant nymphs or whatever. Goldoni describes visiting the old man who was scribbling musical phrases on his desk and dipping into his breviary.

All of which is complementary to the qualities of his musical phrasing.

As composer his mind was furnished with the thoughts of Dante's Paradise and with the gaiety of his home city. At any rate the qualities registered in his music extend from one of these frontiers to the other. And the greatest of European composers, J. S. Bach, was sufficiently interested in six of his (Vivaldi's) concerti to transpose them for his own use, without perhaps having improved them. The work of fitting this music to modern orchestra for the Siena Festival was admirably performed by Casella, Frazzi, and Virgilio Mortari under the general direction of Casella. Count Chigi and the Italian authorities propose to proceed to an annual music week devoted each year to the work of one insufficiently known Italian creator or to a group of related composers. Possibly in 1940 we shall hear the two Scarlatti, and in 1941 possibly, on the bicentennial of Vivaldi's death, a second week of Vivaldi, amply justified by the results of this year's performance.

It all means a much more serious presentation of old Italian music than we have yet had. It means a much more intelligent study of the enormous treasure of Italian musical composition.

Both the eminent musicologue S. A. Luciani[1] and the violinist Rudge[2] have raised another basic issue, namely the distinction and proper criteria for "*musica vocale* and *musica verbale*."

Which merely means: can one understand the words when they are sung? And this question can be divided into two æsthetic questions, namely: Has the musician preserved or has he ruined the rhythm and phonetic qualities of the poetry?

Or, on the other hand, did the poet know his job well enough to write with such qualities of sound and movement that his words are worth preserving or illustrating and emphasizing? In the twelfth century the troubadours tried to fit words and music to each other. Dante animadverted on this subject.

When it came to a question of theater and sung drama, along about the year 1600 a.d. Vincenzo Galilei, Giulio Caccini and a literary circle in Firenze tried to make opera that would keep the verbal values as such. Then came stage music which used the voice mostly as an "instrument to rival the flute," etc. The words, then usually of no great interest in themselves, gave way to vocalization and the intellectual qualities of opera, or at any rate the literary values of libretti are often dubious. Rossini attained a very

---

[1] *Mille Anni di Musica*, volume I, published by Hoepli of Milan.
[2] Article in *Meridiano di Roma*, 3 Sept. 1939.

high degree of mastery; in fact I know of no opera where the words and orchestra are so well combined as they are in the *Barbiere di Seviglia*.

On the other hand the French café-concert songs usually emphasize their words and the sharp meaning of the phrases.

The ideal or an idea, or call it merely my desire, if you like, is an opera where the singer sings great poetry to a fine music which emphasizes and illuminates the significance of the words, and, to do this, makes them clearly audible and comprehensible to the listener.

I have made a few attempts in this direction. No one is compelled to like my music, but I have at any rate set some of the greatest European poetry, namely that of Villon, and of Guido Cavalcanti with a few bits of Sordello. When the Villon was transmitted by the London radio, I sat in the electrician's kitchen in Rapallo and could understand every one of the words.

Antheil and Tibor Serly both wanted to work on these lines: but it is very difficult to find poetry sufficiently well written to stand such musical treatment. Especially in English, the amount of poetry that can be sung without either distorting the words or damaging the musician's invention is limited. Shakespeare wrote for declamation. He wrote a few lyrics to be sung in his plays. He solved the problem of using the voice merely as instrument by writing in such meaningless syllables as "Hey, nonny nonny" on which the singer could turn loose, without damaging the sense of the rest of the poem. The syllables have no meaning in themselves but have good sounds for the singer, and guide the musician in rhythm. In Italian there is a vast amount of libretto writing that is probably singable. But literary snobbism may or may not have obscured it.

However all this battle field is now again laid open.

If the Italians start again listening to two kinds of singing it can hardly fail to stimulate discrimination, and with the proper exposition of seventeenth century and, let us hope, also of sixteenth and fifteenth century music, we should have a musical reform in Italy or a new and valid movement in which fine musical line and strongly active invention will replace the sloppiness of the XIXth century composition.

At any rate, thanks to Count Guido Chigi Saracini and his associates, the Sienese annual week of music has started something and opened up possibilities. It is to be followed with increasing attention by critics of music in general, from all countries.

5   From Rapallo: An Ezra Pound Letter

THERE IS ONE FIELD of discussion in which the Japanese intellectuals can be of great use to us. I repeat "of great use" because you are outside the immediate effects of the problem and can discuss it with greater calm, as, indeed, a purely intellectual and æsthetic problem without coming down to political and economic implications. It is a question of the kind Fenollosa opened for us when he began about 50 years ago telling the Occident that Japan is not merely an inferior form of China. And he continued repeating that theme.

Firstly: Japan is different from China.

Secondly: As regards the Chinese elements in Japanese art and culture, Japan continued to preserve some of the best Chinese skills and customs when China had fallen into her decadence.

From the fragmentary notes he has left us we can at any rate see that *Kumasaka* is basically Japanese. The ghost in that play carries admiration to every western romantic. The gist of what three or more races have meant by chivalry, *Ritterschaft* and *bushido* finds concentrated expression in that Noh drama.

Homeric Passage

Kagekiyo contains the one Homeric passage in such part of the Noh as remains in the Fenollosa manuscript. This is akin to our classic *epos*, whether of Greece or the Nordics. It binds in with the episode of Confucius' father holding the portcullis on his shoulder while the men under him escape. These things are the universals of heroism. If I am to be of any use to you in establishing a better communications service between the Orient and the Occident you must let me speak very plainly.

I believe that the 君子 of one nation finds it quite easy to converse with the 君子 of another. And the form of those characters suggests to me that the 君子 is the ancestral voice speaking through the mask of the child of the present. Though I do not find this explanation in available dictionaries. The better the child of the present's quality and the more up to date he is, the more does he seem to me to be the edge of a very old sword.

He converses with the 君子 of another nation not by effacing his racial characteristics but by intensification of them.

I ask you not to mistake the amiability of my tone of voice. I find with many of my young compatriots that when I try to speak clearly and with proper precision, they think I am scolding them. Nothing of the sort. There are plenty of occasions for being correctly indignant without being supposed to be indignant on other occasions.

Not Detracting

If I tell you that you can use Confucius and Mencius in talking to Occidentals to better advantage than by talking Buddhism I am not detracting from the virtues of Zen concerning which I know very little, save from the great charm of some of the Noh into which I believe Zen is infused.

To cut the cackle, Tami Kumé had very great personal charm; he wanted to save us by Zen and plastic abstractions. But on the other hand Occidental Buddhists are nearly always a bore, at any rate they have been invariably so in my personal experience of them.

The ethic of Confucius and Mencius not only inspires respect but it serves as a road map through the forests of Christian theology. I don't know that the sage Jesuit translators intended it for that use, but that use can be made of it. At no point can the Christian find in it anything opposed to the best of his own doctrine. The Chinese imperial councilors on the other hand and I believe your own dignitaries, found Christianity helplessly immoral, anti-statal and anti-familial. And they have thereby given considerable satisfaction to the few Occidentals who know of the said disapproval. Voltaire, you may remember, said: "I admire Confucius. He was the first man who did not receive a divine inspiration."

Men with less gift for verbal incision but with my kind of mind are apt to think that both Buddhists and Christians make positive statements about things of which very few men can have any certainty. At any rate they offer two different sets of positive teachings about heaven, about souls, survival after death, etc., which are in quite apparent contradiction.

As to that very clever and somewhat westernized author Lin Yutang I do not think he knows his Confucius. He has quite obviously been annoyed by silly and stilted Confucians, who are, I doubt not, as much a nuisance in the East as are stale Christians with us. But I cannot blame St. Ambrose for today's archbishop of Canterbury.

It is quite possible that I over-simplify, but it is also possible that from the greater distance I get a glimpse of some main proportions.

Greek Philosophy

It is with regard to similar main proportions that I now appeal to the Japanese historian and philosopher. If you take Francisco Fiorentino's *Storia della Filosofia* (by which he meant Occidental philosophy) or any other good Western summary, you will find "Greek philosophy" fairly clear in its guesses and then quite elaborate in its details. You will find "mediæv-al philosophy and/or theology" somewhat more puzzling. Usually consid-ered rather inferior to the Greek, now rather out of favor. I can't think it deserves total neglect. There was a lot of hard mental work done in the millenium between St. Ambrogio and St. Antonino but I don't think our historiographers have yet given us a competent analysis of the period. I don't know how far the subject enters your system of study. But as a Japanese lexicographer, Dr. Motoichiro Oguimi, had started making a Greek-Japanese dictionary at the age of 79 and completed it at the age of 94 (incidentally a form of courage which we can admire), I don't see why I should despair of effective collaboration.

In reply to T. S. Eliot's speculation as to what I (personally) believe and in opposition or at least deprecation of Mr. Eliot's *Idea of a Christian Society* (published by Faber, London), I have taken leave to doubt whether we Europeans and descendants of Europeans in America really believe anything that is not at root European. We kid ourselves into "accepting" or saying that we believe certain formulae, or we refrain from attacking them, because, like George Washington we believe that they are useful for keeping the lower classes in order. "The benign influence" and that sort of thing. It is therefore my wish that if the Japanese student starts browsing among rare Latin theologians, he would try to sort out which parts of their writing are due to Greek thought, which parts to Roman, and which parts to the Jewish scriptures. He will also find, a little later, a number of fine minds from the north of Europe, as John Scotus of Ireland, Grosseteste, bishop of Lincoln, or Albertus of greater Germany. At the present moment I have a definite bias. I find the Platonics enthusiastic, the Latins orderly and I enjoy the contact with such minds as the three Europeans just mentioned as with Ambrogio or Antonino (Italian). But I also find an element of disorder and obfuscation.

These quite good minds indulge in all sorts of contortions to get sense out of nonsense, they (as the men of Athens most emphatically did not) spent a great deal of time inventing allegorical meanings, often very in-genious, for statements about winged-bulls and strange animals never encountered in ordinary farming or hunting. There is also a tendency to shift and to avoid civic responsibility.

There is the "pie in the sky" offer, sometimes in our time derided. I quite sincerely wish some dispassionate Oriental would look into this matter and try to sort out these four elements and put fair values upon them.

Did the total European mind lose 1200 or 1500 years in these exercises, say from the fall of Rome down to the day Signor Galileo invented his telescope?

And if so, why did the Europeans do it? And who and for what cause planted this seed of Confusion, and why for that matter did the races of Europe after Luther and Calvin take to giving Near Eastern names to their children?

With Calm

You, far from our immediate struggles, can treat this matter with calm and distinction; if I start going into it I might fall into the snares of power psychology or even of monetary psychology, and this, your admirable poet Kitasono Katue would find, I fear, unpoetic on my part.

Two other points occur to me that are not exactly part of this article and are, yet, kindred to it. Firstly: Very few young men get round to thinking that the idea of good government is perhaps the highest idea that we can ever translate into action. At the age of 23 no one was less given to thinking of such subjects than was the present author.

Secondly: If your students take to *Kulturmorphologie* in the wake of Leo Frobenius or of your present correspondent they might find significance in the fact that Aristotle began his list of intellectual faculties with TEXNE, that is the skill that enables a man to paint a good picture or make a good pair of shoes. Poor "Arry" was scarcely cold in his grave before the professors had removed that faculty from their edition of his works.

Note the text of the *Nicomachean Ethics,* and then that of the *Magna Moralia* wherefrom I observed the discrepancy. Thence, as I see it, dates the decline of Western thought and the inferiority of our writings on ethics when compared to those of Confucius and Mencius. A paragraph to this effect disappeared from my *Kulch* in the printing house. My publishers thought it would do me no good at Oxford.

6   From Rapallo: An Ezra Pound Letter

I FEEL a little lost writing for an unknown public which must, in some sense, be a "newspaper public." Most of my criticism has been written for a nucleus of writers and I have to considerable extent known their beliefs or known when I was infuriating them by attacking particular literary imbecilities. I know the Japanese reader must be friendly or he wouldn't be finding me in print at all, but I haven't the least idea when I may tread on his toes or when I am likely to bore him to death by repeating what he has already read six times.

Back in 1917 or thereabouts I received and replied to a Dadaist greeting from Switzerland. Then Picabia printed magazines in New York. Then in Paris, about 1922, he printed a unique issue of *Pilhaou-Thibaou*, saying good-bye to Dada. By 1923 all the Surrealists were lined up in *The Little Review*, so that neither these movements nor their particular terminologies can now have for me any great news value.

From 1912 for a decade I did my best to tell the ignorant Britons and Yankees that there had been some very good French poetry, and that English poetry, so far as the technique went, had mostly stopped along about the state of Gautier's *Albertus*, and never caught up with his *Emaux et Camées*.

I doubt if anybody gave the frogs more conscientious free advertising than your present correspondent. And, with that past, I claimed, and still claim, a right to be judged impartial in saying that at a given date poetry in English (largely by American writers) began to be "more interesting" or to have, at any rate, an interest which contemporary French poetry had not. This is not to say that Eliot is a better writer than Cocteau.

I might, however, get round to claiming that Cocteau is an exception and a survival. And on the other hand, to be just, I shall also claim, or admit, that Cocteau shows awareness to certain contemporary pressures, extending in his mental range from moods contemporary with Barbey d'Aurevilly to moods contemporary with Mr. Cummings. In his *Antigone* he is quite aware of economics, though he doesn't use up many words on the topic.

You are all, doubtless, tired to death of "red" poetry, and Marxist dogma laid out in bad verse. We have had socially conscious poetry or near-beer or crass propaganda, etc., etc., and no one has better distinguished between it and the real thing than has Kitasono Katue. Nevertheless in 1933 I managed, despite the hostility of the British fool and the diffidence of my publishers, to get the *Active Anthology* printed. Opening it now, after seven years, I can still take satisfaction in having got 49 pages of Basil Bunting printed where only the book-worm can efface him.

Mr. Cummings has said, "You can't sell the moon to the moon." I believe the above mentioned anthology contains more poets who are aware of money, as a problem, than any other anthology ever has, though the better the poet (in Europe) the more certain you can be to surprise the old fogies and Aunt Sallies of my generation by dragging up passages definitely concerned with the ethics and tragedy of money.

Ovid, Propertius, Dante, Lope de Vega, and Shakespeare, and notably Byron, are all perfectly good browsing ground for the economist, for the student of money as distinct from the bloke who has got a floating kidney from psychology or sociology.

Dante swats Philippe le Bel for debasing the currency, Shakespeare turns his phrase onto usury not in the *Merchant of Venice* alone. Catullus alludes to his purse and puns on a mortgage. Hood cursed gold and Lanier, trade. Nothing of this kind, so far as I have [seen], occurs in Fenollosa's notes on Japanese poetry.

Nevertheless, for what it is worth, since 1928 in English, the better the poet, the more certain you are to find him considering the age-old infamy of the money monopoly, of monopoly, of attempts to starve mankind in general, by the trick of trapping and withholding the power to buy.

In Bunting's case this sort of sensibility has broken into some of the strongest verse of our time. Perhaps the poems are too long for quotation in full, so I give a few strophes of the "Morpethshire Farmer." Bunting sees him on the railway platform, driven from his land and compelled to emigrate into Canada.

> Must ye bide, my good stone house
> To keep a townsman dry?
> To hear the flurry of the grouse
> But not the lowing of the kye*
> Where are ye, my seven score sheep
> Feeding on other braes!
> My brand has faded from your fleece
> Another has its place.
> Canada's a bare land
> For the North wind and the snow,
> Northumberland's a bare land
> For men have made it so.
> Sheep and cattle are poor men's food,

Grouse is sport for the rich,
Heather grows where the sweet grass might grow
For the cost of clearing the ditch.
A liner lying in the Clyde
Will take me to Quebec.
My sons'll see the land I am leaving
As barren as her deck.

NOTE: * *Dialect for cattle.*

No one since Burns has used the old simple meters with such force. Bunting is aware not only of the tragedy and the infamy back of the tragedy but of the mode in which it works.

His range is not limited to the "old style," as can be seen from the ultra modern "They say Etna" ending in the idiom of newspaper headlines:

MAN IS NOT AN END-PRODUCT

MAGGOT ASSERTS

Bunting has learned to write a most elegant hand in Persian in process of translating Firdusi, and among his longer poems is a condensation of "Chomei at Toyama." A man's adventures are not necessarily part of his writing, though the figure of the poet may gain popularity from them. In this respect Bunting is all that the romantic can desire. He has been jailed in three countries for never having done any harm. Once in Paris, because two corners back of Mt. Parnasse cemetery that confused him at two o'clock in the morning are so exactly alike, complete with café and awning, that I mistook the one for the other in broad daylight when trying to gather evidence of his character. And as the concierge of the wrong one said: "It is very lucky that his key did not fit the door on the second floor, because the gentleman in that room is very nervous and always has a revolver under his pillow."

Bunting is, so far as I know, the only pacifist who did six months after the last war was over. As a Quaker he would not even say that he would fight if there was a war for him to fight in. He has an unfailing flair for excited areas. Years ago he left Italy in search of peace and arrived in the Canary Islands where a special little revolution broke out even before Spain at large was enkindled. Last May he had, I heard, left America for his native England. Some people's luck is like that.

I suspect him of being the best English-born poet of our time, though J. P. Angold is running a close second. From which you will find my elderly taste differing from the London tea party fashions.

When I want the gist of what is being done in England in the mind and the arts, I wait for the next copy of Ron Duncan's *Townsman*.

I take it that reformers' papers, such as *Action*, the *Social Creditor*, and the *British Union Quarterly* are outside the scope of this correspondence, but I believe that the more active young writers in England are reading them. All this is a long way, or a long time, from the day a Russian philosophical student with undigested Germany in his insides, said to me (about a.d. 1910) "Boundt, haff you gno BOLIDIGAL BASSHUNTZ?" (Anglice: Have you no political passions?) I hadn't.

And now my old friend Doc Williams (Wm. Carlos) can hardly tolerate my existence because I am not a bolshevik, and I find it hard to excuse Wyndham Lewis' last volume from sheer difference with the opinions expressed. And Mr. Joyce is no longer with us, in the sense those words would have conveyed in 1917, and Johnnie Hargrave calls Mr. Eliot's Christianity, "A lot of dead cod about a dead god." All of which goes to show that the Tower of Ivory "has gone West." At any rate temporarily, both for us old duffers of the 1910's and for the youngsters.

7   From Rapallo: An Ezra Pound Letter
Why There Is a War in Europe

KUMASAKA'S GHOST returns from a fine sense of honor. When the men who made wars led them in person, risking their own person in battle, the point of honor remained, but after two centuries or more of mercantilism, we must seek other motives. To this end I would placard every school room with three lines from the Hazard circular of 1862.

"THE GREAT DEBT THAT CAPITALISTS WILL SEE TO IT IS MADE OUT OF WAR, MUST BE USED TO CONTROL THE VOLUME OF MONEY. TO ACCOMPLISH THIS THE BONDS MUST BE USED AS A BANKING BASIS."

The present war in Europe has, in one sense, been going on for a hundred and ninety years. In another sense it was wholly unnecessary. It may date from the day when Paterson held out the bait for shareholders of the proposed bank "of England" in the words: "The bank hath profit of the interest on all the moneys that it creates out of nothing." The war dates certainly from England's interference with American colonial paper money in 1751.

In 1723, the Pennsylvania Assembly had authorized the issue of 15,000 pounds in paper bills, to be loaned on security of land or silver. As the Pennsylvania system developed, such issues were redeemable in a given time at so much per year. A farmer could get money up to half the value of his land, but had to pay it back in 10 years or in 16, after which he could have a new loan.

David Hume errs in saying "the land itself is coined." What was "coined" was not the land but the triple components—land, farmer's capacity to work and his likelihood of doing so, and a ready market. That is, the colonists needed the product of the soil. The paper money was a useful ticket or handy means of reckoning and recording how much work had been done or how much grain (or whatever) grown and delivered to market, hence of recording how produce ought ethically to be handed over to whomever held the ticket.

This did not suit the game of the London monopolists. But, until W. A. Overholser issued his 61 page brochure, the histories neglected this item. London's attempt to reassert money monopoly led to the first American revolution (1776).

American history for the following 90 years should be considered as a series of revolutions and set-backs. John Adams conceived a sane republican (or statal) system. America freed herself from the British Crown; the loose confederation of colonies was (a second revolution) cemented under a sane constitution. The revolution was betrayed by the financial corruption of members of Congress in Washington's time. These swine bought up depreciated certificates of pay due to the soldiers of the revolution, and then passed national laws forcing the Government to pay them the full face value of this paper (out of the pockets of the people).

Banking and funding systems were set up, whereon John Adams wrote in his old age:

> "Every bank of discount is downright corruption taxing the public for private individuals' gain.
>
> And if I say this in my will the American people would pronounce I died crazy." (Citation from my *Canto* 71).

Jefferson warned us that "If the American people ever allow private banks to control the issue of currency, first by inflation and then by deflation, the banks and corporations that will grow up around them will deprive the people of all property until their children will wake up homeless on the continent that their fathers conquered."

Jackson and Van Buren led the people against the monopolists. Jackson delivered the nation from debt. That is, the people beat the banks between

1830 and 1840. Record of this decade has, or had, almost entirely disappeared from American text books.

During the Civil War of the 1860s, the nation was betrayed by a ganglia of Sherman, Ikleheimer, etc., working with foreign (mainly English and Jewish) financiers.

The so-called democratic (or statal system) intended by the founders of the republic was killed. Very few people noticed its death. Jefferson's prophecy was largely but imperceptibly fulfilled. The American people are only now lifting one torpid eyelid. Schemes for the nomadic life had already gone into effect, people wandering about landless sleeping in motor-trailers.

This was brought about by a system in which the Government borrowed the nation's credit and paid interest on it to private concerns. Ikleheimer's circular calculated there would be from 28 to 33 per cent profit. The usury in some banking systems amounts to 60% and so fecund was the new continent that the traffic stood it; with cycles of crash and crisis, which were, nevertheless, followed by recoveries and partial recoveries.

We hear little, and you at a distance certainly hear less of these internal rumblings. When the swindle becomes international, Rota's condemnation of half a century ago covers the situation; he said:

"The mercantilist system placed the happiness of nations in the quantity of money they possess. And it consisted in a clever strategy for stealing the greatest possible amount of money from other nations."

Italy, having benefitted by Rota's *Storia delle banche* may have preceded other nations in realizing the force of this sentence. At any rate she was, in our time, the first Occidental nation to believe that among the first rights of a man, or a country, is the right to keep out of debt.

This point of view both pained and shocked the international usurers.

The tension became unbearable in 1938 when Dr. Schacht openly stated (during Hitler's visit to Rome) that "money which is not issued against exchangeable goods is mere printed paper."

The German word is "*Verbrauchsgüter.*" Gold is exchangeable when people suffer from superstition. It is not edible. You cannot wear it save as ornament. Very few treatises on economics begin with a definition of money. Curious, but you may verify it by long sojourn in any national library.

Now, on whatever substance money is printed, it gives or is assumed to give its possessor the right to take (in exchange for it) a determined quantity and quality of any sort of goods offered for sale in market.

At a certain point the money swindle and the gold habit merge. And a nation that gives too much of its grain or silk or wool to people who dig up gold, or who manage a money issue, is likely to find itself in want. Some lands are fountains of metal (if aided by engineers), other nations are mere tanks. France was a full tank.

Last spring in Washington I said and printed the statement: "War against Germany in our time, would be war against an honest concept of money."

One of the elder members of Congress replied: "Well, most of the gold in the world is in the United States, in the British Empire and in Russia, and I reckon that any attempt to diminish the power of them that have it, will meet with fairly serious resistance."

I might put this in another form: Any nation which surrenders the control of its purchasing power to any other nation or any group or agency outside its own control, will fall into slavery.

Decent Americans protest against our selling you munitions AND at the same time lending money to China so as to make sure you will have a use for those munitions. The men whom I most respect in Europe see behind the present European slaughter an attempt to break down both Germany and the Allies and reduce the whole people of Europe to a servitude under a money control. The more extended the conflict, the longer it lasts, the greater the debt that will be created and the greater the burden of interest that would be due to the lenders of money, the "creators of credit."

8   Letter from Rapallo: In War Appear Responsibilities

WITH THE HITLER INTERVIEW of June 14, the continental war aims are once more made clear in their essential fairness and, for a victorious army, their mildness. Had our universities not betrayed us over an 80 year period, the phrase "freedom of the seas" might still arouse an intelligent glow in the American thorax. There once was a man named John Adams. There once was an American system whereof at least a minority of Americans had an inkling. We were betrayed, sold up the river, hog-swoggled in 1863 by J. Sherman, Ikleheimer and Ikleheimer's London correspondents, but the public has not yet found it out. The bonds were issued as banking basis. Someday we (in the plural) will wake up, but whether our guts have still the tensile strength to take action remains to be shown.

In the meantime there is a question of responsibility both for wars at large and for this war. Herr Hitler has been exceedingly mild in his remarks on British politicians. When I was in America in June 1939, it was known that Churchill and his gigolos meant to "get into the government" (of England) and start a war. Technically they didn't "get in" until the war had been started, but the intention was there and indelible. They have already had part of their war. Count Potocki can bear witness to what I told him at lunch in May, 1939. I am glad to have a few statements in print and dated. France and England were rotten. Not being a military expert I forebore to make prophecies. All I could say was that I could see nothing to prevent another Sudan.

Most of Europe has spoken. A number of English patriots have been jailed for believing that their country should not go to war until prepared. Several Englishmen had demurred at the embezzlement of mandated territories, which embezzlement was part of the Lazard-Churchill (and should we say Kuhn-Loeb?) program.

At any rate a Monroe Doctrine can and should be bilateral. When Monroe followed Adams and Jefferson in the belief that we should keep OUT of Europe, he emphasized what was then the less obvious side of the problem. Fatty degeneration of American politics and of American political exposition has been unchecked for too long. It is time we dug up the creed of the American founders. It is time we knocked the dust off a few perfectly valid ideas (call 'em ideals if Wilson hasn't permanently declassed that term).

Roosevelt has done nothing to maintain the freedom of the seas. With 140 million Americans behind him, he couldn't defend the American post-bag. He has spent ten billions on needless gold, at the cost of the American people. Four billions out of that ten has gone in what appear to me to be excess profits to the sellers of gold, all of which is added onto our American taxes or written up as mortgage of America to an anonymous set of uncleanliness. A little of the once-vaunted American acumen would suffice to start asking: who got it?

I advocate at least that much acumen.

Vanity and provincialism! Millionaire play-boys in key embassies! When it comes to being ridiculous, can you beat busy Bullitt telling Mandel (alias Rothschild), Reynaud, a bunch of Jews, Annamites, Senegalese and freemasons that they are of the blood of Jeanne d'Arc? (Vide his harangue delivered a few days before Paris fell.)

Newspapers run on borrowed money have contributed to this state of vagueness. Take it that Churchill is senile and that his colleagues are, as

Reynaud and Mandel, shop-fronts for Lazard, Neuflize, Honneger, Roth-schild, Sieff, Beit, Goldsmid, Mocatta etc., you have not yet the full list of persons responsible. Meaning responsible for the million dead in Poland, Flanders, Norway, etc. All of which slaughter is due to provincialism, to hoggishness, greed and to a love of monopoly which was not exclusively European.

Nothing effective was done or tried in America to stave off this conflict. All the official pressure was used in the wrong direction. Whether Amer-icans have yet examined the Polish dossier, I cannot from this distance make out, but the facts are written and implied on thousands of pages of news-print. "Forces" in America puffed up or helped to puff up the Poles. They backed the gold-swine and the bank-swine. There were surprises and they failed to conceal their astonishment. When a little American horse-sense finally appeared, the "forces" were peeved. We are not yet out of the woods. There are still Anglomaniacs and usuro-maniacs in America who like us to stick our hands into the fire. For England?

No! most certainly not for England. England has been worm-eaten since 1700. Her vitals were being gnawed over a century ago when Cobbett wanted to cure her. There is a whole literature of velleities, of attempts at English reform. Eight months ago I was thought loony for saying that France probably suffered less from the invasion of 1870 than had the English during the past 20 years from perfectly stinking misgovernment.

What have we in our recent American record that might serve to enlighten them? During the last year a marginal reform has been put into operation. Wallace, the goat of Roosevelt's administration, has got in the point of a gimlet. A trifling amount of money, called "stamps" and limited in its application, has been issued against easily available goods. But, in the wake of Lloyd George, this concession has been used as an implement of degradation. The people have been given back a little of their own purchas-ing power on condition they consent to be paupers and ask the bureaucracy for it.

You have to go back to the most rancid melodrama for a parallel. The wicked guardian, having robbed the orphan of her fortune, tells her it is her duty to be thankful for stale bread and a cot in the attic.

Lost in the Congressional Record for January 23, 1940 are these pas-sages:

"Whereas there has developed in the method of conducting the fi-nances of the U.S. the custom . . . of borrowing financial credit . . . thus increasing public indebtedness."

"Whereas the credit thus lent to the government is in reality based on the real credit of the people, which belongs to them. . . ."

But until the reader has patience to read at least the few phrases of J. Adams that I have been able to quote in my *Cantos*, I know of no brief way of showing him how long sanity has-existed in America (among a few people) and how thoroughly it has failed to percolate into the general consciousness. The people have finally fumbled at a general muzzy notion that at least some wars are economic. In the spring of 1939 one American editor had the nerve to print my statement that:

"War against Germany in our time would be war against an honest concept of money."

Shortly before his death Robert Mond (brother of the late Alfred, Lord Melchett) sat on a sofa in Rome, which sofa is known to me, and said with hith well known lithf: "Napoleon wath a good man. It took uth 20 years to cwuth him. It will not take uth 20 years to cwuth Mutholini. (Took us 20 years to crush Napoleon, will not take us 20 to crush Mussolini.) And the economic war hath commenthed." This is a fact. Statement of it does not involve antisemitism. It in no way implicates the 300 just Jews known to me, or three million unknown. But it does prove a state of consciousness in one member of known set of English financiers.

There are known dynasties in Bank of England directorships: Goschen, Kleinwort, Brandt, etc. The Anglo-French combination is sometimes for brevity's sake written "Lazard." After this war had started the Bank of England directors met and doubled their salaries, as proof of purity, patriotism etc.? One old lady shareholder protested, but her protest in no way moved Montagu Norman. The American reader on his part might however start looking for the American representatives of these "forces." The relation of home office to branch office seems to me of minor importance. In 1863 the main offices were in London. It is there in the record. John Sherman wrote to Ikleheimer, Morton, and Ikleheimer wrote on to Rothschild in London. The "capitalists," as they are called in the Hazard report, did indeed see to it that a great debt was made by our civil war, and used to control the volume of our American currency.

Over 20 years ago C. H. Douglas asserted potential plenty. The Loeb report, one of the best achievements of the New Deal, proved it. Whereon the rage of international usury knew no bounds. They argued: "If plenty exists, we cannot control it. Therefore it must not exist. Curtail crops! Maintain monopoly! War is the greatest sabotage of all possible."

But the Germans wouldn't play ball. Even now, instead of smashing all

the French factories, they have to a great extent merely captured them. I beg
you observe the record of loans for August 1939 from London to Poland,
Greece, Turkey, Rumania. I ask you who has tried to extend the conflict.

I assert that from the start England was mucking round in Bulgaria, and
only the genius of Mussolini and the good sense of King Boris prevented
hell breaking loose in the Balkans.

Financiers make wars for the sake of creating great debts and for the
sake of monopoly. They and their henchmen are advocates of destruction.
They have manifestly advocated the destruction of Paris. If Paris were
destroyed, suckers would borrow money and ask "credits" to rebuild it.
Even "La Voix de la Paix," a French free anti-government radio voice was
on June 15 displaying his ignorance of the nature of debt, money and credit.

9   From Rapallo: An Ezra Pound Letter

I HAVE NEVER FATHOMED what a level-headed Japanese reader feels when he
finds an Occidental slamming the said Occidental's government, or his
president and the heads of departments.

It should be said by way of preface that a president is, in theory, a
servant of the people, and that as long as he accepts office on that theory, his
employers are licensed to grumble when he makes an ass of himself or talks
nonsense. This may explain why "Woodie" Wilson so hated the American
system and tried so hard to wreck it. It may explain why many of us
consider Franklin Roosevelt a president and proved servant of Jewry rather
than a respecter of American law and traditions.

What his pretended (and in fairness one must add his very probably
intended) reforms have, in the main, amounted to is the spending of ten
billion dollars of America's money for gold, paying 35 dollars an ounce for
it instead of 20 dollars and 67 cents, thus putting four billion dollars of extra
or unearned or unjust profits into the pockets of an anonymous lot of
vendors of an almost useless and certainly unneeded metal. Hence, quite
probably, the misery of the American farm population, and the mortgages
on American farms.

* * *

Naturally the bleeders who sell gold are delighted with the administration.
The American, who is American by race, birth, and long tradition, grits his
teeth, turns tomato-red, curses, exhausts his vocabulary of vituperation and

ends up (or at least my New England host last year ended up) by saying: "He is ... is ... etc. ... a little Lord Fauntleroy."

One of my adolescent memories is that of an ex-senator in Wall Street abusing Theodore Roosevelt, but never have I known American hate of anyone equal to that I found in America last year directed against the executive. But I had no means of gauging how widely this hatred was diffused. The Democrats whom I met seemed to dislike Mr. Roosevelt's politics, and especially his economics, even more than did the Republicans, but on the other hand he had friends.

*   *   *

With the American mail now cut down to air service I am not going to pretend a knowledge of American feeling in July, 1940. In May, 1939, I had the pleasure of saying to the Polish Ambassador in Washington: "God help you if you trust England." Several other remarks that I managed to get into print at that time, though they were not welcome, would now find a greater acceptance than they then did.

The German publication of documents has reinforced some of them. However, it may still be news in the Orient that already in June, 1939 it was known in Connecticut that Churchill, Eden and Co. meant to get into the government and start war.

*   *   *

I take it The Japan Times expects news from me, and not prophecy, even if the news takes several weeks to reach Tokyo, and if I differentiate myself from certain types of journalist, let us say the Knickerbockers, D. Thompsons, Lippmanns, and Gunthers, by occasionally setting a contemporary act or fact in perspective with history. For example, the Berlin papers almost err when they describe the British firing on the French fleet as "without precedent." In some senses the precedent is inexact. In 1812 the U.S.A. was not a recent ally of England. They were merely at peace with England. A British frigate got within close range (I think it was 50 yards) of an American frigate and opened fire.

"Democracy" is now currently defined in Europe as "a country governed by Jews." However, the British navy has never been Jewish. And indeed the Anglo-Saxon vocabulary translates the word sae-mann (which is now spelled seaman) simply as pirate.

*   *   *

No one will make head or tail of the "apparent contradictions" of democratic governments until there is a handy manual of the press of England, France and the U.S.A. No profession is less written about than the profession of journalism. When the Russian revolutionaries got into the Czarist archives, they published a lot of papers (The Raffalovitch Papers) with the title *"L'abominable venalité de la presse."* Raffalovitch finally decided that the French press wasn't worth buying, as no one believed it. The luminous line in the 500 pages of his correspondence is: "I recommend we give him ten thousand roubles, as is paid to the *Times* and the *Telegraph*" (of London). *The Morning Post* before its lamented demise printed a set of my communications, but demurred at quoting this suggestion of Monsieur Raffalovitch.

The Regime Fascista recently told us that in 1930 a certain Meyer advised Jews not to bother with newspapers. He said, "get into the news agencies," that is where papers get news. America was fed by these agencies, and has therefore been a long time in discovering Europe. I mean Europe since 1920. I doubt if Mr. Rip van Wendell Willkie has yet heard of the Europe now here. At any rate he hadn't heard about our Europe a year ago, when writing for that last and lowest of all periodicals, *The Atlantic Monthly*.

And of course Mr. Willkie won't hear of Europe in American papers, for the very good reason that a year ago only five of them were running at a profit. That means that the rest were on borrowed money.

Hence one smiles when Mr. Roosevelt talks about a free press. A newspaper in the U.S.A. is free to print what its creditors and advertisers want printed. I doubt if any American daily paper will go deeply into the merits of, let us say, canned food in America.

A journalist whom I respect very considerably once described to me an interview with his owner; the latter saying: "What do you think you are, a sort of ambassador? Do you know what runs this paper? Do you know what pays for your keep? Women's underwear!" When I was in London in November, 1938, a friend saw about 20 people arrested for demonstrating against the reception of Carol of Rumania, who was, however, given the full front page of a pictorial daily with the heading "A Regular Fellow," complete in opera cloak and boiled shirt.

An explanation of British and American dailies will convince you of the importance of certain advertisements.

The last poster that caught my eye on the way to Victoria station was: IF CHRIST CAME TO LONDON. He hasn't.

* * *

I keep on saying that it is very hard for one people to understand any other. People do not define their terms. The injunction is fairly old . . . but even if people attempt to do so, they do not realize how little certain words mean to men who are not accustomed to using them or who have not got used to their meanings.

The continent of Europe is full of talk about *"autarchia"* translated as "autarchy." It would save a lot of American and English time if they would translate this word as "the right to keep out of debt."

Scoundrels are often men who do not WANT the public to have its time saved. If they are working a swindle, they do not want the public to find it out UNTIL they have got away with the swag. Hence the very great non-receptivity in the news "service" or system run by usuriocracy and monopolists.

* * *

Henry Adams warned his brother Brooks Adams that he might be martyred. Brooks didn't much care, and he died at a ripe old age, but the public is still nearly unaware of his books, in especial of *The Law of Civilization and Decay* and *The New Empire.*

I know of no American author from whom the Tokyo reader can learn so much Occidental history from so small a number of pages. Go to it. Pirate him. Read him. Perhaps men who read him in 1897 and 1903 found him less lively than you will, reading him now. He was not a fanatical monetary reformer or insister on monetary pact and the known history of money, as is your present correspondent, but he had covered most of the rest of the ground. He knew and said very plainly that the old Roman empire flopped because it failed to protect the purchasing power of agricultural labor. Italian agriculture was ruined by the dumping of cheap grain from Egypt.

I doubt if any author has formulated so many of the bases of empire. The root of sane government is Confucius and Mencius; but the formulae are not fully exposed.

In the stress of the present Anglo-Jewish war on Europe the term *"valuta-lavoro"* has emerged in Italy. That is one sign of Italian strength and sanity. So far as I know, Brooks Adams was unknown in Italy, and General J. F. C. Fuller is among his very rare English readers. Certain facts re-emerge, certain laws continue to be independently rediscovered by people who have never come into contact with records of them.

You find Hitler almost quoting Confucius; you find Mussolini almost citing Jefferson. The answers to the statal problem are known. Every time a dynasty has endured for three centuries we find certain laws at its base. You must defend the purchasing power of labor, in especial, of agricultural labor.

B. Adams starts sanely with the antithesis: money-lender and peasant. Whether the Orient has learned anything from the effects of Indian usury, I do not know. Every now and again we get a gleam, that is, three or four lines of print, showing a very acute sense of money, both in Japan and in China. Perhaps your records have not been so often and so successfully destroyed as have those of the Occident.

* * *

It may even be that my original intention in this article is unnecessary. I started to warn you against accepting "shop-fronts." The European press is full of talk about Reynauds, Blums, Pierlots, Churchills, all of whom are labels pasted over the very solid facts of the firms running the gold exchange in London, the Bank of England, the Banque de France. I suppose the name Sassoon has a meaning in Tokyo, or at least across the water, in Shanghai. You may have a more immediate contact with the reality than have the London and Paris neighbors of Sieff (Moses Israel), Melchett, Lazard, etc.

As no American seems to know whom Mr. Morgenthau bought the ten billion of gold from, perhaps some Oriental will have the ingenuity and patience to start finding out. No one would be more delighted by full and detailed information on this point than would your present correspondent. I have been through eight volumes of U.S. Treasury reports but they merely say how much, never FROM WHOM.

10   From Rapallo: An Ezra Pound Letter

THE RADIO this morning (July 17) announced fusion of Oriental and Occidental cultures as part of the new Japanese program. Hardshell conservatives will fear a general discoloration of culture, the sudden acceptance of the faults of both cultures, such, indeed, as Fenollosa found imminent years ago and withstood. A serious fusion means rigorous selection of the best works of both hemispheres and an historiography that shall give the most pregnant facts with greatest clarity of definition.

I can, I believe, claim something like seniority, or at any rate a long diligence in the search for the former. At fifteen I started an examination of international literature for my own needs. And from 1910 onward there is

printed record of my results, however imperfect. I have had a little collaboration. Eliot however gave up his Sanskrit. Bunting learned to write a
beautiful Persian hand. Aldington remained inside the language groups I
had examined. Prof. Breasted thought my idea of a quarterly publication of
such results of American research as attained value as literature, that is
such as had more than specialist's philological interest, was "a dream
floating above the heads of the people." By which he meant the American
University system wherein he held very high status as Assyriologist. I see
no reason for Japan's taking over the stupidities and flat failures of American scholarship. Tokyo has the liveliest magazine of young letters in the
world (**VOU**). New York once had it, that was twenty years ago. Paris often
had it before then. Editorial Yunque of Barcelona has just started a very
good bilingual series of poets (*Poesia en la Mano*) beginning with J. R.
Masoliver's excellent translations from Dante, Spanish text facing the original.

If I recommend eight volumes of my own essays and anthologies to the
Kokusai Bunka Shinkokai as a starting point, it is not, as might be supposed, from immodesty, but simply because I do not know of any other 30
years or 40 years persistent effort to sort out the Occidental books most
worth attention. There are encyclopedias, compilations giving names of
ALL the known writings, etc., but not attempts to show the best books in
relation to each other.

The very great labors of the Leo Frobenius Institute cover a different
field. Your universities will of course take note of them.

The hang-together of art and the economic system is not yet very
generally understood. I keep insisting that an "epic is a poem containing
history." That may explain why epic poets need to know economics. It does
not touch the lyric writers so closely. However, a "fusion or union of
cultures" implies a mutual regard for two historiographies. Here your
universities can save their students a great deal of time by importing Brooks
Adams' *The Law of Civilization and Decay* and *The New Empire.*

I think, in fact, that you might start your study of our new historiography from those books, though to understand American cycles they must be
amplified by brief compendia of the writing of the American founders, John
Adams, Jefferson, Van Buren, and by a narrative containing facts which I,
personally, have found in Overholser, Woodward, Beard, Bowers, and not
(oh very emphatically not) in the text books used in American beaneries.

I cannot condense four of the essential factors further than I have
already done in my "Introductory Text-book" offered herewith.

Introductory Text-book [In Four Chapters]

Chap. 1. "All the perplexities, confusion and distress in America arise, not from defects in their constitution or confederation, not from want of honor and virtue, so much as from downright ignorance of the nature of coin, credit, and circulation."—John Adams.

Chap. 2. ". . . and if the national bills issued, be bottomed (as is indispensable) on pledges of specific taxes for their redemption within certain and moderate epochs, and be of proper denominations for circulation, no interest on them would be necessary or just, because they would answer to everyone of the purposes of the metallic money withdrawn and replaced by them." —Thomas Jefferson (1816, letter to Crawford).

Chap. 3. ". . . and gave to the people of this Republic THE GREATEST BLESSING THEY EVER HAD—THEIR OWN PAPER TO PAY THEIR OWN DEBTS."—Abraham Lincoln.

Chap. 4. "The Congress shall have power: To coin money, regulate the value thereof and of foreign coin, and to fix the standards of weights and measures." *Constitution of the United States*, Article I Legislative Department, Section 8, p. 5. Done in the convention by the unanimous consent of the States, 7th September, 1787, and of the Independence of the United States the twelfth. In witness whereof we have hereunto subscribed our names. —George Washington, President and Deputy from Virginia.

This "text" was followed by a half page of notes and bibliography. Thus:

> The abrogation of this last mentioned power derives from the ignorance mentioned in my first quotation. Of the three preceding citations, Lincoln's has become the text of Willis Overholser's recent *History of Money in the U.S.*; the first citation was taken as opening text by Jerry Voorhis in his speech in the House of Representatives June 6, 1938; and the passage from Jefferson is the nucleus of my *Jefferson and/or Mussolini*.
>
> Douglas' proposals are a subhead under the main idea in Lincoln's sentence; Gesell's "invention" is a special case under Jefferson's general law. I have done my best to make simple summaries and clear definitions in various books and pamphlets and recommend as introductory study, apart from C. H. Douglas' *Economic Democracy* and Gesell's *Natural Economic Order*, Chris. Hollis' *Two Nations*, McNair Wilson's *Promise to Pay*, Larrañaga's *Gold, Glut and Government* and M. Butchart's compendium of three centuries' thought, that is an anthology of what has been said, in *Money*. (Originally published by Nott.)

There again I have nothing to retract. I left copies of the above work with a number of senators and congressmen last year in Washington, also with a few historians. The more they knew already, the more nearly saw the bearing of my four chapters. I doubt if anyone can further, or to advantage condense, the thought of John Adams than I have in Cantos 62/71, and I have made a start on Jefferson in my *Jefferson and/or Mussolini*. Both of which volumes can be explained. There is no reason for someone in Tokyo refraining from issuing a commentary, but I doubt if an adequate history of the U.S. can be written without INCLUDING the essential ideas which I have there set together. The compendia of *histoire morale contemporaine* made by Remy de Gourmont and Henry James, I have at least indicated in my *Make it New*.

At this point I would offer a word of warning to Japanese alumni of American, or other Occidental universities. With the exception of Frobenius' *Forschungsinstitut* in Frankfurt, our universities are NOT, they most emphatically are *not*, in the foreguard of Western thought. There is a time lag of 20, 40 or 60 years in what they teach in economics, history and literature. They may be more lively in departments of material science. At any rate most of their Japanese alumni were taught ideas belonging to Western decadence. And that decadence was nowhere more notable than in Western tendency to erect museums rather than temples.

Now the museum is all very well in its way. The juvenile student can see bits and pieces of what has been achieved in the past, which may keep him from narrow provincialism both of place and of time.

In the study of comparative literature, T. S. Eliot has acutely observed that, "existing masterworks constitute a plenum, whereof the divers parts have inter-related proportions and values. The relations of extant works are modified by new work that is really new."

It is also true that the real writers of any epoch collaborate, sometimes consciously and voluntarily, sometimes unconsciously and even against their own will.

Yeats and I collaborated voluntarily. Yeats and F. M. (Hueffer) Ford involuntarily. Cummings is possibly unconscious of collaboration, etc. However, a museum is made up of fragments. An attempt to present the literature of a country or continent is bound to appear fragmentary or at least made up of heteroclite matter of different degrees of importance. Even more so when we come to translated literature. There is no uniform merit in translations, any more than in works. One nation may have an epic. Another a set of plays. But one dimension is common to all masterworks, namely, they contain the quintessence of racial quality. I have seen Villon in Paris 500 years after his lines were written.

I have seen Boccaccio and Goldoni in Italy, and it is commonplace that "London is full of Dickens." By which laconic phrases one means that the "news" printed by these authors is still the event of the day in their countries.

Whatever I have compiled either in essays or in anthologies has been in an attempt to set together maxima of achievement, that is, work in which at least some of the qualities of writing and concept have attained the highest known degree. And my results are I think largely confirmed by the findings of England's most distinguished resident critic, T. S. Eliot (born American). And to a certain extent I think Yeats and F. M. Ford would have agreed with us, however long it may take the literary bureaucracies and the book trade to admit it. In several cases even the book-trade has had to give way 20 or 25 years after the fact.

I am therefore recommending my own finding re comparative literature. I am recommending Brooks Adams and subsequent "new" economists in the field of history. I have elsewhere cited various other compendia. Germany is talking of Karl von Stein and of Ruhland instead of Marx. The thought of an epoch does not present itself in all departments. La Tour du Pin, Fabre, Frazer, Burbank, may seem names picked up at hazard. Strictly scientific names are world-known—it is only when you get to the border-line between material (practical) science and culture that the vital writers may lie hidden for half a century before coming into their own. In the fields of history or economics the vital writers may be half absorbed and super-seded before being known to more than three hundred readers. After which they crop up again later as "sources," the "source" for practical purposes having very little importance save for retrospective scholars, very little, that is, in proportion to the immense importance of getting the right solution, whether for an anti-tubercular serum, or for an economic (monetary) process.

John Adams remarked that "very few people have the chance to choose their system of government." It is extremely difficult to make a thorough reform of studies that have become fixed or waterlogged through a century or more of university habit. There is, on the other hand, a grand chance of effecting an up-to-date system, if you deliberately set out to present a relatively unexplored foreign culture, and can do so without superstitions, at any rate looking clearly at definite facts either established or provable, and not caring a hang whether these facts have been acceptable to the controllers of the educational (videlicet mis-educational or obfuscatory) system in the countries which you elect to investigate.

If Japan can produce a better, that is clearer and more incisive, set of brochures showing the real thought of the founders of America's social form, than now exists in America, so much the greater your glory. The best and most revolutionary book on Botticelli was brought out by one of your citizens. It was, or at least appeared to me to be, extremely original in its treatment of Botticelli's details as comparable with Oriental treatments. The impartial and alien eye really saw what the familiar native eye had taken for granted. So much for suggested imports to Japan. When it comes to exports, we in the Occident wonder whether a Japanese history exists; or at any rate we fear that no translation of your history exists that will tell us as much of Japan as the TONG-KIEN-KANG-MOU in De Moyriac de Mailla's version tells us of China. You can't order such works over night. De Mailla's French makes literature of even rather dull passages. Klaproth's *Nippon o Dai Itsi Ran* does not. It is merely well printed. We want to know more about you. There is a gap between *Kagekiyo* and the new dredger-plus plywood veneers.

What I really know of Japan I have got from Fenollosa's notes on the Noh and from a handful of "very much over-civilized" young men to whom the Noh was familiar. I cannot suppose this to be a "working knowledge" but I believe it to be a much more "real" knowledge than I should have got by starting at the "practical end" and omitting the fragments vouch-safed to me.

In struggling against enormous odds (meaning financial odds) for a mutual understanding between Japan and the Occident, there is still the danger that a Japanese educated in the U.S.A. might occasionally believe a statement printed in English or American newspapers without first looking carefully at the date line, and name of the agency supplying said news. It cannot be too firmly understood that "some" agencies and newspapers exist mainly, or even wholly, for the purpose of causing the stock markets to wobble, their "political" purposes being a mere cover for this means to putrid profit. I personally feel that some of you might get your European news via the U.S.A. even if as many of your students have gone to Germany (have they?) as to the U.S.A. *Re* which possibility I register the simple statement made to me two years ago by an American publisher. (Parenthesis: my friends often urge me to be "reasonable.") The publisher said: "Facts unfavorable to Germany and Italy are news; facts favorable to Italy and Germany are propaganda."

Against which I set a revealing statement made by Otto Dietrich (Terramare pamphlets no. 13): "The Führer will never create an office unless thoroughly convinced of the suitability of the person selected for it."

Perhaps the spiritual descendents and unconscious followers of Confucius do him more honor than physical descendents who spend their time borrowing money.

11   From Rapallo: An Ezra Pound Letter

IT IS IMPOSSIBLE to explain contemporary Europe to Japan without a long economic preface, possibly a longer preface than the average reader has patience for. One can roughly indicate the cycle of Occidental infamies since the founding of the Bank of England about 1696 A.D., via the suppression of paper money in England's American colonies, Cobbett's struggles against the ruin of agriculture in England, industrialization, the ruin of land owners by financial chicane, etc. Suffice it to say that by 1935 we were all fed up with the fall of empires, kingdoms, etc. It was all "old stuff." Governments had flopped, Austria was, later, a minor collapse, but for over a century and a quarter no man had laid hands on a Rothschild. That item was NEWS with a big "N," but not one European journalist in a hundred had sense to know it, and not one in a thousand could print his perception if he had one. Three hundred million or whatever golden schillings or whatever had gone into Skoda gun works, to make trouble, via Vienna. The reply was the *Anschluss*, the incorporation of Austria in the German Reich.

In one sense history, not merely ideological history, is built out of phrases. It is built out of crystallizations of words into very brief groups, say five, six, or a dozen words. These words become fact. And it is impossible to exaggerate their force, because they cannot come into existence save as proof of a state of understanding. I mean clear understanding, not mere confused apprehension or suspicion.

Hjalmar Schacht made history in 1938: "*Geld, dem keine Verbrauchsgüter gegenüberstehen, ist ja nichts als bedrücktes Papier.*" Money that isn't issued against commerciable goods is mere printed paper.

Of course you have to know quite a bit of economics to understand why this sentence is history. Aristotle left certain terms undefined, or at any rate failed to "educate" the Occident and give it a clear (when I say clear, I mean clear) understanding of certain properties of money. Some people continued to think of money as "a universally accepted commodity delivered in measured amounts." By 640 A.D. the Tang dynasty had got round to using paper money, that is, "an admonition or memorandum of how much the holder of a certain kind of piece of paper ought to receive in the common market." The inscription of the Tang notes is essentially the same as that on the ten lire notes in Italy today.

Then came the word "credit." By 1623 the Sienese Bank, the Monte dei Paschi, had discovered the basis of sound credit, namely the abundance of nature and the responsibility of the whole people. Jefferson knew that it was unnecessary for the U.S. Government to pay two dollars (out of the people's pocket) for every dollar's worth of goods or services delivered to the government. In other words he knew that the state need not rent its own credit from a clique of individuals either American or foreign. Nevertheless even today men go on confusing mandates or orders to deliver what exists and promises to hand over something which may exist next year or the year after. I hope the Japanese student will find two words, one for each of these paper implements, and then refrain from using the two words indifferently and confusedly. If you do this, the Occident will come to sit at your feet.

In the meantime, very informative work is being printed in Italy. I need hardly say that the Axis Powers are the most interesting phenomena in the Occident at this moment, A.D. 1940, year of the Fascist Era XVIII. *Gerarchia*, a monthly magazine founded by Mussolini, contains on p. 345, the month current, the words *"problemi economici, cioè sociali"* ("Economic problems, that is to say social").

This also is history. It shows the final penetration of a whole realm of ideas that scattered economists and reformers have been hammering at, and trying to hammer into the public mind for the past 20 years.

There is, indeed, need for a drastic and burning revision of the rubbish taught in ALL Western universities in the departments of history and economics. Beginning with Brooks Adams the live thought of half a century runs through authors who are practically excluded—I mean 100% (one hundred per cent) excluded—from the frousty beaneries of the U.S.A., England, etc. C. H. Douglas, Gesell, Chris. Hollis, McNair Wilson, Overholser, Larrañaga, Butchart's compendium, do not figure among the authors revealed to our students. An Italian minority, chiefly *non-universitaire*, I should say, is served by a flock of periodicals which do treat these subjects, often in an "unreadable" manner. However, as you are enjoying a new Italo-Japanese amity society, you might do worse than to fill its reading room with copies of *Gerarchia, Rivista del Lavoro* and publications of this sort. C. Pellizzi is now editing *Civiltà Fascista*, but for brevity's sake it is now possible to make a short cut via Odon Por's *Finanza Nuova*, an 80-page summary of NEW financial ideas (published by Le Monnier, Firenze, 10 lire). Apart from brief restatement of ideas and experiments elsewhere, the opening pages of this book give the clearest, and for the first time so far as I know, an adequate statement of the basic differences of theory, and, be it said, the superiorities of Corporate State finance over other proposals and experiments. You cannot understand the new Europe without knowledge of the Italian Fascist revolution and you cannot understand that revolution without distinguishing two components in it: the men who, led by Mussolini, regenerated Italy, and the men who, seeing that they could not prevent the regeneration, went along with it for what they could make out of it. Por is distinctly in the first group.

"There had been retouches, but not root changes, because the state intervention did not get down to bed rock, but left the hegemony to predatory groups."

"Autarchy set going as constructive reply to the disintegrating power of money-ocracy, was quickly seen by the latter to be a deadly attack, to be resisted by all means whatsoever, including war. . . ."

". . . . it is at any rate clear that it is not the national aggregates that are fighting . . . but financial cliques prodding the peoples to fight."

"Why does Plutocracy fight autarchy?" asks Por.

"In the first place autarchy aims at producing enough goods for national needs. Money no longer dictates production, but an autarchic-cooperative order does the dictating and money depends on this order for its volume and value."

I wonder if I can translate that sentence any more clearly? Por goes on:

"In short, the cooperative autarchy abolishes money as merchandise as it has abolished labor as merchandise."

The Italian word is *merce*. We might say: Under autarchia neither money nor labor [is] something a clique can sweat profits out of.

"The state having established its rule over the economic system extends this rule over the financial."

"If you consider that the Bank of England is owned by international financiers who are very hard to identify, and that the British Government has not the power to direct the bank's actions always and everywhere; and that the Banque de France is owned by private capitalists and that many seats on its board of directors are, as it were, hereditary in the plutocratic families: Rothschild, Neuflize, Hottinguer, Wendel, Duchemin, etc. who control the key industries, including the arms business, you can measure the meaning of the reorganization of the Banca d'Italia."

"It has become really national because no international interest can get to work inside it. . . ."

"The credit of a corporatively organized country is limited to its real riches."

"These consist in its physical resources in their natural state bettered by modern processes of labor, plus the vital activities of the population and the state of the sciences; of the culture and the intellectual and moral education of the people and the efficient ordering of its institutions. The true wealth is not money. Money is the means accepted to actuate production and stimulate the exchange of riches . . ."

"No sector of the economy can get stranded; all the necessary monetary means to develop the nation's wealth will be provided without having resource to foreign financings."

All this may seem to be nothing but very plain common sense. Japan may have arrived at this state of sanity and progressed beyond it, for all I know. But you may take it from me that Europe, in general, had not done so by September last year. Even among the bright reformers in various "progressive sectors" such as the U.S.A. (New Deal); Alberta (Social Credit, sabotaged by Monty Norman and the London bleeders); New Zealand (amply reviewed by Por in a later chapter of his *Finanza Nuova*), some of the essential parts of the mechanism had been omitted.

It is for the above very simple ideas that the Axis Powers are fighting against mouldy superstition. That much you can take as news item, whether you agree with me or not, as to the value of the ideas in themselves.

12   From Rapallo: An Ezra Pound Letter

JAPAN is to be congratulated on bringing Mr. Matsuoka to her Foreign Office. Having sat at Geneva he knows just how rotten the League was. He knows to an atom the kind of swindler who made it. He knows the mentality that was in it, and is in the Carnegie peace swindle. He knows to what degree the latter sniveling gang of pacifists has refrained from using its endowments honestly and how well it has blocked any research into the real causes of war. And this knowledge of his might be of world use.

* * *

Funk's plan is a complete answer to the infamies proposed by Streit and Co. But that doesn't mean that Funk's plan will get any adequate publicity in America. You might think it would . . . you might think my compatriots would be able to see the sense of collaborating in a new world order instead of keeping their collective heads in a bag, but if so, you have neglected to note the thoroughness of the obfuscation, various strata of which date from 1863, or 1873, or 1920.

* * *

The work of the Vanguard Press in flooding America with cheap editions of Marx, Lenin, Trotsky and Stalin might have been harmless, might even have been useful, had the Americans known their own history. But they have not known their own history; do not know it, and are not in the process of learning it.

As to their learning anything from their papers . . . they have been and are being served by men who sell news that is wanted. Unwanted news just doesn't "sell."

Rip van Wendell Willkie reads, and has read, the same news sheet as Roosevelt and Morgenthau . . . that is to say, he is pre-conditioned by news-baths carefully prepared by Reuters, Havas, etc. . . . namely, by the propaganda of Rothschild, Lazard and the rest of the most poisonous dregs of humanity. This has been going on for some time.

If Japan gets a "bum" deal, it will be due quite as much to the American people's real ignorance as to any ill-will or even to the blind greed of a minority.

Boak Carter has tried to tell 'em (the Americans) some of the story. The more cats he lets out, the more difficulty he has of getting any time on the air, or of even holding a column.

A quite dear old friend writes me that she is not exactly praying, but concentrating her will every evening to stop Hitler (about whom she knows nothing). She is not a venomous woman and she likes German opera.

A quite bright New York journalist thinks I am in danger of being imprisoned here in Italy for the sentiments expressed in a quotation which I have had stamped on my writing paper. He does not recognize the quotation as being a motto of Mussolini, despite the fact that it is followed by the "m" now used all over this country to indicate citations from the writings or speeches of Il Duce. The quotation is: "LIBERTY IS NOT A RIGHT BUT A DUTY."

* * *

You Japanese are said to be very ingenious. Go on. Invent something. Find me a mental gimlet that will let a squirt of light into the indubitably active "minds" of America. "Listen-in to Tokyo!" Yes, brother. And the sooner Tokyo starts TELLING the American people its own history, i.e. the history of the U.S.A., the sooner the American people will find out. For, of their own motion and initiative, they are NOT finding it out.

God alone knows what we Americans know of Japan. None of us reads Japanese. Some tens of and hundreds of thousands of us can read German, French and Italian.

* * *

Note to your own honor that Italy billed their taking of Somaliland as the FIRST time the British Empire had lost a colony. Spain said, "the first time in 300 years." A day later came Japanese opinion to the effect that it was the first time SINCE the American Revolution, when we Yanks took out 13 colonies all at once! (Nevertheless, it took us five years, not two months.)

APPENDIX I

Tami Koumé, *The Art of* 靈 *Etherism, or Spiritico-Etheric Art*

I AM AN ARTIST; I must live in my art; my life is in my art. This being the case, I can ill throw my pencil for a pen, in order to set forth in so many words the principles as well as the inner meanings of my life-problem, the Spiritico-etheric Art.

However, for the enlightened public, who are not yet well acquainted with my art, but kind enough to be curious to know what that is in reality, I would fain forgo the advantages, and try to describe the nature and content of the art in which I have been spiritually awakened, through truthful speculation, and by means of entire devotion to the cause of the all-great and mystical Universe.

We are now standing at the critical moment of humanity. We must be saved by something. Hence who would venture to say that the Universe should d[eny?] the cries vehemently uttered by the chosen few, who participate in the saving councils of Nature? There are [a] few born now, whose spiritual and intellectual capacities represent the ages of [a] thousand years hence; for nature does not bring forth children useful only for the present age.

In last May, 1920, I have exhibited my artistic creations on my own account, to show the content of my art-life; in other words, I have attempted to reveal the processes that have led my art from artificial creations "to super-artificial-growing-creations."

Now these "Super-artificial-growing-creations" stand as a sort of medium between self and the universe, while self is a kind of medium in like manner between the universe and the growing creations; and so I have provisionally styled this art then a mediumistic school. But this term, convenient as it is, [is] apt to be misunderstood as to the essential significance thereof, on account of its already enjoying a peculiar technical usage of its own; besides, it is rather too superficial to be applied to my spirit-saving art.

Upon this I was forced temporarily to coin a new term, which is but a symbol of my art, by which symbol, 靈 (which I make bold to pronounce Reitherism or 靈 Etherism) the essential features of my art-life, it is to be hoped, might be made somewhat plainer. Let me here remark *par excellence* that this sign being the symbol of my art, has no conventional pronuciation, but only serves to signify the inner meaning of my art, and may thus be pronounced as above indicated, because it is an artistic representation of my art-life.

Historically speaking, the art that applies colouring matters on the surface, has been called painting, whose development, it is quite needless to repeat here.

The more advanced painting of the present age has so far progressed as to be able to delineate mental phenomena. But those schools of painting are unable to exhibit anything decisively and analytically as to the origin of all things, and the substance of the mind.

They only deceive themselves and others through unsatisfactory self-affirmations. I, who found it impossible to conform to this state of unreason, have at last arrived at this my art, Reitherism, or Spiritico-etheric Art, through purest and truest intuition, and by means of sincerest speculation and pious devotion, even willingly risking physical safety. I was thus saved.

Reitherism is an artification of human life.

Reitherism is a beautification of all things material and immaterial.

It is again a beautiful manifestation of Spirit.

Those who are possessed of a beauty-consciousness, will all acknowledge that, in general, Art means an all-round consciousness-operation that goes for creating beauty artificially. It is a philosophical representation of this truth.

The birth of art is either an *Anschauung* or an intuitive operation. Art is or should be an Artificial creation, that represents its objects through its own cells. Hence Art is again purest philosophy that deals with the Universe or human life, by imparting its own life to the objects or subjects it has to do with.

The conclusion of art is beauty itself. Beauty consciousness, æsthetic consciousness, is a bodily experience of the life-forms of the good.

Good is the primary intuition or direct-perception that is to be harmonized and incorporated with the truth.

In the sense of truth, Art is the mental form of humanity. It is universally a self-contemplation and self-reflection.

In fine, the true, the good, and the beautiful, or truth, goodness and beauty, must form a trinity in unity.

The essence or essential quality of beauty is inexpressible.

True Art is a radiation of high toned or high flooded sense of beauty, that is impressed on practical life of humanity. The ecstasy of faith seems to be the same with an eternal purification of the rapture felt in the moment of love.

The essence of beauty is not to be touched outside the region of self-knowledge. If it is so, old æsthetics is but a puppet logic, for it cannot go beyond shadowing forth superficial differences of nature.

In the puppet logic, art is defined to be an enjoyment of life. Such views are boastfully entertained by the ignorant, who consider themselves (i.e. men) most high-stationed in the universe, as lords of creation, thus deceiving themselves and others, under the shadow of old antiquated æsthetics, or so-called science of beauty. In fine, man has no right to define art an enjoyment of human life.

If there are any enjoyable elements in art, they are, must be, the essential nature of art herself, not her definable meaning, much like the æsthetic impressions accompanying the ecstasy or rapture of faith.

* * *

The littleness of self or ego, cannot but be felt by those who have become conscious of their own intrinsic nature.

Many and various problems that men cannot solve by means of the progress of science and development of reason, must not be struck away or blotted out as merely unthinkable or incomprehensible.

At least, I myself cannot blunder away the essential power, great and mystic, of the Universe, which we bodily experience irresistibly—and this by lukewarm reasons of science or psychology. No; God forbid!

In such mood, we cannot but exclaim admiringly, when we gaze upon the millions of bright, shining heavenly bodies, "O God, how splendid!"

We thus cry to that irresistible might of Nature, and this superartificial power, "O God!" However we have become conscious of these grand phenomena, so as to extort from us such rapturous exclamations, we cannot deny the Absolute Power called God, pervading the whole Universe.

However, the "God" I admire is not the God of monotheism or polytheism; neither is he the impersonal God of pantheism, though in his essential nature he somewhat approaches the latter. Positively it is not the God of Atheism, said to be one with the Universe.

I deem God to be one with the Universe, but that is so in theistic point of view. Yes; I intuit the existence of God, great and mystical. To recognize the Universal Consciousness or Cosmic soul, is to acknowledge God. The narrow and poor intellect of man can only touch some portion of Universal Consciousness, great and mystic, merely by negating himself.

Men are not aware of the preciousness of negating themselves. But yet those who are awaking to the salvation of their own souls, are approaching the precious state of self-negation daily more and more, nearer and nearer, by self-discipline and deep sincerity—this is not denied by God himself.

Now simple or pure ego I call the state in which human personality, with its minimum conscious condition, is harmonized and interfused with the consciousness of the Universe. But, what is the state of simple ego, or pure ego, here introduced rather mystically? That is the state of realization or bodily experience of spiritual enlightenment, rational and exalted, attained by inspiratory judgement and reasonable speculation—a state, free from all doubts, and impure ideas, transcending little human personalities, wherein reigns naïvety and simplicity.

In this state, minimum human consciousness being present, consciousness manifestations in the cerebral cells subsiding, superhuman powers of extraordinary spirituality are dominant.

Such artists who are conscientious enough to live in truth and purity, should bravely renounce all those petty ingenuities, learned from conventions, and listen to the voice of conscience, for these petty ingenuities only tend to deceive others as well as the artists themselves.

Although we are determined to part with the shallow self-affirmatory modes of representation taught to us from historical education, so pertinacious are we men, that we feel much grudge to do away with those skills which have been our companions years long. But those earnest artists who have once listened to the precious voice of conscience, cannot but renounce all grudge to live the pure and true life of enlightened artists.

If not so, chefs d'oeuvre themselves are not much better, nay far worse, than those rough lines drawn by children expressive of their love toward nature. They are simply productions of time devoted to ingenuity.

True Art must be love towards humanity, born necessarily for saving the disquietude men entertain in respect to the present existence.

For us who endeavor to live in the soul-saving art, there is no need of a temple or church occupying and enclosing a portion of space. All phenomena pervading the infinite universe; nay, one single constellation glittering in the firmament, one single flower emitting sweet fragrance in the field—these are a thousand times better than myriad volumes of printed books, being a direct teaching of God bestowed on us mortals.

The works of Cézanne and van Gogh are manifestations of love apprehended necessarily from Nature. The still lifes of Cézanne are smiling lives, while van Gogh's plants are portions of breathing Nature. They cannot but feel, as though inanimate nature were his or her brothers and sisters.

Yes! all things are our brothers and sisters. All things, men, animals, plants, nay mountains, rivers, desks, papers, all are so. At least I perceive them to be so. One's own work—what does it consist of? It is a synthesis of himself, the canvas, and colouring matters. In other words, the work here produced, is an animated object, as it were, which has absorbed my spirit, and got combined with paints on the canvas to be manifested thus.

In one's own productions one's life dwells, and animate some of the elements (spiritual elements) that go to constitute one's self. One's own works produced on such faith are one's brothers, kith and kin, to be sure!

One's work of art is, so to speak, a fragment or detachment of one's own life. Therefore works of art that are not in earnest, and falsely represented, are so many useless cuttings-away of the artist's life! An artist, if he fears death, cannot execute (growing) works. But, to think of death without any (growing) work, this is far more unbearable indeed!

Such artists who fear death, and at the same time fear the appearance of their growing works—these have no right to exist in the noble world of art. I have said, all things in Nature are our brothers.

Yes! so they truly are. All things in Nature are the workings and manifestations of *Ether*. Men too, in the beginning of their existence, are but simple cells. The germinal cells have, each of them, specific cell-mind, which I christen provisionally *Spiritual element*.

The spiritual element, which pervades the universe, according to its different operations, sometimes makes organic manifestations, and sometimes inorganic manifestations. Strictly speaking, the distinction between *organic* and *inorganic*, is, simply, based on the point of view from human standard. They are simply the two faces of that infinite, absolute thing called the Universe.

I shall now speak of my realization of the truth. I repeat, the so-called Spiritual element is the cell-mind of Ether, which not only pervades all spaces, but even fills up the spaces between atoms. All objects emit subtle emanation called *aura* or auric *atmosphere*, which is nothing but the proceeding of this spiritual element.

Just as in our visual nerves, vibrating etheric rays strike the retinas to produce colour-impressions; so this spiritual element, by acting upon the cerebral convolutions, can make the nerve centre in the brain produce the auric atmosphere, as above referred to.

The minutest elements in the sensory organ or sensorium are the sensitive cells. Again the minutest elements in the inner sensory centre of the cerebral convolutions are a mass of nerve-cells. In a highly sensitive condition of these nerve-cells, the sensory centre is enabled to have communion with the external (so-called) spiritual-elements.

So even the colour-forms, that are not reflected on the retina of the eyes, can be seized at the Fornix of the brain. Some persons, in whom their spiritual sensation is highly developed, can insensibly represent or perceive them; just as forms that are not made visible by means of prismatic spectrum, can be seized by ultra-violet rays of the spectrum. Our ⌐¬ school artists are too highly ultra-sensitive to be merely ingenious to draw visible things.

The recent tendency to give theoretical explanations to the movements of colours or lines, is a dreadful one, apt to specimenize (specify) art, or restrict the significance of it.

Æsthetic symbolisation, or artistic representation, is not mnemonic (of the memory) symbolization constituted by means of speculation or meditation, nor is it a conventional specimen either. This is a symbolization reached by the inbringing of feeling, *"Einfühlung,"* through which the artist's spiritual character as well as his or her philosophy is manifested, or æsthetically symbolized.

* * *

The life of art is eternal and everlasting. As long as the Universe stands, as far as all things exist, art is a changeful representation of Nature, running along the orbit of the whole Universe.

Art, though deemed by Moderns to have been brought to a stand-still, or deadlock, has in truth, only finished her first stage, now just on the point of entering on the second stage, which would only commence her true career.

We who have not yet been saved by conventional art based on sense perceptions, must henceforward be saved by the images reflected on the Fornix of the brain.

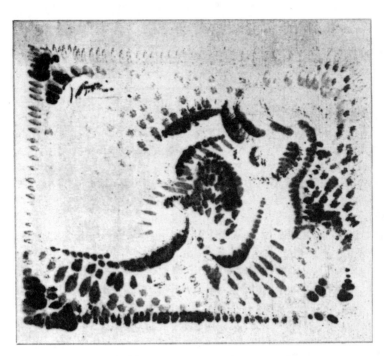

APPENDIX II   VOU CLUB

IN HIS ESSAY "VOU Club," Ezra Pound introduced to Western readers some contemporary Japanese poets. In his generous opinion, their poems were "better work than any save those of E. E. Cummings," admiring in them the Japanese eye which was "like those new camera shutters that catch the bullet leaving the gun." In his estimation their thought went from one peak to another "faster than our slow wits permit us to follow."

Pound's essay appeared in the *Townsman*, vol. I, no. 1 (January, 1938), as an introduction, with the "Notes" by Katue Kitasono, to thirteen poems by eight of the VOU Club members: "Upon the Tragedy of a Flower on the Calm-latitudes or of a Passenger Aeroplane" and "Secrecy of a Duet" by Takeshi Fuji; "The End of Evil Fortune" by Chio Nakamura; "The Road of Flowers" and "Glassy Hour" by Takeshi Koike; "Young Swan" and "Love's Magnetism" by Toshio Sasajima; "Finger Top of Waltz" and "Outflow of Waltz" by Koichi Kihara; "A Battle of Roses" by Minoru Yasoshima; and "Poems" by Katue Kitasono. Reprinted here are Pound's "VOU Club" and Kitasono's "Notes" from the *Townsman*, in addition to six poems by VOU poets, as well as James Laughlin's "Modern Poets of Japan" from *New Directions* 1938.

As Pound had suspected, there certainly were other clubs of poets in Japan at that time. Among the "active" poets in the Tokyo area were Junzaburō Nishiwaki, Shiro Murano, Ichiro Ando, Ikuo Haruyama, and Fuyuhiko Kitagawa, to name a few. But also as Pound had guessed, the VOU Club was a center of intellectual attention at that time, rapidly increasing its membership during the years 1935-37.

Almost twenty years later, Kitasono recollected the old days and wrote an essay, "The VOU Club," upon the request of Michael Reck, who visited him in Tokyo. Reck later included this essay in his book, *Ezra Pound: A Close-Up* (New York: McGraw-Hill, 1967).

Ezra Pound, *VOU Club*

IT IS NOT A CASE of asking what would any set of eight European and/or American poets look like if asked to translate *their* poems into Japanese. It is a case of saying that for half a century after Papa Flaubert started writing, any man who wanted to write English prose had to start by reading French prose. And it may be that from now on any man who wants to write English poetry will have to start reading Japanese. I mean modern Japanese, not merely studying Chinese ideogram, as I have been advocating for the past twenty years.

Not as translations but as *actual writing*, these poems are better work than any save those of E. E. Cummings at his happiest. They may even serve to introduce Cummings and Péret to readers who have thought my more obscure younger contemporaries merely eccentric. Yes. You will have to read Mr. Kitasono's introduction twice, and the poems three or four times. The Japanese eye is like those new camera shutters that catch the bullet leaving the gun. You will not understand some sentences as you read them, but only after having got to their ends, see that they reach round and tuck in their beginnings, so that sense is there nicely boxed. I myself feel rather like a grizzly bear faced by a bunch of weasels. It is the Mongoose spring, the chameleon's tongue quickness. All the moss and fuzz that for twenty years we have been trying to scrape off our language—these young men start without it. They see the crystal set, the chemical laboratory and the pine tree with untrammelled clearness. As to their being a or the most active new club of poets in Tokio, I doubt if any one city contains two such clubs. I know that nowhere in Europe is there any such vortex of poetic alertness. Tokio takes over, where Paris stopped.

Make no mistake, the thought is not absent from these poems. The Japanese poet has gone from one peak of it to another faster than our slow wits permit us to follow before we have got used to his pace.

Ezra Pound

Katue Kitasono, *Notes*

THESE POEMS collected here were all written by the members of the VOU Club. This club was planned in a stroll of fifteen minutes or so under the platan-trees at Ginza Street, August 1935. After a week the VOU Club consisting of fifteen members was born as a most active, new club of poets in Japan. Almost the half of these poets belonged before to the "Club d'Arcueil," which was made in the spring of 1931 by four young poets and two poetesses. The magazine *Madame Blanche* was published under my editorship.

At that time we were profoundly influenced by the personality and the attitude for art of Erik Satie. In the memory of this harmless great artist we used the name of the place where he had lived for our Club. The movement of this club rapidly exerted an influence over young poets, and the members increased next year to more than forty, making an epoch in the poetical world.

It was by an inevitable result of the tendency of the age that the "Club d'Arcueil" should dissolve at last without a serious reason and the *Madame Blanche* ceased to be published at No. 19.

Now the most interesting subject to us is about the relation between imagery and ideoplasty. Contemporary young poets are all vaguely conscious of, and worry about this part. Some of them went over again to its extremity and returned. Others gave up exploration and found out a queer new country, remaining only as amateur thinkers. But anyone whose standing ground is in literature can do nothing for it, if he ignores the system of literature.

The formation of poetry takes such a course like below:

(*a*) Language   (*b*) Imagery   (*c*) Ideoplasty

That which we vaguely call poetical effect means, generally, ideoplasty which grows out of the result of imagery. Man has thought out to make a heart-shaped space with two right angles. This great discovery on plastic, and also that of the conics in mathematics, are two mysteries brought by man's intellect.

The relation between imagery and ideoplasty makes us suppose the heart-shaped space which is born by the connection of the same mysterious two curves. We standardized these two curves and got a necessity.

What we must do first for imagery are collection, arrangement, and combination. Thus we get the first line, "a shell, a typewriter, and grapes," in which we have an æsthetic feeling. But there is not any further development. We add the next line and then another æsthetic feeling is born. Thus all the lines are combined and a stanza is finished. This means the completion of imagery of that stanza and then ideoplasty begins.

This principle can be applied to poems consisting of several stanzas. In that case ideoplasty is formed when the last stanza is finished.

Though it cannot be allowed as orthodox of poetry that imagery is performed by ideoplasty, this violence is dared often by religionists, politicians, and satirists. Morality poems, political poems and satirical poems are written, almost without exception, with such an illogical principle.

The phenomena in our life proceed, through our senses to our experiences, perceptions, and intuitions. It is intuition rationally that provides the essentials for imagery, and it is the method of poetry that materializes intuitions perceptively and combines. Consequently, exact imagery and ideoplasty are due to an exact method. Pure and orthodox poetry cannot exist without this theory.

I fear that the contemporary Japanese literature has not been appreciated rightly in the western world, because of the books written not with ability but with amateur energies. The true understanding is not to be led by those to wear gloves and take the pen. It must be carried out by those who, standing on the literary fact of Japan, bravely suffer for laying the eternal literary foundation on the new land.

For a long time we have desired our poems to be read by superior poets of Europe and America. To our gratitude an opportunity has been given by Mr. Ezra Pound whom we respect heartily.

I see those poems have been deprived of the most part of the nuances of Japanese by the imperfect translation. But each of us did his best to translate his own poems. Though this first attempt may not succeed, we cannot neglect its literary and cultural meaning.

Katue Kitasono

POEMS

I

Under the the umbrella of concrete, yesterday, we laughed at tomato for its
  carelessness.
Their thoughts have gone rotten by a bucket, and they talk of rope-necktie.
A shot is cabbage in the sky over the office.
Dear friend, now is all right the heel.

To-day a duck they dug out in a brush of philosophismus
My laugh is nearer to the condition of Dachshunde-like cylinder than the
  cucumber-shaped ideas of Aquinas.
I put on gloves emeraldgreen and start with a book *Membranologie* under
  my arm.
Is there a shop to sell clear bags?

To-morrow beside a bucket a necktie I shall wear for the sake of General
  clothed in vegetable costume.
A weary city is likened to a brush.
Be-gone! a wandering head.
Be-gone! in a fling like an explosive, over the rock through a Geissler's brass
  pipe.

II

In leaden slippers I laugh at the fountain of night, and scorn a solitary swan.
A parasol of glass she spreads, and wanders along the lane the cosmos
  flowering.
Over the cypress tree I image, to myself, a hotel marked with two golf-clubs
  crossed;
And move my camera on the sand of night.

In the street, there shining the spindle-shaped amalgam stairs, the
  telephone-bell is ringing on the desk.
In Congo by a barber a parrot is trained and sold at Kabinda.
Then by cheerful young sailors her head is replaced by a leaden one:
Just a glimpse of it a watchmaker catches under cocoanut-trees, where is
  seen a dome tightly closed.

On the table I toss the gloves of antelope, and the gloomy fellows I ignore.
A typewriter packed in a raincoat of oil-skin is dead and gone on the *Le
  Temps.*
She, spreading the parasol of glass, pursues a nightingale, in the space

between the *Le Temps* and the cosmos flowers.
Or the new age is born.
Under the hydroplane, "Hambürger Flügzeugbau Ha 139," a duck throws
    into confusion the battle line.
Among the cosmos flowers vibrate machineguns.
By the drain a young washerman blows up.
O the clearer, the better is the sky over the street.
Flash on the concrete a bright wire and shovel.

—Katue Kitasono

UPON THE TRAGEDY OF A FLOWER ON THE CALM-LATITUDES OR OF A PASSENGER AEROPLANE

Sliding down the stair-cases of plants,
Tearing off the soft stripes of calm-latitudes,
A round-bodied mannequin's yellowish bare foot
Suddenly crushes a chalky structure with a bang of a gun.
Then, the fountain of soda-water is opened,
And the inner-side of the zoo comes slowly to be seen.

—Takeshi Fuji

FINGER TOP OF WALTZ

I switch on a gilded turbine of glass,
Give an anticorrosive of asphalt upon the air current ascending,
Pave the street with white-gold lines, and ballasts toss.
The mind of sky brightens canvas shoes,
Since then a system of necktie became milkwhite colour.
A single sound of cloud has dissolved,
When came out a sound of lens.
Finger tops of a boy who praises verdure, stepping emergency stairs of
    afternoon.

—Koichi Kihara

YOUNG SWAN

One stamp is going down on the white canal Along its
side the red culture tosses chairs and its a pageant
In this time the dahlia venerates my mind But high
steady forest Enjoy this tablet Many windows are more
beautiful than the goods Take care I'm nothing But at
last I'm a blue manifesto for her.

—*Toshio Sasajima*

THE END OF EVIL FORTUNE

Summer falls crushing
My dear jar of champagne
Your love affair is dispersed over the sky, and in vain,
So the empty conception
Which has now burnings the perfume, colour,
And there grows the white empty grass
And it is a dream of one cigarette only
O oblivion, all must he reject on the ground
Now glistening the valley, so bitter the slips of glasses
Nor shabby the shining sun
Death is ugly
Tomato is crashing too
Tomorrow is not so good as aujourd'hui
In broad day camouflages the clothings
I am sorry to feel the Zephyr
Cucumber drifts
Silhouette of present state
O I honour your fortunelight.

—*Tio Nakamura*

GLASSY HOUR

Coming back from the sea, the morning after a long absence.
Training the gymnastics, a sun-dial and a priest.
In front of the theater, a clipping-man is standing.
Aiding by a swallow, an envelope, from a hospital, is gnawing the
    apples, and runs after the side of Obelisk.

—*Takeshi Koike*

James Laughlin, *Modern Poets of Japan*

THE POEMS that follow are the work of a group of young Japanese poets, members of the Vou Club, translated into English by themselves. I am particularly glad to be able to publish them because of two dissociations which they can effect. They will show first of all that militaristic imperialism has not wiped out artistic activity and secondly that there is live poetry in Japan. We might not have known it, as little, apart from the classics, filters through to the Occident except the very bad modern imitations of the classics—such as the poems written by the emperor's third cousin's grandmother for his birthday.

The first thing to think about in stating these poems is the fact of the ideogram. The Japanese language, derived from the Chinese, is still very much a picture language. In spite of the intrusion of the phonetic characters the Japanese can still see in many of the words which he writes the picture of the thing itself. What is the result in terms of poetry? Naturally there is more verbal reality, a closer relationship between the thing and its name, some of the essence of the thing in the name.

But of course that quality is not carried over into a translation. So we can only surmise that the oriental poet and poetry reader are, in this respect, "better off" than we are, and let it go at that.

What we can, to some extent, judge is the greater tension. If I understand Japanese syntax aright it has, to an even greater degree than an inflected language like Latin, a minimum of dead words—that is, words which have no charge of meaning apart from their purely grammatical function—articles, prepositions, etc.—all the useless little words which clutter up a positional language like English and thin out the vigour of the poetic line.

I think anyone must concede that one of the most important factors in poetry is verbal inter-activity—word working upon word, the sense-aura of one word fusing and contrasting with those of the words near it. The dead little words of English lessen this activity by separating the meaning-bearing words. Thus in English we only get in small segments of the line—in adjectival and adverbial phrases for the most part—the kind of tension that we often get in a whole line of Latin, where there will be perhaps only one word out of seven that does not carry a meaning. The same sort of thing, I think, is possible in Japanese; certainly these poems confirm that thesis.

And the poets of the Vou Club are very well aware of the rich possibilities of their medium. They would not perhaps use the word "tension" but they have coined the word "ideoplasty" to express the esthetic effects which the close juxtaposition of verbal images makes possible. Here is what the leader of the group, Katue Kitasono, has to say about ideoplasty and about the group's general conception of poetry. Occidental poets will not waste any time they may spend studying Kitasono's statement, so I print it in full.

[selection from Kitasono's previous "Notes"]

There is one other fact that the American reader should know before he applies himself to these poems—that there is a very strong French influence in Japan. Tokyo knows a great deal more about what is going on in Paris than New York does. All of the important books of Eluard have been translated into Japanese ideogram. None have been published in New York.

And so the thoughtful reader will think about the relation of ideogram to Surrealism. He will also want to think about the following statement, which I quote from Kitasono's last letter: "The experiment we are now making on poetry is to express our polygonal ideas vividly as by painting. The poetical movement of the Vou Club might be defined as directed to natural-scientific realism."

The name "Vou," by the way, means nothing special. Kitasono writes that it is "not even so significant as a single grape-leaf. The word Vou shall be bestowed its quality and its value by the club's strong will and its solid action."

"Strong will and solid action" sounds rather bad, sounds like Fascism and poets in uniform. But this is not the case. The real outlook of the poets can be appraised from a few of the biographical notes which accompanied the manuscript: "Haruki Sohu . . . walks with a stick as slender as a feeler. Tio Nakamura . . . she raised the most charming voice when she was near being drowned in the sea last summer. Eiko Sirota . . . so poor at sums that she cannot add up the money she must pay for the cakes she had, but very proud of that. Syuiti Nagayasu . . . when tired of work he goes to the street and enters a lonely coffee-house, and sometimes goes home from there."

[The above introduction, accompanied by a selection of poems by **VOU** poets, appeared in New Directions 1938. In New Directions 1940, poems by Kitasono and Ueda Toshio further appeared.]

Katue Kitasono, *The VOU Club*

THE VOU CLUB was born in 1935. The members at the start were Kitasono Katue, Iwamoto Shuzo, Miki Tei, and eleven other poets. The initial number of the magazine **VOU** was issued on the 5th of July in the same year, containing four essays on poetry, fifteen poems and the translation of a letter of Jack Vasse.

I can remember the moment in which the strange name VOU was adopted by us. It was on the table of a small coffeehouse on the Ginza street. We had been satisfied with none of the names introduced there, each of them having its own meaning restrictive to our activities, when we hit upon the meaningless spell[ing] which Iwamoto was scribbling automatically on a scrap of paper, and thus we became VOUists.

The VOU poets wanted to create a new trend of art in Tokio entirely different from those which were already born after the First World War. To begin with, we needed to break up every traditional and conventional art in Japan. We decided that we should be as ironical in our artistical attitude as Erik Satie who fought for modern music.

In **VOU**'s third issue we printed Abstraction-Creation Art Non Figurative, and Boethy's essay in the fourth issue. I specially mention this, because I wish to suggest the direction of art of the VOU group at this time.

In the beginning of 1936 the members of our group counted 21, several composers, painters, and technologists having joined us. In May of the year we held the VOU Club demonstration at the hall of the Denki Club, in which we read eight manifestos and recited poems of our own. This attempt was rather a failure as there came up only a few opponents.

I had sent copies of **VOU** to Ezra Pound, who soon sent to me from Rapallo a copy of *Guido Cavalcanti* and a letter with his affectionate hail that the VOU group would remain forever in the youth of twenty-one. He gave us as many opportunities of touching the avant-garde of England and America as he could. If **VOU** still keeps the youth of twenty-one (as I am sure of it), it's much indebted to his sensible suggestions.

In 1937 through Ezra Pound I knew D. C. Fox, member of Forschungsinstitut für Kulturmorphologie supervised by Leo Frobenius, and I published the very interesting essay "Paideuma" in **VOU**'s sixteenth issue. It was in this same issue that the VOU poet Fuji Takeshi treated of T. E. Hulme's *Speculations* in his article "The Direction of Poetry as a View of the World."

In February 1937 I sent to Pound sixteen VOU poems with my notes, which were printed the next year in the first number of *Townsman* started by Ronald Duncan, with Pound's introductory notes for them. This was the first appearance of VOU poems in Europe, and the next year James Laughlin in America printed fourteen VOU poems with his notes in New Directions. The war between China and Japan already began in July 1937. We hoped it would soon be finished, but on the contrary it was marching to the death fight of the Pacific War. The government began to stiffen even on art. Some of the surrealists were imprisoned. In 1940 we were forced at last to abandon publication of the magazine. I succeeded somehow or other in keeping VOU poets from arrest.

On December 8th 1941, I heard, in the library of the Nippon Dental College (the librarian of which I have been from then till now), the radio news of the attack on Pearl Harbor. Fortunately there came an interval in which the pressure on culture was a little slacked, and I could reissue the magazine under the title *New Technics,* with the contents just the same as before. It lasted four numbers and then ceased as the army persecuted again every movement of international tendencies. We diverted ourselves in cultivating the classical field of Japanese literature. I began printing the literary pamphlet *Mugi* (*Wheat*), which was continued until the beginning of 1945 when Tokio was exhaustively bombed out.

In August Japan surrendered. I caught on the radio the Emperor's voice in the Ichijoin Temple in Sanjo, a small town three hundred kilometers from Tokio. VOU poets came back from the war by twos and threes, and in 1947 we revived the magazine **VOU**. After numbers 31 and 32, the inflation in this country forced us to give up the next issue.

It was by the backing of [the] Asagi Press that we could begin publication of the newly titled *Cendre,* which was put out six times until 1949 when Asagi got into depression. In January of this year [1950] we again put the title back to **VOU** and published the thirty-third and thirty-fourth issues aided by the Shoshinsha Press.

VOU's orientation: everything humanistic is a boredom. Tears, cryings, loves, crimes, ironies and humors, all attract us in no ways. We only find a little of æsthetic excitement in erasing every humanistic vestige from art.

"Everything tends to be angular"—T. E. Hulme.

Michael Reck, *Memoirs of a Parody Perry*

NEARLY A HUNDRED YEARS after Admiral Perry hove into Tokyo harbor, I myself landed in Japan—with no letter from the U.S. President, like Perry, but at least some notes of introduction from the American "minister of the arts without portfolio," as Horace Gregory had so aptly described Ezra Pound. I slipped in unnoticed, one among thousands of hapless draftees bunked six-deep on a troop ship. Except for my precious notes of introduction, I was merely a parody Perry—a Till Eulenspiegel, no bemedalled emissary.

For several years before, I had been visiting the most distinguished American poet, appropriately enough (for him? for the country?) confined in a "bug house"—Saint Elizabeths Asylum for the Criminally Insane in Washington, D.C. The Master could be seen from 2 to 4 p.m. only and he allotted each regular visitor his or her "day." Mine was, I believe, Tuesday. As Dr. Thomas Szasz has convincingly shown, Pound was often far more lucid than his incarcerators. If he was crazy, then every person with a one-track mind and a Mission is crazy.

Pound might have been called, varying Hokusai, "the old man mad about culture." He felt that his Mission was, quite simply, to keep civilization from sinking. If the aim seems quixotic, we might remember what he had done for English-language literature in the nineteen-tens and -twenties. Making connections, bringing people together, so that "CONVERSATION / should not utterly wither" (*Canto* 82) was part of his Mission, and each of us who had been taken into the "tribe of Ez" was expected to carry out his little mission. When I left for Japan, the very decidedly portfolio-less minister of arts supplied addresses.

First was 1649 Nishi-Ichi, Magome, Ota, Tokyo, home of the leader and doyen of the VOU movement, Kitasono Katue, poet and collagist denominated "Kit Kat" by Pound, who could never resist a pun. Kitasono had founded the VOU group of poets back in the thirties. Now he would meet regularly with his coterie at home, beneath towering stacks of Western avant-garde magazines. Seated round him on the straw-mat floor, they read their poems and the Master provided acerbic comment. "No smoke rises from that chimney," he would say if a poem did not please him.

Hyperbole, unbounded fantasy, words used as gesture rather than literally, mocking at sentimentality—these surrealistic props were VOU's stock in trade. Kitasono regarded both his art and his surroundings as if from a vast distance; the thick spectacles seemed to stand for an attitude. He spoke little English, but surely read a great deal. Kitasono's wife was the English speaker for the household—as when I commented that Japan was nigh to becoming a Little America and, after struggling to find words, she said most demurely: "mod-ern won-der-land!" EP bombarded "Kit Kat" with letters in a Poundese so terse and allusive it was often difficult even for a Poundian—and, not surprisingly, Kitasono told me that he could not understand much of them.

Pound had praised Heinrich Heine's "clear palette"—by which he meant that Heine could treat emotional matters with no smudges of sentimentality—and I suppose that he saw in "Kit Kat" the same clarity of vision. His punning epithet did define a certain felinity in Kitasono, who approached both his verse and his plastic art with suave indirection, as though on padded feet.

2-11-15 Midorigaoka, Meguro-ku, Tokyo. Fujitomi Yasuo, then and now professionally a poet and vocationally a middle-school English teacher, was publishing a poetry magazine called *Sette*, in English and Italian—using his own typewriter as a printer! A copy went to Pound and he sent me Fujitomi's address. We met regularly and it was on my instigation that Fujitomi began translating Cummings. He subsequently produced many volumes and founded a magazine called *i* devoted exclusively to Cummings. This was what Pound's mission of bringing people together meant in practice.

Fujitomi and I labored together making a rough translation of Pound's Sophoclean adaptation, *Women of Trachis*, since Pound had wanted it eventually done as a Noh play. Our translating sessions were often a struggle—I holding out for brevity and Fujitomi for grammar. The project unfortunately came to nothing, as my time in Japan ended before we had finished.

In June 1954, Fujitomi and I visited Ernest Fenollosa's grave at the Miidera, a temple overlooking Lake Biwa near Kyoto. We wandered up and up through a great cryptomeria forest of the temple preserve to find Fenollosa's resting place, Lake Biwa stretching immensely below. All the Orient seemed before me, as it had been for Fenollosa. I wrote Pound of my visit and he recorded it in the last line of his *Canto 89*—I suppose implicitly comparing the exploration of the American West (Fremont's expeditions into the Rockies) with my exploration of the East, the cultural frontier of Pound's own time:

> I want Fremont looking at mountains
>   or, if you like, Reck, at Lake Biwa . . .

Then there was 10 Kakinokizaka, Meguro-ku, Tokyo. During the

1910's, a young Japanese dancer named Michio Ito had appeared in London salons, asking everywhere the same question—so he told me forty years later: "What is art?" Did he ever find out? Alas, I forgot to ask him. In all events, he had danced the Guardian of the Well in the first performance of Yeats' *At the Hawk's Well*. Ito told me that he had learned to dance like a bird by watching the hawks in the London Zoo. Pound had known him in London and, looking back, recorded a snatch of his conversation in *Canto* 77:

> "Jap'nese dance all time overcoat" he remarked
> with perfect precision . . .

I had been seven months in Japan before a fair wind finally blew me to Michio Ito's dance studio—my Japanese finally seeming sufficient to supplement the elliptic English I expected of him. I found him no longer speaking epigrammatic pidgin English but a nearly perfect American. Between the two world wars, he had lived in New York and Hollywood. He discoursed on balance. He told about seeing an old man amid the dust and noise of the street in Cairo, surrounded by a group of intent children and drawing with a stick on the ground. After seeing him do this every day, Ito approached him—he was teaching them astronomy. The old man had told him that 6,000 years ago in Egypt there had been a civilization with perfect balance. Ito said, "I have spent my life studying why it was lost and how to find it again."

The pudgy white-haired gentleman stared into the air, remembering his friend of forty years before, and intoned: "if I saw Ezra today I would give him a massage and say: . . . 'relax.'" And he recounted how he had gone backstage to converse with Spanish dancers who had just given a spectacular performance. "And you know," he told me, "they had absolutely nothing to say." The moral of the tale being, I suppose, that art is doing, not talking about it. Perhaps, indeed, he had found out.

"Bliss it was in that dawn to be alive"—I suppose. Well, paradise comes, as Pound observed in the *Cantos*, "spezzato"—in bits and pieces. My memory is of an Ezraic generosity wide as the oceans—at least spanning oceans—and a keen curiosity that swept Japan into its vast net. Light would come from the East, Pound believed: the particularity of its perceptions reflecting the physical immediacy of the ideogrammatic characters. He abhorred abstract thought and—like Bertolt Brecht—believed "the truth is concrete" (the phrase is Brecht's). The concreteness of truth—this is what Pound found in the Far East. He never traveled to the Orient but for a while it so happened that I saw Japan as his surrogate. Being "Reck at Lake Biwa" has left a lot to live up to.

POSTSCRIPT: In Place of a Note to Letter 71

USEFUL BOOKS need no explanation; they speak for themselves as this one does. But there may be some justification in underlining a new facet of Pound in his role of *Father and Teacher* and to add a touch of humor to an otherwise very serious text.

Pound must have been pleased when Katue Kitasono, alias "Kit Kat," assured him that young readers in Tokyo liked the description of life and customs in the Tyrol. The fact that neither Pound nor I could read Japanese made my rudimentary drawings of haystacks and rakes all the more valuable as pictographs.

To Mary Moore of Trenton, on January 17, 1938, Pound wrote: "My own daughter has just made her literary debut in Japan." Such explicit statements are rare in his correspondence. A day earlier he had fired off a typically cagey long letter "to the Rt/ Rev the POSSUM and Omnibosphorous WHALE the one to hand to tother in ConSybbletashun."

Everyone knows that the Possum is T. S. Eliot and that after his conversion to the Anglican Church, Pound playfully addressed him as the Right Reverend. The "Whale" was Frank Morley, a fellow editor at Faber & Faber who worked in close consultation with Eliot. He was sailing for New York, hence the "Omnibosphorous"; in a subsequent letter, "a wallowink on the Adlandik." Morley, sometimes honored with the title of "Son of Narwahl," vied with his two friends in inventing a language for their private zoo filled with panthers, elephants, rabbits and cats, bats and lesser animals. Their letters can not be paraphrased, though more often than not, they need explaining. We can only hope to read them soon in their entirety.

Pound's promoting of unknown young authors is legendary. Modesty ought to forbid my transcribing parts of the letters concerning me, but it is to his credit:

> ... interesting to translate. Child of twelve/ stylistic influence if any, Miss Martineau's *Norway* (Italian translation of that to explain where a Norwegian child came from). And with all the FAKE naive stuff, a little real is a comfort/ to say nought of the perfectly good bits that Frazer hasn't got into the *Golden Bough*. If a child wrote it it must be comprehensible to other infants? I don't think there can be any more cause the child has been uprooted and sent to a place to get kulchur. . . .

I have simplified the spelling. The "Norwegian child" is Henny Bull

Simonsen, and the effect of Miss Martineau's book was such that our friendship endures to this day.

While I was getting kulchur in Florence, Pound was suggesting possible illustrators for *The Beauties of the Tyrol*. Edmund Dulac was one of them. He made it quite clear I was not a young prodigy; Mozart and Shirley Temple notwithstanding, he had a real horror of young prodigies. He asked the gentlemen at Fabers that the contract be made with the "authoress to whom I cheerfully deed over translation fees as encouragement. . . ." There seemed to have been no doubt in his mind that the booklet would make Fabers' fortune! But Mr. Eliot, after due consideration, answered, yes, it was a nice little book, well written and life well portrayed, but there was just one objection: "it couldn't SELL."

"I takes my possum as he cooks it" (EP to TSE, 25 Nov. 1937) was not always the case. Not when the Possum was not possum enough to hide his tracks and betrayed careless reading of his friend's letters. He had somewhat ironically wondered if Pound had become proficient in Swedish, or whether he had translated from an Italian translation from the Swedish.

W. C. Williams' story that my mother was a Swede curiously rankled and Pound may have detected a lingering echo. So the final comment was: "Waaal naow Protopherious . . . the error was I didn't send it to Larry [Pollinger, the literary agent] who would have saved you the error of thinking it wouldn't SELL." And he bets that when it does get printed, it will sell TWO copies for every copy Faber has sold of his (E.P.'s) own work, with the exception perhaps of *Selected Poems* to which Eliot had written the preface. In closing, the seemingly nonchalant riposte: "Oh yes, *en passant/* the Tyrol has never been Swedish/ perhaps you mix Gustavus Adolphus with the late François whiskers Giuseppe." That ended the matter, and Pound has taught us not to overestimate juvenilia, be it his own or anyone else's.

What we get in this collection of letters to Japan is the persistent effort of an adult and responsible artist to create a better understanding between distant nations and the establishment of culture as a concrete value, a measure of exchange. If the possession of a small island threatens bloodshed, let the contendants trade off land for such a commodity as a traditional and highly refined form of art. An island like Guam in exchange for one hundred films of Nō plays, for instance. Men paid to talk peace might examine such simple solutions?

—*Mary de Rachewiltz*

NOTES TO LETTERS

1

Yone Noguchi: Yonejirō Noguchi (野口米次郎) [1875-1947]. In an undated letter of 1914 to his mother, Pound wrote: "Yone Noguchi dined with me on Tuesday; interesting *littérateur* of the second order. Dont like him so well as Sung, or Coomaraswami. Still you neednt repeat this, as the acquaintance may grow and there's no telling when one will want to go to Japan."
The Pilgrimage: a book of verse by Yonejirō Noguchi, illustrated with wood-block prints by Utamaro, published by Elkin Mathews in 1909.

2

Mathews: Elkin Mathews had published Pound's *A Quinzaine for This Yule* (1908) [A2], *Personae* (1909) [A3], *Exultations* (1909) [A4], and *Canzoni* (1911) [A7].
The Spirit of Romance: was published by J. M. Dent & Sons (1910) [A5].
Yeats: W. B. Yeats

4

Mary Fenollosa: wife of Ernest Francis Fenollosa (1853-1908), American scholar and Orientalist who taught philosophy and economics at Tokyo Imperial University (1878-86) and other universities in Japan, while he studied Japanese and Chinese art, religion and literature.

Along with fellow Americans in Japan—Edward Morse, Percival Lowell, William Sturgis Bigelow, Lafcadio Hearn and John La Farge—Fenollosa and his circle greatly contributed to the rediscovery of the value of Japan's classical artistic heritage at a time when it was being neglectfully cast aside in favor of Westernization and modernization. *See* Van Wyck Brooks, *Fenollosa and His Circle* (N. Y.: E. P. Dutton, 1962).
Sarojini: Sarojini Naidu (1879-1949), a Bengali poet. Educated in England, she is the author of *The Golden Threshold* (1905) and other poems written in English. Mary Fenollosa had met Pound at Naidu's home in London on September 29, 1913. *See* Omar Pound and A. Walton Litz, eds., *Ezra Pound and Dorothy Shakespear: Their Letters 1909-1914,* pp. 264-70; and D. G. Bridson, "An Interview with Ezra Pound," *New Directions* 17, ed. James Laughlin, p. 177.
"My City, My beloved . . .": i.e. New York City. Quoted from the first line of Pound's poem, "N. Y.," included in *Ripostes* (1912).

5

Franz Hals: Frans Hals (1581?-1666), Dutch portrait painter.
banshee: a supernatural being in Irish and Scottish folklore, supposed to give warnings by its wails of an approaching death in the family.
Mr. Hirata: Kiichiro Hirata (1873-1943), translator, essayist, and scholar of English literature. After studying at Oxford University, he taught at Tokyo Kōtō Shihan

Gakko and other universities. Author of *Studies of Recent English Literature*, and *Essays of Tokuboku* ("Tokuboku" is his pen name).

Romaji: Roman letters.

"Kinuta": a Nō play included in Fenollosa and Pound, tr., *The Classical Noh Theatre of Japan*; so are "Nishikigi" and "Hagoromo."

"Yōrōboshi": "Yoroboshi," a Nō play. A blind child beggar at Tennōji in Naniwa turns out to be the son of the man in the seventeen-day Buddhist practice at the same temple. The son, having been enlightened, is led by his father's prayers to describe the beautiful scenes of Naniwa as he envisions them in his mind, and dances. The two return home.

"Sumidagawa": In search of her son, the mother comes from Kyoto to the bank of the Sumida River, only to find his tomb; there at night she tries to embrace his ghost in vain.

7

Verdun: a city on the Meuse River, in the north-eastern part of France; site of significant battle of World War I.

8

Itow: Michio Ito (イ尹 藤 道 郎) [1893-1961], a Japanese dancer; played the part of the Hawk at the performance of Yeats' *At the Hawk's Well* in Lady Cunard's drawing room on April 2, 1916, for which Edmund Dulac designed and made the costumes and masks. In writing this play, Yeats had been inspired by the Japanese Nō plays in English translation in Ernest Fenollosa's notebooks.

9

the "cloud-bridge": Hashigakari, the bridge between the stage and the retiring room in the Nō theatre.

11

Lustra: was published by Elkin Mathews (1916) [A11].

Certain Noble Plays of Japan: with an introduction by W. B. Yeats, was published by The Cuala Press (1916) [A12].

Miss Bisland: Elizabeth Bisland (1861-1929), later Mrs. Elizabeth B. Wetmore, who edited the letters of Lafcadio Hearn; a friend of Mary Fenollosa's.

Tagore: Rabindranath Tagore (1861-1941), Bengali poet, dramatist and mystic; acquaintance of Pound and Yeats. His "hiding, incognito, somewhere in Southern California" is spurious. Awarded Nobel Prize for Literature in 1913.

13

book on poor Gaudier Brzeska: *Gaudier Brzeska*, published by John Lane (1916) [A10].

Egoist: edited by Harriet Weaver and Dora Marsden.

Quest: edited by G. R. S. Mead.
Poetry Review: edited by Harold Monro.

15

play . . . about Fox: Michio Ito had performed "Fox Dance" in 1915.

18

Coburn: Alvin Langdon Coburn (1882–1966), American photographer who resided
at the time in London; *see* his *Autobiography,* ed. Helmut and Alison Gern-
sheim. A photograph of Pound by Coburn was reproduced as frontispiece for
Lustra (1916). Pound had listed him as a faculty member in the "Preliminary
Announcement of the College of Arts" (1914).

22

East Stroudsburg: a town on the upper Delaware River which Pound had been
acquainted with in his youth.
Dalcroze: Emile Jaques-Dalcroze (1865–1950), Swiss composer and music teacher;
inventor of eurhythmics, a system whereby music is coordinated with body
movements. He founded the various Instituts Jaques-Dalcroze throughout Europe.
Kyōgen: Japanese traditional comedy which developed with the Nō, and is often
performed with Nō plays on the Nō stage.
"Shojo," "Kagekiyo," "Hagoromo": Nō plays, included in Fenollosa-Pound translations, *Certain Noble Plays of Japan* [A12]. "Your book" refers to '*Noh' or Accomplishment* [A13].
"Busu": a piece of Kyōgen. During the master's absence, his two servants find out
that the "busu," which they have been told to be poison, is actually black sugar.
They eat it up, and break their master's favorite hanging scroll and a bowl as well.

25

Kandinsky: Wassily Kandinsky (1866–1944), Russian abstract painter and mystic;
see his *Concerning the Spiritual in Art* [*Über das Geistige in der Kunst*] (published in 1914 in English translation as *The Art of Spiritual Harmony*).

26

Picabia: Francis Picabia (1879–1953), French Dadaist and "sur-irrealist" painter;
acquaintance of Pound's in Paris.

27

Capt. J. Brinkley: John Brinkley (1887-1964), son of Francis Brinkley and uncle of
Aya, wife of Gonkuro Koumé (younger brother of Tami); worked for the League of
Nations in Paris.

30

Gakushūin: (学習院), educational institution established in 1877 in Tokyo mainly for the children of Japanese nobility. It is now open to the public, and includes a co-ed university, high school and other levels.

Barney: Natalie Clifford Barney, who held the "Friday *salon*," was "*l'Amazone*" of Remy de Gourmont's *Letters to an Amazon. See* Charles Norman, *Ezra Pound* (New York: MacMillan, 1960), p. 269.

32

Fenollosa: see note to letter 4.

Umewaka Minoru: Minoru Umewaka (梅若実) [1827–1909], a Japanese Nō player; gave lessons to Fenollosa. *See* letter 5; *see also* Fenollosa and Pound, *'Noh' or Accomplishment.*

Dr. Mori: Kainan Mori (森槐南) [1863–1911], a Japanese scholar of Chinese language and literature; gave lessons to Fenollosa.

Dr. Ariga: Nagao Ariga (有賀長雄) [1860–1921] graduated from Tokyo Imperial University in 1882, where he was a student of Fenollosa. Doctor of jurisprudence in international law; taught at Tokyo Imperial University and Waseda University. Author of a number of books on literature, sociology, and pedagogy as well as international law; later became a member of the Privy Council. He was an assistant-interpreter for Fenollosa while the latter was in Japan, and the translator of Fenollosa's *Epochs of Chinese and Japanese Art* after it was posthumously published in 1912.

that earth quake: "The Great Earthquake of Kanto" which struck Tokyo and Yokohama area on September 1, 1923. According to the statistics, the magnitude was 7.8–8.2; deaths totalled 99,331, with 43,476 missing.

C. H. Douglas: Major Clifford Hugh Douglas (1879–1952), British economist and originator of the theory of Social Credit, which holds that maldistribution of wealth due to insufficient purchasing power is the reason for economic depressions and World Wars. Published articles in A. R. Orage's *The New Age.*

Gesell: Silvio Gesell (1862–1930), Minister of Finance of the second Munich Republic (1919); monetary reformer and author of *The Natural Economic Order.*

Cavalcanti: Guido Cavalcanti Rime, published in 1932 [B27].

ABC of Reading: published in 1934 [A35]

33

Jean Cocteau: French poet and long-standing friend of Pound's from his years in Paris (1920–25).

35

Izzo and Camerino: Carlo Izzo, an Italian translator of Pound's poems, and his friend Aldo Camerino, sent out a group of letters in the fall of 1935, and launched "a movement tending to establish a regular exchange of technical, mostly pro-sodic, information . . . between literary people of different countries"; *see* Charles Norman, *Ezra Pound*, p. 332.

Bunting: Basil Bunting, British poet.

Laughlin: James Laughlin, publisher of New Directions.

Zukofsky: Louis Zukofsky, American poet.

Angold: J. P. Angold, a British poet; author of an unpublished book on economics called "Work and Privilege" which Pound tried to translate into Italian; *see* David Heymann, *The Last Rower* (New York: Viking Press, 1976), p. 140.

welsh scholar: W. Moelwyn Merchant?; Hugh Gordon Porteus?

36

Jefferson and/or Mussolini: published in July 1935 [A41].

37

Ken Yanagisawa: (柳沢健) [1889–1953], Japanese diplomat and poet; author of *Orchard, Journals of South Europe,* and *Twilight on the Indian Ocean.*

Ginza: the most fashionable street in Tokyo at that time.

UNKER and Bopoto: see Kitasono's letter to Pound (30 January 1937).

38

Alberto Carocci: Italian publisher.

Utai: the rhythmic chanting of Nō texts.

Rihaku: Japanese name for the Chinese poet Li Po.

con espressioni di alta Stima: with expressions of high esteem.

40

Hajime Matsumiya: (松宮順), Councillor of the Japanese embassy in Italy, 1936–38.

ABC: ABC of Reading [A35].

W. E. Woodward: see selection of letters from Pound to Woodward in *Paideuma,* vol. 15, no. 1 (Spring 1986), pp. 105–20.

41

Suma Genji: a Nō play whose "suspense is the suspense of waiting for a supernatu-ral manifestation—which comes"; *see The Classic Noh Theatre of Japan.*

Active Anthology: [B32].

Make It New: [A36].

The Chinese Written Character: [B36].

Ta Hio: [A28].

D. C. Fox: Douglas Fox, assistant to Leo Frobenius at the Forschungsinstitut für Kulturmorphologie in Frankfurt; edited numerous works of Frobenius. *Paideuma* was the name of the journal the institute published.

43

Margaret Lenoa: Margaret Gerstley Lenoa corresponded with Pound on staging Nō plays, etc.

Meierhold: Wsewolod Emiljewitsch Meyerhold (1874–1942), Russian actor and director.

44

Pauthier: M. G. Pauthier, French translator of Confucius.

kana: Japanese syllabary.

Cathay: published in 1915 [A9].

45

Globe: Milwaukee magazine to which Pound contributed articles on politics and economics during 1937–38.

Uncle George: Representative George Holden Tinkham of Massachussetts; he met Pound in Italy.

l'uomo più educato: "the most experienced, or knowledgeable man."

Ronald Duncan: British poet and editor of *Townsman* (London); "no relation" of the American dancer.

Satie: Erik Satie, who lived in Arcueil, a southern section of Paris.

Sasajima: Toshio Sasajima (佐々島 敦夫), a member of the vou Club.

Nakamura: Chio Nakamura (中村 千尾), a member of the vou Club.

KOIKE: Takeshi Koike (小池馬克), a member of the vou Club.

Cummings: e. e. cummings.

Morrison: Robert Morrison, a Protestant missionary in Asia who compiled a six-volume Chinese-English dictionary (published in Malacca, 1815-22).

48

MAO SHE CH-HÍNG TSËEN: Mao Shi chêng chien (毛詩鄭箋), the text of the Confucian *Book of Odes* edited with notes by Mao Heng (毛亨) and Mao Ch'ang (毛萇), later annotated by Chêng Hsüan (鄭玄) in the later Han period, and reputedly the most authentic version of the *Odes*.

Kwan Kwan Tsheu KEW: 關關雎鳩 . The first line of the first poem (a folksong of Southern Chou) included in the Confucian *Odes*, meaning " 'Kwan, kwan' sing the [two] eaglefishers." "Kwan" means "pass," but it is used here as onomatopoeia of the bird's cry.

49

as superior man . . . : Pound's translation from the fourth and sixth lines of the same poem in the Confucian *Odes* above: 君子好逑 左右流之

old latin bloke: P. Lacharme, *Confucii Chi-King, sive Liber Carminum,* ex Latina, P. Lacharme interpretatione, edidit Julius Mohl (Stuttgart and Tübingen, 1830).

Hemingway's "They all made peace": **VOU** no. 19 (July 1, 1937) contains Kitasono's

Japanese translation of the poem by Hemingway (pp. 33–4).

Butchart: Montgomery Butchart, author of *Money*, one of Pound's select economic texts.

50

Jennings' appalling translation: The Shi King: The Old "Poetry Classic" of the Chinese by William Jennings (1891).

51

beautiful book: Kitasono's book of poetry, *Letters of the Summer* (夏の手紙) [*Natsu no Tegami* in Japanese]; *La Lettre d'été* referred to in Kitasono's letter of 6 September 1937.

Brinkley: Francis Brinkley (1841–1912), an English Japanophile journalist. Visited Japan as a naval attaché to the English Embassy in Tokyo in 1867; in 1881 bought the *Japan Mail* and became its president and chief editor. In 1892, also began writing for the London *Times* as its Tokyo correspondent. Author of *Guide to English Self-taught* (1875); *History of the Empire of Japan* (1893); *Japan and China* (1903); *New Guide to English Self-taught* (1909); *History of the Japanese People from the Earliest Times to the End of Meiji Era* (1915).

52

nowt red not . . . : (莫赤匪狐 莫黑匪烏   ). "Red is the fox, black is the crow." Pound later translated the line (rightly) as "All red things foxes, each black a crow/(evil in omen)," in Part One, Book 3, *The Classical Anthology Defined by Confucius* (1954), p. 19.

55

Ukiyoe: woodblock print.

56

Bigelow: William Sturgis Bigelow (1850–1926), an American physician and Orientalist who went to Japan in 1882. He later became a Buddhist, and gave his collection of Japanese works of art to the Boston Museum of Fine Arts. *See* Van Wyck Brooks, *Fenollosa and His Circle*.

58

Broletto: Italian quarterly magazine edited by Carlo Peroni.

Maria's booklet: Maria Pound's essay, "Gais or the Beauties of the Tyrol," was eventually published in the *Reijokai* (令女界) in Japanese translation by Kitasono; *Reijokai*, vol. 18, no. 1 (January 1, 1939), pp. 98–111.

Guide: Guide to Kulchur [A45].

59

beautiful Townsman: refers to *Townsman,* vol. I, no. 1 (January, 1938) which contained Pound's introductory essay "vou Club" and a selection of poems by its members translated into English. Their poems were to be published in *New Directions* 1938, edited by James Laughlin. *See* Appendix.

62

Peroni: Carlo Peroni, editor of *Broletto.*

What does vou stand for?: According to Yasuo Fujitomi, when Kitasono and Shozo Iwamoto were talking in 1935 about their new magazine in a coffee house, Iwamoto unconsciously and idly wrote with water from his fingertip on the table V and O and U. Kitasono thought vou had no meaning in any language, and they decided then that it be the title of the magazine.

UTAI: (謠) is the vocal part of the Nō play, and has nothing to do with vou.

our Purcell music: Pound had organized performances at Rapallo of ten trio sonatas for two violins and continuo by Henry Purcell (1658-95), based on an edition by W. Gillies Whittaker and published by L'Oiseau Lyre in Paris.

sheets of galley proof: for *Guide to Kulchur* [A45].

63

Youngmen's Noh Plays: Nō plays performed by young men.

65

Kagekiyo and Kumasaka: two Nō plays.

very small Western college: Olivet College (Michigan); *see* Pound/Ford, *Letters,* ed. T. Materer, pp. 152–4.

Claude Bowers: member of the National Institute of Art and Letters in the U.S.; author of *Jefferson and Hamilton* and *The Tragic Era,* books Pound strongly recommended. U.S. Ambassador to Spain in 1938.

Fox: Douglas C. Fox, Leo Frobenius' assistant.

Delphian Quarterly: edited by Mary W. Burd; printed article by Olga Rudge on Vivaldi, as well as numerous articles and letters by Pound, including "Reorganize Your Dead Universities" (April 1938 issue).

66

Tong Kien Kang Mou: T'ung chien kang mu (通鑑 綱目) [*Tsu gan kō moku* in Japanese] (59 vols.), abridged by Chu Hsi (朱喜) from *Tzu chih t'ung chien* (資治通鑑) [*Shijitsugan* in Japanese] (294 vols.) by Su-Mao Kuang (司馬光) of the Sung Dynasty.

sort of notes left by Emperor Tai-tsong: cf. Canto 54, "And the Emperor Tai Tsong left his son 'Notes on Conduct'."

the first government note: According to Mêng Lin (盂麟) of the Ching (清) dynasty, the currency notes had been used since the time of Kao Tsong in the

T'ang period in China. But, according to more recent studies, the first government note (文 子) appeared in 1023 in the Sung period.

Prof. Mori: see notes to Pound's letter of 24 May 1936.

Mr. Matsumiya: see Pound's letter of 1 January 1937.

67

Miss R/: Olga Rudge.

Isida: Ichiro Ishida (1909–   ), Japanese composer and friend of Kitasono; among his works is *Piano Pieces: Northern Country.*

68

Manyosyū: Manyōshū, the oldest Japanese anthology of poetry compiled toward the end of the Nara period, in the latter half of the eighth century. It comprises about 4,500 poems written by various classes of people, from Emperor to common soldiers, living in various districts in Japan, from the fifth century to 759.

Waka: literally means Japanese poetry. In ancient times the word *"waka"* was used, to distinguish it from Chinese poetry, to denote *chōka, tanka, sedōka,* and other forms of Japanese poetry, with the rhythmic pattern based on the combination of 5 and 7 syllables, but it now denotes particularly *tanka,* the most popular form among them, with 5, 7, 5, 7 and 7 syllables.

Uta: literally means poetry or song; it often denotes *tanka.*

Kokinsyū: Kokinwakashū (Anthology of Japanese Poetry, Ancient and Modern), compiled between *c.* 905 and *c.* 914 by Ki no Tsurayuki, Ki no Tomonori, Oshikōchi no Mitsune, and Mibu no Tadamine, by command of Emperor Daigo (888–930). It comprises about 1,100 poems, most of which are *tanka.*

Sinkokinsyū: Shinkokinwakashū (New Anthology of Japanese Poetry, Ancient and Modern), commissioned in 1201 by ex-Emperor Gotoba (1180–1239) and completed in 1221. Among the six compilers was Fujiwara Teika. It comprises about 2,000 poems. [All the dates supplied by Kitasono in parentheses for the three anthologies are uncertain.]

A Guide to Japanese Studies: Kokusai Bunka Shinkokai, eds., *A Guide to Japanese Studies: Orientation in the Studies of Japanese History, Buddhism, Shintoism, Art, Classic Literature, Modern Literature* (Tokyo: KBS, 1937).

K. B. S.: Kokusai Bunka Shinkokai (国際文化振興会) [Society for Promoting International Cultural Exchange].

70

Cactus I/: Cactus Irland

Wyndham L/: Wyndham Lewis.

new portrait of me/: portrait in Tate Gallery.

72

K2°: "K secondo" or "duo"; K two times.

Girl's Circle: Reijokai; see Pound's letter to Kitasono, 18 January 1938, and Kitasono's letter to Pound, 10 February 1939.

Porteus: Hugh Gordon Porteus wrote, ". . . the most fruitful experiments with language are likely to continue to emerge from those who concern themselves with *images* and their relations. . . . Nothing more novel and exciting has been done lately, along these lines, than by the poets of the Japanese **VOU** group. . . ." *Criterion*, vol. XVIII (January, 1939), pp. 397.

73

Charles Henri Ford: American avant garde poet (1910–?); author of numerous books of poetry, editor of *Blues* (1929–   ) and *View* (1940–   ). Ford's *The Garden of Disorder and Other Poems* (European Press, 1938) was reviewed by Kitasono in **VOU** no. 26 (April 26, 1939), pp. 17-8; Kitasono also translated into Japanese W. C. Williams' "Preface" to the book and Ford's note on international chain poems.

Chain poem: Charles Henri Ford was also a contributor, along with Kitasono, to the chain poem printed in *New Directions* 1940, together with his introductory "How to Write a Chainpoem."

74

ALL *the Noh plays ought to be filmed*: in a later letter (31 October 1939) to Iris Barry, curator of the film archive of the Museum of Modern Art in New York City, Pound wrote:

Dear Iris

Cant remember everything all the time.

I forget whether the film of Noh Play, "AWOI NA UYE," that Shio Sakanishi had shown to me in Washington is from your collection.

In any case I am starting rumpus to get ALL the NOH filmed. Ought to be done SOON, otherwise all the IN and YO will get messed and some god damned Jap Wagner smeared over the whole business.

I wonder if you cd/ get the Museum to colly/bo/rate by putting in an order, either via Dr. Sakanishi (Congress Libr/) or direct to the

KOKUSAI BUNKA SHINKOKAI

Meiji Seimei kan, Marunouchi, Tokyo

If you can write to them, merely say that Museum is interested in my proposal and that you wd. of course be ready to take copies of all films made with properly qualified Noh actors.

I hear that Shigefusa Hosho is good. Forget who did the Awoi, but it was a good show.

some of the phono discs do NOT seem to me very good.

Whether Fox can get Forschungsinst/ to place similar order, I dunno but do mention matter to him.

I hope to be publishing a boost for the idea in Japan, shortly.

and so forth.

A *"Tong Kien Kang Mou" of Japan:* A general history of Japan like *T'ung chien kang mu,* from which de Mailla translated into French his *Histoire Générale de la Chine, ou Annales de cet Empire.*

Nipon O Dai itsi ran: Nippon Odai Ichiran (日本王代一覧) [A Chronicle of Japanese Emperors], 4 vols., edited by Nobuyoshi Fujiwara, covers the period from Emperor Jimmu to Emperor Gotoba.

Klaproth: Heinrich Julius Klaproth (1783–1835), an Orientalist who taught Asian history and geography in Paris, edited and translated the 1834 edition of *Nipon O Dai Itsi Ran, ou Annales des Empereurs du Japon.*

75

Mr. Moori: Yasotaro Mōri (毛利八十太郎), editor of *The Japan Times,* and translator of Soseki Natsume's *Botchan* into English.

76

my latest and shortest book: What Is Money For? [A46].

Rothschild: family that controlled an international banking firm; founder was Meyer Amschelm Rothschild (1743?–1812).

Sassoon: family that controlled a large trading firm in England; founder was David Sassoon (1792–?).

78

"poeta economista": "poet economist."

my beloved young novelist: Maria Pound.

"Shinbu" "Miaco" . . . know: referring to Canto 58. The sources are de Mailla and also Klaproth, tr., *Nipon O Dai Itsi Ran, ou Annales des Empereurs du Japon* (Paris, 1834), pp. xiv, and 399; *see also* John J. Nolde, *Blossoms from the East: The China Cantos of Ezra Pound* (Orono, Maine: National Poetry Foundation, 1983), pp. 323–26.

79

Igor Markewitch: Igor Markevich (1912–83), Russian composer and conductor who stayed in Italy during World War II.

82

McN. Wilson: R. McNair Wilson, American historian; author of *Promise to Pay,* one of Pound's select texts on the truth of economics.

Kuhn Loeb and Co.: New York banking firm involved in international finance.

De Wendel: French family involved in international finance.

Vivaldi week in Siena: the *Settimana musicale* (September 16th to 21st) of the Siena Academy, under the auspices of the Accademia Musicale Chigiana, devoted entirely to the music of Vivaldi, under the direction of Alfredo Casella; Olga Rudge and Pound greatly contributed to its inspiration and conception, and managed to interest Count Chigi in the project. This germinal event sparked the renewal of interest in the music of Vivaldi witnessed in our century. *See* essay 4.

Odon Por: Hungarian-Italian economist; author of *Politica economico-sociale in Italia anno XVII–XVIII*, which Pound translated in 1941: *Italy's Policy of Social Economics 1939/1940* [A49].

Dr. Sakanishi: Shio Sakanishi (坂西 志保), curator of the Japanese Section at the Library of Congress. She showed Pound the film of Nō plays in the Library during the summer of 1939, which impressed him greatly. Shio Sakanishi, "An Uninvited Guest: Ezra Pound," *Eigo Bungaku Sekai* [英語文学世界] (November and December, 1972). *See also* note to letter 74.

83

Shotaro Oshima: (尾島庄太郎) [1899–1980]; Japanese poet, translator, and professor of English literature (1949–70). While teaching English at Waseda University (1935–70), translated many of W. B. Yeats' poems into Japanese; author of *A Study of Modern Irish Literature* (1956); *W. B. Yeats: Man and his Works* (1958); and *English Literature and Poetic Imagination* (1972).

Poems: Among Shapes and Shadows: Shōtarō Oshima's book of poems written in English, published by the Hokuseido Press, Tokyo, in 1939; 350 copies were printed, and the copy sent to Pound was no. 199. As Oshima wrote in the preface, "the majority of these poems were written during my stay in England, 1937–1939."

84

"Antonio Vivaldi": probably "Vocale o verbale," an account of the Vivaldi Week performances in Siena which appeared in *Meridiano di Roma* (November 26, 1939) [C1526]; there also appeared on November 25th "Risveglio Vivaldiano" in *Il Mare* [C1525].

Kuan Chia Tung: ? related to Chia Tung, author of *Lays and Relays; Being Selections from the "Lays of Far Cathay"* (Shanghai: Kelly & Walsh, 1894).

Marquis de Laplace: Pierre Simon Laplace (1749–1827), French mathematician and astronomer; author of *Exposition du Système du Monde* (1796).

85

the triangle: the Axis.

vou with yet again my phiz.: **VOU** no. 28 (December 1, 1939) contained a photograph of Pound and Kitasono's translation of "Statues of Gods" [D186], originally published in *Townsman*, II, 7 (August 1939) [C1575].

Beard: Charles Beard, American historian; author of *Economic Origins of Jeffersonian Democracy*.

Woodward: William E. Woodward, American journalist and historian who was on several advisory boards dealing with business and insurance during the Roosevelt administration; Pound sent him several items on economics to pass on

to the president—which he never did. *See* selection of letter from Pound to
  Woodward in *Paideuma*, vol. 15, no. 1 (Spring 1986), pp. 105–20.
Bowers: Claude G. Bowers, American historian and Ambassador to Spain (1938);
  author of *Jefferson and Hamilton* and *The Tragic Era.*
Overholser: Willis A. Overholser, American economic historian; author of *A Short
  Review and Analysis of the History of Money in the United States* (Libertyville,
  IL: Progress Publishing Concern, 1936).
Evviva la Poesia: Long live poetry!
EPOS: epic poetry.

87

Action: newspaper published in England by Sir Oswald Mosley.
British Union Quarterly: journal published by the Mosley Party; formerly the
  Fascist Quarterly.
Social Creditor: published (beginning 1938) in Liverpool, England.

88

a very elegant volume: Kitasono's *The Violets of Fire* (火 の 菫) [*Hi no Sumire*],
  illustrated and designed by Seiji Togo.
Japanese Dance all time overcoat: Michio Ito's remark to Pound, quoted in Canto
  77.
a better article . . . than the J. T. interviewer: see *Japan Times,* November 26 and
  December 4, 1939.
Masaichi Tani: unidentified.
Ainley's face behind that mask: Ito made a comment to Pound on Ainley who
  played the part of Cuchulain in Yeats' *At the Hawk's Well* in London in 1916:
  "He must be moving and twisting his face behind his mask." The remark is
  quoted in Canto 77.
borrowing the old lady's cat: Ito asked Mrs. Tinkey if he could borrow her cat. But
  she "never believed he wanted her cat/ for mouse-chasing/ and not for oriental
  cuisine" (Canto 77).
Did you see the Hawk's Well?: The Ito family produced *At the Hawk's Well* in
  celebration of the 50th anniversary of their parents' wedding. Michio Ito translated the play. Kisaku designed the masks and the stage. Hiroji composed the
  music, and designed the costumes. Osuke conducted the orchestra; Koreya
  Senda played the part of Cuchulain; Michio, the Old Man; Teiko (the wife of
  Hiroji), the Hawk. *See* Helen Caldwell, *Michio Ito: the Dancer and his Dances*
  (Berkeley: University of California Press, 1977), Chapter II.

89

Miharu Tiba: Miharu Chiba (1903–   ), Japanese dancer, dance scriptwriter, and
  music educator; author of *Miharu's Textbook.*
Seiji Togo: (1897–1978), Japanese painter, whose paintings are often phantasmal

and colorful. "A Woman with a Parasol" and "A Woman with Black Muffler" are among his well-known works.

her portrait painted by Mrs. Frost: "Mrs. Ruth Sterling Frost was an American lady who rented Palazzo Contarini in Venice. She was also a painter and did a portrait (unfinished) of me." (Mary de Rachewiltz in a note to the editor.)

91

pamphlet I am sending Iwado: What Is Money For? [A46]?

Por: Odon Por.

Dali: Salvador Dali, the surrealist painter.

The Little Review: edited by Margaret Anderson and Jane Heap (1917–24).

"Agon" is later: T. S. Eliot's Sweeney Agonistes was published in 1932, hence "later."

Crevel: René Crevel (1900–35), French surrealist poet, novelist, and critic.

92

Kokusai Bunka Shinkokai: Society for Promoting International Cultural Exchange.

Bauernfähig: farming skill, capacity.

君子 : chün tzŭ, a true gentleman, a wise man.

94

Hoffmann's bulletin: News from Germany, ed. H. R. Hoffmann.

his side kick Kung/: unidentified.

Mencius: Meng-tse (371?–288? B.C.); Chinese Confucian philosopher. Mencius held that the duty of a ruler is to ensure the prosperous livelihood of his subjects, and that warfare be eschewed except for defense. If a ruler's conduct reduces his subjects to penury, then he must be deposed. Proposed specific reforms in landholding and other economic matters.

Avicenna: Ibn Sīnā (980–1037), Persian philosopher, theologian, physician, mathematician, linguist, and astronomer. Interpreted Aristotle in a neo-platonic light, held that the unity of Mind (or Nous) gave form to all that exists, and that the universe emanated from the divine Active Intellect.

Matsumiya: see note to letter 40.

K. Takashi Ito's British Empire and People: The book was originally written in Japanese as Eiteikoku oyobi Eikokujin (1937) by Takashi Ito (伊東 敬) [1906–   ], then an official of the Japanese Ministry of Foreign Affairs.

Funk: Walter Funk, Nazi economist, appointed Minister of Economy in 1937.

Miaco: Miyako literally means capital, and usually designates Kyoto in Japanese history.

Willkie: Wendell Lewis Willkie (1892–1944), Republican nominee for President of the U.S. in 1940. See "Willkie, the G.O.P. Hope," Japan Times, 12 August 1940.

97

Ponder's Modern Poetry: unidentified.

Salonfähig . . . La Quiete: Salonfähig means "to be fit to be in a salon," literary or
otherwise, to have polite manners, be educated; to have *"savoir faire."* La Quiete
is the name of Pound's daughter's school in Florence.

Servant of the People article: unidentified.

Vaglia: money order.

98

Fosco Maraini: (1912–   ), Italian anthropologist and art historian. Associate
professor at Hokkaido University (1938-41), lecturer at Kyoto University (1941–
45). Author of *Meeting with Japan* (1959); *Japan: Patterns of Continuity* (1971);
and other works.

Matteo Ricci: Italian Jesuit missionary to China (1552–1610); had authentic respect
for the Chinese classics and adopted the dress of the literati; became court
mathematician and astronomer; due to his erudition and demeanor, the Chinese
came to respect Christianity. Translated many Western works of science and
mathematics into Chinese, as well as Christian texts. Sent back to Europe reports
on China. Acted as cultural ambassador between these worlds and as proponent
of a world culture.

Kung fu Tsu, Men-tsu: Confucius and Mencius.

99

P. Tyler: Parker Tyler, an American poet and editor.

Margaret Anderson: editor of the *Little Review.*

Thayer: Scofield Thayer, editor of *The Dial.*

Eddie and Wallie: Edward VIII of England and Wallis Warfield Simpson (who came
from Baltimore).

Guarnieri: Antonio Guarnieri (1883–1952), Italian cellist, conductor, and composer. He gave his first performances at Siena; also directed operas at Vienna,
Milan, and other places in Europe. Pound heard him at the Venice Biennale in
1936.

Itoh's book: see note to Pound's letter to Kitasono, 25 August 1940.

Ban Gumi: program; order of sequence of Nō plays.

Possum: T. S. Eliot.

Duncan: Ronald Duncan.

Angold: J. P. Angold.

Bunting: Basil Bunting.

Funk: Walter Funk, German Minister of Economy.

Riccardi: Raffaello Riccardi, Italian Minister of Finance.

100

Gerarchia: [*Hierarchy*], journal published in Milan; founded by Mussolini.
Di Marzio: Cornelio di Marzio, editor of *Il Meridiano di Roma.*
my econ. Book: ABC of Economics [A34].
Tuan Szetsun: unidentified.
enclosure: unidentified; probably something on Itoh's *British Empire and People.*

101

two articles: Setsuo Uenoda, "Language Trouble," and Tatsuo Tsukui, "Japan's New Structure and Cultural Aspects," *Japan Times Weekly* (October 17, 1940), pp. 229–30, 236–40, 242.
Basho and Chikamatsu: Bashō Matsuo (松尾芭蕉) [1644–94], a *haiku* poet. Monzaemon Chikamatsu (近松門左衛門) [1653–1724], a *kabuki* and *jōruri* playwright.
Tanakas: reference uncertain.
T. T. and S. U.: Tatsuo Tsukui and Setsuo Uenoda.
lingua franca: common language.

103

L'OROSCOPO DEL 5: "The horoscope of December 5—This Thursday lacks lunar configurations, it will be dominated by a magic aspect between the Sun and Jupiter which will favour good business, but we will have to watch expenses, especially if caused by the fair sex." (Translated into English by Mary de Rachewiltz.)
Li Ki: Chinese book of customs and rituals.
Chiang K/Cheker: supporter of Chiang Kai-shek.

104

Lahiri's book: Amar Lahiri, *Japan Talks* (Tokyo: The Hokuseido Press, 1940).
Roppeita Kita: (喜多六平太) [1874–1971], a Nō player who succeeded to the old name of the Kita School at 21. Author of *Roppeita's Talks on Art* (1942).
Umewaka Minoru: Minoru Umewaka (1827–1909), a Nō player of the Kanze School. Fenollosa took lessons from him.
Mushakoji: Saneatsu Mushakoji (武者小路実篤) [1885–1976], a Japanese novelist and painter.
Y. Yashiro: Yukio Yashiro (矢代幸雄), author of *Sandro Botticelli* (London and Boston: The Medici Society, 1925), 3 vols. (Only 630 copies were printed.)
Neue Sachlichkeit: movement of self-proclaimed "sober objectivity."
Frazier: Senator L. J. Frazier (Republican) of North Dakota. Pound corresponded with Frazier in 1936 about the possibility of compiling a "REAL text book" for the study of American history in the schools.
Volpi: Giuseppe Volpi, Count di Misurata (1877–1947), Italian Minister of Finance (1925–29); translated *The History of Fascism.* He appears in Cantos 76/39, 80/87.

105

Y. Noguchi: Japanese poet and expert on wood-block prints [Ukiyo-e]; *see* letter 1.

"the jew is underneath the lot": T. S. Eliot, "Burbank with a Baedeker: Bleistein with a Cigar," l. 23.

Reese: Holroyd Reese, founder of Albatross Books (Hamburg-Paris-Bologna) and purchaser of Tauchnitz Editions.

Bibliotecario: librarian.

Bernie Pshaw: George Bernard Shaw (1856–1950); saw Michio Ito dance at a gathering at Lady Ottoline Morrell's home in 1918.

106

Maupassant: Guy de Maupassant.

Caldwell: Erskine Caldwell.

107

Gerhart Münch: German pianist, who along with Olga Rudge, violinist, "formed the nucleus of the Rapallo concerts." The Amici del Tigullio sponsored the concerts. *See* R. Murray Schafer, *Ezra Pound and Music* (New York: New Directions, 1977), p. 322, and Canto 75.

108

Janequin: Clément Janequin (1472/75–1559/60), French musician; *see Cantos* 75 and 79.

San Pantaleo: a small church on the hillside of Sant'Ambrogio.

videt et urbes: "and he looks at the towns."

Politica Economico-Sociale in Italia: Italy's Policy of Social Economics 1939/1940 [A49].

109

Matsuoka: Yosuke Matsuoka (松岡洋右) [1880–1946], was appointed Foreign Minister of Japan in 1940, and concluded the Japan-Germany-Italy Tripartite Pact.

Guam: an island in the South-west Pacific; soon to become the scene of a bloody battle in World War II.

U.P.: United Press.

put it on the air: see "March Arrivals" (1941) in *Ezra Pound Speaking.*

Hoshu Saito and Gado Ono: (斉藤芳州), (小野鵞堂), Japanese calligraphers who taught calligraphy in Japanese universities around the turn of the century.

Nott edtn/: [B36].

110

"Buona Pasqua": "Happy Easter."

"*HIGHBROW*": *The Fountain of the Highbrow*, selected essays by Katue Kitasono.

Mr. *Eliot converting the Archbish. of York:* (?) reference to T. S. Eliot's broadcast in the spring of 1941, "Towards a Christian Britain."

113

Studio Integrale: Italian translation of Confucius' *Ta Hsüeh* (*Ta S'eu; Ta Hio; Daigaku*) by Ezra Pound and Alberto Luchini, published in 1942 [B46]. Each page had the Chinese text with the Italian version below.

Mao's comment: Mao Shih Chêng Chien, a Confucian anthology of poetry edited with commentary by Mao.

S. Int. on the better paper: Some copies of the *Studio Integrale* were printed on a "better," thicker, and watermarked paper.

married: Mary Pound married Boris de Rachewiltz; their son is Siegfried Walter de Rachewiltz.

114

Lao, Mao: Probably Lao-tzu (the "originator" of Taoism) and *Mao Shih Chêng Chien,* but it is hard to guess the "interesting plan"; see Kitasono's letter to Dorothy Pound, 15 December 1948.

Je mange, donc je suis: "I eat, therefore I am." A parody of Descartes' dictum, *"Je pense, donc je suis"* ("I think, therefore I am"). Shortage of food was extremely serious in Japan during the post-World War II period. [One form of Pound's stationery had also borne the motto: *"J'aime, donc je suis"* ("I love, therefore I am")].

115

G.H.Q.: General Headquarters (of the Occupation Troops in Japan).

D. D. Paige: editor of *The Letters of Ezra Pound, 1907–1941* [A64].

116

The Rape of Lucretia: libretto by Ronald Duncan for music by Benjamin Britten, who was later to compose a group of Nō-inspired operas.

117

a charming duck: probably alluding to the phoenix myth and to the story of "The Ugly Duckling." "Cendre" means ashes, cinders.

118

Four Pages: a little magazine published by Dallam Flynn, a member of Pound's circle at St. Elizabeths; see Eustace Mullins, *This Difficult Individual,* p. 314.

Sokolsky: George Ephraim Sokolsky (1893–1962), American journalist. In his column, "These Days," which appeared in the *New York Sun* and some 300 newspapers during the 1940s and early 1950s, he crusaded against what he thought to

be the growing menace of Communism. He was one of the visitors of Pound in
Washington, D.C.; see Mullins, p. 315.

Marcos Fingerit: Argentine poet; author of *Antna, 22 Poemas Contemporaneos*
(Buenos Aires, 1929); *Cancionero Secreto* (La Plata, 1937); *Ardiente Signo, con
una nota Liminar de José Luis Sanchez-Tricado* (La Plata, 1940).

119

Kumasaka: a Nō play; see *The Classic Noh Theatre of Japan*, Part II.

Chinese poems: The first two lines written in Chinese are from Po Lê-t'ien. The
longer poem, according to Yasuo Fujitomi, is the Chinese translation of Kitasono's poem, "Dishes," by a Chinese friend of Kitasono. The original Japanese
poem, "Dishes," may be translated into English:

For supper	Every day	They grow
dishes are spread	ephemeral	a grass leaf
like tree leaves	and delightful	a cloud
Rape blossoms	Sound of the dishes	And are filled with
fresh gingers and	sorrowful and hard	the potter's thought
starworts	pierces my heart	like a gust of wind.

Kenneth Rexroth: (1905–1982), American poet, essayist, and translator; among his
works are *One Hundred Poems from the Japanese* (1955), and *One Hundred
More Poems from the Japanese* (1976).

Manyo and Kokin Wakas: Japanese poems in the anthologies, *Manyōshū* and
Kokinshū; see notes to letter 68.

120

Mao Shih: Mao Shih Chêng Chien, Confucian anthology of poetry edited with
commentary by Mao. See Ezra Pound's letter to Kitasono, 21 October 1937; and
Dorothy Pound's letter to Kitasono, 4 May 1947.

122

Thomas Cole: see Kitasono's next letter to Dorothy Pound. Cole's "Conversation
with Ezra Pound," however, is not printed in **VOU** 35. Instead, his poem
"Toward Winter Journey" translated into Japanese by Kitasono is printed in
VOU 34, published 1 January 1950.

123

stills: cinema photographs (frames).

Prof. Hisatomi Mitsugi: Mitsugi Hisatomi (1908–   ) was to publish *Fenollosa: A Record of a Man Who Devoted Himself to Japanese Art* (Tokyo: Risōsha, 1957).

Kayoikomachi: a Nō play. A woman, who daily gathers and brings nuts and firewood to a priest in ascetic practice at Yase, turns out to be the ghost of Ono no Komachi, a Heian poetess. The priest prays for her and her lover, Fukakusa no Shōshō. They receive Buddhist commandments. Confirmed, they are saved from the agonies of hell.

Kocho: a Nō play by Kanze Nobumitsu. A priest from Yoshino watches a plum tree in Kyoto. A woman appears, talks of the *Chuang-tzu*, and disappears. The priest chants a Buddhist script. The woman reappears in the form of a butterfly, enlightened, dances and disappears. *Chuang-tzu* is said to be written by Chuang-chou, or Sōshū in Japanese. *Cf.* Pound's poem, "Ancient Wisdom, Rather Cosmic": "So-shu dreamed . . . a butterfly."

125

Yasutaka Fumoto: (1907–   ), a Japanese Sinologist, who taught at The Third High School, The First High School, Tokyo University, and other universities; author of *The Development of Confucian Studies in the North Sung Dynasty* (1961), and other books on Chinese history of thought.

Prof. Goto Sueo: Sueo Goto (1886–1967), a Japanese Sinologist, and professor at Keiō University; among his books are *Cultural Currents between East and West*, and *Literature and Science*.

126

"The Garret" . . . . : These poems are translated and published in **VOU** 35 (1951), pp. 15–16.

127

Ueda Tamotsu: Tamotsu Ueda (1906–73), professor of English at Keiō University. His translations of *How to Read* and some short poems by Pound were published as *Sekai Bungaku no Yomikata* (Tokyo: Hobunkan, 1953). He is also the translator of *Selected Poems of T. S. Eliot* (1973). His miscellaneous works were collected and published posthumously as *Collected Works of Tamotsu Ueda* (1975).

129

Michael Reck: a disciple of Pound's St. Elizabeths years who travelled to Japan; Pound provided introductions to Michio Ito and Katue Kitasono, as well as to Yasuo Fujitomi (translator of e.e. cummings) with whom Reck attempted a Japanese translation of Pound's *Women of Trachis* (*Traxiniai*). Reck is the author of *Ezra Pound: A Close-Up* (New York: McGraw-Hill, 1967); *see* Appendix 3.

In a letter of March 12, 1954, Pound wrote to Reck the following remarks on how to go about rendering a Japanese version of the TRAXINIAI:
RK/ re TRAX/

           dont bother about the WORDS, translate the meaning. in the spoken parts/dialog, this should be CLEAR, and be what the speaker would SAY if getting over the meaning in japanese NOW.

in the XOROI, go for the FEELING. The two KINDS of language are quite different/ in the first real people are speaking/

saying what carries forward the action/ in the XOROI they are singing (except the few lines marked "spoken")/

Ito cd/ do some fine choreography for the Analolu/ xoros.

The troops have come HOME/ whoops. there is no need for more than one voice, most of the time/ ⟨others repeat contrapunto, one voice @ a time. However Nō-like & for as long as they like.⟩ a lot of voices might blurr the words. The greek will do you no good, unless the jap chorus could get closer to the greek rhythm, than in working from the english/ BUT it is not the least necessary to copy either/

it is a case of getting the equivalent feeling. The form of the play is magnif/ everything fits/ Daysair goes INTO the tragic mask. Herak emerges from it.

TRAX in antithesis to Antig/ and other Soph/ plays in that NO ONE has any evil intentions, NO bad feeling, vendetta or whatso. All of 'em trying to be nice/ BUT the tragedy moves on just the same.

Daysair, Queen and woman/ top of all greek descriptive writing in the Nurse's description of her before the suicide. HERAK/ tough guy who is also a God.

Dont bother with words or linguistic constructions/ the people are alive/ the speech is clear and natural.

Various people fussing about colloquialism. What one wants is what a Jap Daysair, or Hyllos or messenger would SAY, under the circs/ NOT a copy of english grammar/

In the sung parts, be as classic as you like/ drag in phrases from Noh itself if they fit and intensify the situation. (I dont recall any in particular, but there might be some or some that wd/ recall great Noh lines.)

reading in N.Y. with cello and kettle drum acc/ the Xoroi. ⟨sd. to hv. gone well.⟩ B.B.C. transmitting it on or about Apr/ 25. I dont spose Tokyo gets London 3rd/ program.

Ito to do anything he likes. ko GUN fun-TOooo. (He will be sorry to hear that Dulac is dead if he hasn't heard it already.)

⟨Slow mail⟩ D.P. sending two Hud/ in case F.M. dont step on the gas at once. You can ask me re/ partic/ passages, naturally.

The Venus is practically naked behind that gauze curtain/ I dont know quite how naked a jap goddess can be in apparition/ at any rate from the crotch up. She aint eggzakly a Kuanon/ but the willow bough cd/ be brought in definitely. she cd/ hold one. Goacher who is doing the Hyllos for BBC/ has sent on some prize bestialities in other translations. They dont even understand that LAMPRA.

after that phrase Herak who has been cursing D/ for a bitch never utters a reproach. THAT is like the transformation in Noh.

Do they, or do you know that the last message I got thru into U.S. press ⟨1940⟩ was: We shd/ GIVE Guam to the Japs, but INSIST on having 300 sound films of Noh in exchange. (And how damn much better THAT wd/ have been.) Don't lie down on the fight to get sound films of actual Noh. some bloody foundation/ bastids pouring out millions for scholastic fugg.

even "grammar" dont matter if the speech is alive/ it can be ungrammatical IF it is the way people speak/ the way a Queen, or a hobo, speaks NOW in Japan. Day/ is an aristo/

and also sensitive, very delicately. The Hyllos the next role in so far as it requires understanding presentation. That is why I am so glad to have got Goacher for it. They say their BBC Herak/ is a colossus who can roar. The nurse narrates so that is less difficult/

> but Ito might do a choric dance, combine a choric movement to occur silently while she is describing the suicide. IN fact, all the intelligence they have got can be turned on/ and let 'em ENjoy themselves.

. . .

One misprint in *Hud/* PUT there in print shoppe AFTER proofs were corrected/ i.e. read Nemean NOT Newman herdsman.

ALZO/ p. 511, enter Nurse.

> Better she also enter in a tragic mask (small mask, quite different from Daysair's).

> The Minoru will understand difference.

130

seal character: The "seal text" of the Confucian *Odes* was to have been published by Harvard University Press but never appeared.

Vanni: Vanni Scheiwiller, publisher of *All'Insegna del Pesce d'Oro* editions (Milan); Pound's Italian publisher.

german and italian versions of TRAXINIAI: Translated by Eva Hesse [D31] and Margherita Guidacci [D68], respectively. German version was performed in Berlin (1959) and Darmstadt (1960).

projected edition of the Odes: The Harvard University Press de luxe edition was to have included "sound graphs" alongside the seal text.

Scarfoglio: Carlo Scarfoglio, an Italian writer (son of Matilde Serso, one of Italy's leading journalists) who translated the Confucian *Odes* into Italian [D81b].

131

Broletto: edited by Carlo Peroni and published in Como.

Beauson Tseng: Beauson Tseng (曾約農) [Tseng Yüeh-nung], author of *Cul-*

tural Relations between China and the West (1968).

Tcheu's lament: lament of Ch'ü Yuan (屈原).

Kripalani: Krishna Kripalani, translator of Rabindranath Tagore's *Chokher Bali* and other writings.

Warsaw cellarage: Polish trans. by J. Niemojowski, privately circulated (1959).

the charming member of your other profession: the Italian dentist, Bacigalupo.

d'antan: of the past.

Oberti, Carrega: editors of *Ana Eccètera,* a literary magazine published in Genoa.

Boris: Boris de Rachewiltz, Italian Egyptologist and Pound's son-in-law.

Mary's Kagekiyo: Mary de Rachewiltz translated Pound's "Introduction" to 'Noh' or *Accomplishment* along with the play "Kagekiyo" from *Certain Noble Plays of Japan,* published by Vanni Scheiwiller in 1954 as *Introduzione ai Nô* [D60]; the play was reprinted in 1956 in Leo Magnino's *Teatro giapponese* [D91].

132

Di Riflesso: published by Vanni Scheiwiller.

visually I can see: Kitasono was an innovator and enthusiast of "concrete poetry."

133

the Japanese translation of your poems: Ryozo Iwasaki, tr., *Ezra Pound: Selected Poems* (Tokyo: Arechi Shuppan, 1956).

Homyoin, Enjoji Temple: Hōmyō-in (法明院) is in the northern precinct of Onjō-ji (園城寺), commonly called Enjō-ji, more popularly known as Miidera (三井寺).

Laurence Binyon: Robert Laurence Binyon (1869–1943), British poet and art historian; for many years an official in the British Museum in London. He was a friend of Pound's and visited Japan in 1929. Author of *Japanese Art* (1909), *Art of Asia* (1916), *The Spirit of Man in Asian Art* (1936) and *Art of the Far East* (1936), etc.

Vale!: Be in good health, farewell.

Junzaburo Nishiwaki: (1896–?) Japanese poet and scholar; wrote introduction to Ryozo Iwasaki's translation of Pound's "Mauberley." His poem "January in Kyoto" was translated into Italian by Mary de Rachewiltz and published in 1959 by Vanni Scheiwiller; it also appeared in *Edge* 5.

134

Edge: Australian literary magazine founded by Noel Stock in October 1956, to which Pound was a frequent anonymous contributor. Pound's "Five French Poems" appeared in the first issue.

Zielinski: Thaddeus Zielinski, Polish professor of Greek; author of *La Sibylle, Trois Essais sur la Religion Antique et le Christianisme* (Paris: Redier, 1924). *Edge* 2 was entirely composed of a translation of this work into English as "The Sibyl."

W. L.: Wyndham Lewis.

D. P.: Dorothy Pound.

La Martinelli: a booklet published by Vanni Scheiwiller in 1956. It contains reproductions of paintings by Sheri Martinelli, an American painter and "disciple" of Pound at St. Elizabeths, with an introduction by Pound.

Ford: Ford Madox Ford.

Amaral: José Vásquez Amaral's translation of *The Pisan Cantos* into Spanish was published in 1956: *Los Cantares de Pisa* [D219].

Eva: Eva Hesse's translation of *The Pisan Cantos* into German was published also in 1956: *Die Pisaner Gesänge* [D28]; she also translated a selection of Pound's poetry and prose, *Dichtung und Prosa* (1953), which was reissued in paperback in 1956 [D26].

TRAXINIAI in London: First English publication in book form of Pound's *Women of Trachis* appeared on November 30, 1956, published by Neville Spearman [A72]; the play had already been published, however, in the Winter 1953/4 issue of *Hudson Review,* vol. vi, no. 4, ed. F. Morgan. The English edition bears the dedication by Pound: "A version for Kitasono Katue, hoping he will use it on my dear old friend Miscio Ito, or take it to the Minoru if they can be persuaded to add to their repertoire." The addenda include remarks by Denis Goacher, Peter Whigham, S. V. Jankowski and Ricardo M. degli Uberti.

Academia Bulletin: a Pound-instigated leaflet edited by David Gordon, a frequent visitor to St. Elizabeths. Uberti's essay ("Why Pound Liked Italy") appeared in the first issue (1956); *see Paideuma,* vol. 3, no. 3.

Verkehr: communication.

Lorenzatos: Zesimos Lorenzatos, translator of *Cathay* into Greek as *Katah Metaphrasoon apo to Aggliko* (1950) [D51].

Pivot: see [B53] and [B55].

cordialie saluti: cordial greetings.

135

causerie: banter.

Nimbus: ed. T. Hull and D. Wright; vol. III, no. 4 (Winter 1956) [London].

omnes eodem cogimur: "we are all urged toward the same."

translate it into Japanese: see note to letter 129.

Norman Douglas: British author and long-time resident in Italy; author of *South Wind,* etc.

John Espey: author of *Ezra Pound's Mauberley: A Study in Composition* (1955).

Friar: Kimon Friar.

Brinnin: John Malcolm Brinnin (?).

Legge: James Legge, 19th century British Sinologist; translator of the *Li Chi,* etc.

T'ao Yüan-ming: (陶淵明) [To Emmei, in Japanese] (365–427), a Chinese poet.

136

"dérocher": "to cleanse metals with acid."

Noel Stock: editor of Australian literary magazine *Edge.*

prebebde: indication of rhyme scheme (?), or of divinity degree (?).

Kojiro Yoshikawa: (吉川 幸次郎) [1904–80], a Japanese scholar of Chinese
literature, for many years professor at Kyoto University. Among his books is *The
East in the West* (Tokyo: Bungei Shunju, 1955), which contains a reproduction of
a painting by Sheri Martinelli and an essay on his visit to Pound at St. Elizabeths
in Washington, D.C.

h. de campos: Haroldo and Augusto de Campos, poets; translated the *Cantos* into
Portuguese (*Cantares*, São Paulo, 1960).

Eva Hesse O'Donnell: Pound's German translator; editor of *New Approaches to
Ezra Pound* (London: Faber 1969).

García Terrés: Jaime García Terrés, Mexican translator of Pound's poems into
Spanish.

Chiang: Chiang Kai-shek.

Jo Bard: Joseph Bard, editor of *El Dinamismo de una Nueva Poesía* (Puerto de la
Cruz: Instituto de Estudios Hispanicos, 1957) and novelist; Pound had met him
in Rapallo in 1928.

137

parcel: see [D60], [B46], [D 59], [D61] and [A68].

etiam atque-etiam vale: "further and even further may you be well."

138

Nippon: Japan.

140

Cole Rice: Karel Vaclav Rais (1859–1927), a Czechoslovakian poet and novelist.
Elmer Rice is an American novelist and playwright.

Fletcher's widow: Mrs. John Gould Fletcher, wife of the American poet whom
Pound knew during the years of the Imagist movement in London.

Hagoromo: a Nō play.

Kiogen: Kyogen, a comic interlude set between Nō plays.

146

grandson of Leo Frobenius: Sebastian Frobenius; the story appears in *Alto Adige*
(December 7, 1958), the day following the visit.

my daughter works on Junzaburo's poems: Mary de Rachewiltz was translating
"January in Kyoto" into Italian.

Del Pelo Pardi: Giulio Del Pelo Pardi, classical scholar, agrarian archæologist and
inventor of a system of soil conservation and shallow ploughing.

148

Okada: Tomoji Okada (1880–1965), former director, London Branch, Yamanaka and Co.

to honour E. F. in manner stated: Pound had written of Fenollosa in the "Introduction" to the translation of Nō plays: "When he died suddenly in England the Japanese government sent a warship for his body, and the priests buried him within the sacred enclosure at Miidera."

your information: Tomoji Okada, under the direction of Kichirobe Yamanaka of Yamanaka and Co., had the remains of Fenollosa which had already been buried at Highgate Cemetery, London cremated in 1909; Okada then asked Yasotaro Kato, an art dealer, who was on his way to Japan through the Siberian Railroad, to take the ashes to Japan and lay them to rest at Miidera, the temple in Otsu where Fenollosa had studied Buddhism and which he had especially loved. See Tokutaro Shigehisa, "Fenollosa's Ashes and Japan," *Comparative Literature* (Tokyo), vol. 2 (1959); and "A Letter of Ezra Pound," *Fenollosa Society of Japan Newsletter*, no. 5 (1982).

vol/ on Art: E. F. Fenollosa's *Epochs of Chinese and Japanese Art*, published by William Heinemann in 1912.

NOTES TO ESSAYS

1

Dowland: John Dowland, (c. 1567–1626), English lutenist and composer.

Ogden: Charles Kay Ogden (1889–1957), author of books on "basic English," including *The ABC of Basic English* (1932), *Basic English* (1933), *The Basic Dictionary* (1939) and *Basic by Picture Stamps* (1941).

2

the magnificent "Runner": see Leo Frobenius, *Prehistoric Rock Pictures* (New York: Museum of Modern Art, 1937).

totalitarian: see "Totalitarian," *Guide to Kulchur.*

Anschauung: "outlook."

P. Bottome: Phyllis Bottome (1884–1963), English novelist; author of *Private Worlds* (1934), *The Moral Storm* (1937), etc.

Active Anthology: [B32].

J. F. C. Fuller: John Frederick Charles Fuller (1878–1966), Major General (1930); author of *War and Western Civilization, 1832–1932* (1932); *Armaments and History* (1945); *The Second World War* (1949), etc.

Sickert: Walter Sickert (1860–1942), English painter.

3

正名 : "the clear definition of terms"

誠 : "sincerity"

Funa-Benkai: a Nō play.

Arrow Editions: New York publisher of *The Chinese Written Character as a*

Medium for Poetry [B36b].

Shigefusa Hosho: (宝、生重爽) [1900–1974], Head Master of the Hosho School of Nō.

Michitarô Shidehara: (幣原道太郎) son of Premier Kijūrō Shidehara (1903-   ); studied in the U.S. and worked for Kokusai Bunka Shinkōkai. Translator of the Nō program specially arranged for the delegates to the seventh conference of the World Federation of Education Associations held in Tokyo in 1937; the Nō plays were performed by Shigefusa Hosho's troupe and were accompanied by an exhibition of Nō costumes and masks; *see* essay 3.

4

David Nixon: violinist; *see* M. de Rachewiltz, *Discretions.*

an abortive Vivaldi society: its establishment in Venice was attempted by Giorgio Levi.

Count Chigi: Count Guido Chigi Sarracini, patron of the Sienese *Accademia Musicale* and sponsor of the Vivaldi Week; *see* Murray Schafer, ed., *Ezra Pound and Music.*

Cobbett: Walter Wilson Cobbett (1847–1937), English violinist, businessman and patron of music.

Goldoni: Carlo Goldoni (1707–93), Italian playwright, author of the libretto for Mozart's *La Finta Giardiniera* and other operas.

Frazzi: Vito Frazzi (1888–   ), Italian composer who taught composition at the Conservatory of Florence, and later at the Accademia Musicale Chigiana in Siena; *see* Murray Schafer, ed., *Ezra Pound and Music.*

Virgilio Mortari: (1902–   ), Italian pianist, music critic, and composer; educated at the Milan Conservatory; associated with the Vivaldi Week of the Siena Festival since 1939. Among his works are: "La Figlia del Diavolo" (opera, 1954), and *La Tecnica dell' Orchestra Contemporanea* (1950), etc.

S. A. Luciani: Sebastiano Arturo Luciani (1884–1950). Italian musicologist, associated with the Siena Accademia Chigiana. Olga Rudge and he founded the Centro di Studi Vivaldiani; edited, along with Olga Rudge, *Antonio Vivaldi: note e documenti sulla vita e sulle opere* (1939); *see* Murray Schafer, ed., *Ezra Pound and Music.*

Vincenzo Galilei: (c. 1533–1591), Italian composer, viol player, and singer; father of Galileo Galilei; composer of *Madrigali Monodiche* (1585) and lute pieces, among others.

Giulio Caccini: (1558–1615), Italian singer and composer at the Medici court in Florence; composer of the opera *Euridice* (1600). Both Galilei and Caccini were members of the *Camerata Bardi*, a group of musicians and literati who attempted to revive ancient Greek music and drama in the new form of opera.

Villon: Le Testament [E3h].

Cavalcanti: [E3a].

Sordello: [E3a].

Antheil: George Antheil (1900–1959), American pianist and composer; accompanied violinist Olga Rudge in numerous Paris performances of Pound's music; helped Pound edit *Le Testament; see* Pound's *Antheil and the Treatise on Harmony* [A25] and Murray Schafer, ed., *Ezra Pound and Music.*

Tibor Serly: (1900–1978), Hungarian-American composer and violist; studied with Kodály; friend of Bela Bartók, whose music he brought to Pound's attention; composer of a symphony, a viola concerto, orchestral works, songs, etc.; his music was performed several times during the Rapallo concerts, and he performed at one himself (March 3, 1935). Serly "amplified" Pound's violin sonata "by extensions"; *see* Charles Norman, Ezra Pound, pp. 282–3, and Murray Schafer, ed., *Ezra Pound and Music.*

5

Ritterschaft and Bushido: chivalry in German and in Japanese.

君子 : "kunshi" in Japanese ("chün tsŭ" in Chinese); the Confucian ideal of man: "a true gentleman."

Lin Yutang: Lin Yu-tang (林語堂) [1895–   ]. Chinese linguist and novelist; his *Moment in Peking* (北京好日) [1939] was on the best seller list in America.

Francesco Fiorentino: (1834–84), author of *Storia della Filosofia, Scritti Varii di Letteratura, Filosofia e Critica* (1876) and *Il Risorgimento Filosofico nel Quattrocento* (1885); *see* "The New Learning: Part One," *Guide to Kulchur.*

St. Ambrogio and St. Antonino: St. Ambrose (340–397), bishop of Milan; St. Antonino da Firenze (1389–1459).

Motoichiro Oguimi: (1845–1941), Japanese Christian minister and educator; compiler of *The New Testament Greek-Japanese Dictionary,* published by Kyōbunkan, Tokyo, in 1940.

John Scotus: Joannes Scotus Erigena (*c.* 810–*c.* 877), Irish Neoplatonic philosopher; author of *On the Division of Nature.*

Grosseteste: Robert Grosseteste (*c.* 1175–1253), English theologian and astronomer.

Albertus: Albertus Magnus (1206–1280), scholastic philosopher with wide and accurate knowledge of physical sciences of his time.

Nichomachean Ethics: see "And Therefore Tending," *Guide to Kulchur.*

6

Pilhaou-Thibaou: [C623 & C623a], "*supplément illustré*" to *391,* containing contributions by Pound, Picabia, Jean Cocteau and Erik Satie.

Active Anthology: [B32].

Hood: Thomas Hood (1799–1845), English poet.

Lanier: Sidney Lanier (1842–1881), American poet.

Firdusi: Firdausi (*c.* 920–*c.* 1025), early Persian epic poet.

A Russian philosophical student: Slovinsky; *see* "Murder by Capital."

Lewis' last volume: The Hitler Cult (London: Dent, 1939).

Hargrave: John Gordon Hargrave (1894–   ), English artist and writer; leader of a faction of Social Credit movement in England; author of the novel *Summer Time Ends.*

7

Hazard: Rowland Gibson Hazard (1801–1888), American manufacturer, writer, member of the Rhode Island House of Representatives (1851, 1854, 1880), and of the State Senate (1860). His financial articles, which gained for him a wide reputation, were written during the Civil War, and some of them were collected and published as *Our Resources* in 1864.

Paterson: William Paterson (1658–1719), the founder of the Bank of England. Shortly after the Revolution of 1688, when William and Mary found the royal coffers empty, Paterson and his colleagues proposed to establish the new Bank of England. See Earle Davis, *Vision Fugitive: Ezra Pound and Economics* (Lawrence: University Press of Kansas, 1968), pp. 85–6.

Hume: see "Essay on Money."

W. A. Overholser: author of *A Short Review and Analysis of the History of Money in the United States* (Libertyville, IL, 1936); contained material on usury in the U.S. during the 1860s.

Sherman: John Sherman (1823–1900), American statesman, Senator from Ohio (1861–77, 1881–97) and Secretary of the Treasury; *see* "A Visiting Card."

Ikleheimer: Ikleheimer, Morton and Van der Gould, a New York banking firm; *see* "A Visiting Card" and "Gold and Work."

Rota: author of *Storia delle banche* [The History of Banks] (Milan, 1874).

Schacht: Hjalmar Schacht (1877–1970), German banker, President of the Reichsbank (1923–30, 1933–39); *see* Canto 52.

Verbrauchsgüter: articles of consumption, expendables.

printed the statement: see "Ezra Pound on Gold, War, and National Money," *Capitol Daily* (May 9, 1939) [C1509].

8

Count Potocki: Jerzy Potocki, Polish Ambassador to the United States, with whom Pound dined in Washington in May, 1939; Pound remarked: "God help you if you trust England."

Lazard: family of international bankers; Lazard Frères, founded during the gold rush in California, traded in gold between San Francisco and Paris via New York and London.

Kuhn-Loeb: U.S. immigrant dry-food merchants who later became prominent investment bankers in New York. The firm "Kuhn, Loeb and Co." was founded in 1867 by brothers-in-law Abraham Kuhn (1819–1892) and Solomon Loeb (1828–1913). James Loeb (1867–1933), American banker, planned and helped to publish Loeb Classical Library.

Bullitt: William Christian Bullitt (1891–1967), then American diplomat. U.S.

Ambassador to Russia (1933–36), and U.S. Ambassador to France (1936–41).

Mandel: Georges Mandel (Jeroboam Rothschild) (1885–1944), French statesman, Minister of the Interior in Paul Reynaud's government.

Reynaud: Paul Reynaud (1878–1966), French statesman; as Minister of Finance in 1938, pursued extreme deflationary policy; became Premier in March 1940; appointed Marshal Pétain Vice Premier in May 1940; resigned on June 16, 1940, giving way to Pétain.

Neuflize . . . Mocatta: Jewish families prominent in various fields. Sieff: Israel Moses Sieff, British industrialist, "reputed anonymous owner of . . . the Daily Mirror" (Edwards and Vasse, Annotated Index to the Cantos, p. 199), appears in Canto 74. Beit: Alfred Beit (1853–1906), South African financier and co-founder, with Cecil Rhodes, of Rhodesia. Goldsmid: English family, settled in London in the eighteenth century. Abraham Goldsmid (1758–1810) was a prominent financier; Isaac Lyon Goldsmid (1778–1859) made a large fortune by financing railway construction. Mocatta: old English family of Marrano origin.

Cobbett: William Cobbett (1763–1835), English journalist, social reformer and politician; published the Political Register, a radical reformist journal which decried the pitiful conditions of the working classes, and Parliamentary Debates; elected member of Parliament after the Reform Bill of 1832 was passed.

Wallace: Henry Agard Wallace (1888–1965). Secretary of Agriculture (1933–40), Vice-President of the U.S. (1941–45), Secretary of Commerce (1945–46); leader in the New Deal administration; author of Agricultural Prices (1920), New Frontiers (1934), Technology, Corporations and the General Welfare (1937), and other books.

Lloyd George: David Lloyd George (1863–1945), British statesman; leader of coalition government (December 1916–1922); leader of the Liberal Party (1926–31).

Mond: Jewish family of chemists in England. Lord Alfred Mond (1868–1930), "head of the mushrooming chemical trust, Imperial Chemical Industries," bought the English Review; see Eustace Mullins, This Difficult Individual, Ezra Pound (New York: Fleet, 1961), pp. 41–42; see also Canto 104. Robert Ludwig Mond (1868–1938), his brother, was a scientist and archæologist. See "A Visiting Card."

Montagu Norman: Montagu Collet Norman (1871–1950), English banker, President of the Bank of England (1920–1944).

Loeb report: report by Harold Loeb (1891–   ), The Chart of Plenty: A Study of America's Product Capacity (New York: Viking, 1935); author of The Non-Production of Wealth (1933), Production for Use (1936), and Full Production Without War (1946).

King Boris: Boris III, Czar of Bulgaria (1918–43).

9

Fauntleroy: hero of Little Lord Fauntleroy (1886) by Frances Hodgson Burnett; (Shōkōshi, in Japanese translation).

my New England host: Pound stayed with Theodore Spencer during his visit to the
  U.S. in 1939.
Raffalovitch: Arthur Germanovich Raffalovich (1853–1921), Russian economist,
  was a Russian publicity agent in France, which exposed him to the charge of
  bribery.
Meyer: Arthur Meyer (1844–1924), French journalist, co-founder of *Le Gaulois*
  (1865).
Mr. Rip van Wendell Willkie: Wendell Lewis Willkie (1892–1944), American
  lawyer and business executive; Republican nominee for President of the U.S.
  (1940); *see* Canto 77, l. 257.
Carol of Rumania: Carol II (1893–1953), King of Rumania (1930–40); renounced
  right of succession to throne in 1925, deserted wife, and went to Paris to live in
  exile with Mme. Magda Lupesu. Deprived of the throne in 1940 through German
  influence, he fled to Spain, Cuba, and then Mexico.
Brooks Adams: (1848–1927), American historian; direct descendent of John Adams
  and brother of Henry; author of *The Law of Civilization and Decay* (1895; 1897);
  America's Economic Supremacy (1900); *The New Empire* (1902); and *Theory of
  Social Revolutions* (1913). Pound championed *The Law of Civilization and
  Decay,* which emphasized the role played by money and usury in the rise and fall
  of civilizations.
"voluta-lavoro": labor money.
J. F. C. Fuller: John Frederick Charles Fuller (1878–1966), British soldier; served in
  Boer War and World War (1914–18); Major-General (1930); author of *War and
  Western Civilization, 1832–1932* (1932); *The Last of the Gentlemen's Wars: A
  Subaltern's Journal of the War in South Africa, 1899–1902* (1937); etc.
Blum: Léon Blum (1872–1950), French statesman; *see* Canto 80.
Pierlot: Hubert Pierlot (1883–1963), Belgian statesman.
Morgenthau: Henry Morgenthau (1891–1967), American statesman, Secretary of
  Treasury (1934–1945).

10

Prof. Breasted: Professor of Romance languages at University of Chicago; *see Guide
  to Kulchur,* p. 62.
Overholser, Woodward, Beard, Bower: Willis A. Overholser, author of *A Short
  Review and Analysis of the History of Money in the United States* (1936);
  William E. Woodward (1874–1950), author of *Money for Tomorrow* (1932);
  Charles Austin Beard, author of *An Economic Interpretation of the Constitution
  of the United States* (1913) and *Economic Origins of Jeffersonian Democracy*
  (1915); Claude G. Bowers, author of *Jefferson and Hamilton: Struggle for Democ-
  racy in America* (1925), and *Jefferson in Power, the Death Struggle of the
  Federalists* (1936); *see also* Pound's letter to Kitasono, 13 January 1940.
Jerry Voorhis: monetary reformer and U.S. Congressman from California, whom
  Pound met in Washington in 1939; *see* David Heymann, *The Last Rower,* pp.

85–6; and also Earle Davis, *Vision Fugitive: Ezra Pound and Economics,* pp. 194–6.

Chris. Hollis: Christopher Hollis, author of *The Two Nations: A Financial Study of English History* (1935).

Karl von Stein: (1757–1831), Prussian statesman.

Ruhland: Gustav Ruhland (1860–1914), author of *System der politischen Ökonomie* (1939).

La Tour du Pin: Patrice de La Tour du Pin (1911–75), French poet, author of *La Quête de Joie* (1933), *Comme de Poesie* (1946), *La Contemplation Errante* (1948), and other works; *see Guide to Kulchur,* pp. 96 and 264.

Fabre: Jean Henri Fabre (1823–1915), French entomologist, author of *Souvenirs Entomologique,* 10 vols. (1879–1907).

Frazer: James George Frazer (1854–1941), Scottish anthropologist, author of *The Golden Bough,* 12 vols. (1890–1915).

Burbank: Luther Burbank (1849–1926), American horticulturist.

Otto Dietrich: (1897–1952), German journalist and politician. Since 1938 he was Press-Chief of German government and State-Secretary in German Ministry of Propaganda.

11

Skoda: firm founded by Emile von Skoda (1839–1900), a Czechoslovakian manufacturer.

Monte dei Paschi: i.e. the Siena Bank; *see* Cantos 42 and 43.

C. H. Douglas . . . Butchart's compendium: Pound is referring to the list of books in his "Introductory Text Book." C. H. Douglas, *Economic Democracy;* Silvio Gesell, *The Natural Economic Order;* R. McNair Wilson, *Promise to Pay;* Willis Overholser, *History of Money in the U.S.;* P. Larrañaga, *Gold, Glut and Government;* Montgomery Butchart, *Money.* Christopher Hollis is the author of *The Two Nations: A Financial Study of English History,* to which Pound is much indebted.

Gerarchia: Hierarchy; journal founded by Mussolini.

Rivista del Lavoro: Review of Labor.

12

Reuters: Reuters, the German news agency founded by Paul Julius Reuter (1816–1899); of Jewish parentage, he became a Christian in 1844.

Havas: French news agency founded in Paris in 1835 by Charles Havas.

Boake Carter: Boake Carter (1898–1944), radio broadcaster (CBS); author of *Black Shirt, Black Skin* (1935) [dealing with Italy and Ethiopia]; *"Johnny Q. Public" Speals! The Nation Appraises the New Deal* (1936); *I Talk As I Like* (1937); *Why Meddle in the Orient?* (1938); *Why Meddle in Europe?* (1939); *Boake Carter's Answer to Anti-Semitism; The Truth About Judah in Relation to the Anglo-Saxon-Celtic People* (1941).

Ezra Pound to Hajime Matsumiya, Secretary of the Japanese Embassy,
Rome
TLS-2   15 Dec. 1937

Dear Mr. Matsumiya

or if Sig. Matsumiya is no longer in Rome, perhaps his successor will
read this as it is more urgent than permits communication via Tokio.
I am happy to say that just at this moment I have had a very interesting
manifesto of Japanese poets printed in *Townsman*, London. I hope they
will send you a copy. I am sorry you never got round to sending me
your own manuscript.
In view of the accident to the American Gunboat. I think it perhaps
⟨would⟩ ease the strain if someone would explain to the american public
that the Emperor is not exclusively a political Emperor. If they had any
inkling of the religious phases of his position they might understand it
better.
     I mean they should be told that if not exactly a Pope, the Papacy is
the only European institution representing some of his attributes.
     I don't myself understand all this very clearly, but in the interest of
concord, I think this phrase might be useful.
     There are some civilized Americans, at least some of us are more
civilized than them.
I hope to see you again when I come to Rome. The new microphotographic and photostat process, using Leica films and enlarging them, op-
ens a totally new possibility for bilingual texts.
                                        I mean we can NOW print
ideogramic texts, and any oriental scripts as cheaply as we do our own
printing in alphabet, and texts faced by translation into English or
French, German, Italian, CAN now be produced at a rate which will permit their sale to students.
     It is quite possible that someone in Tokio could start this exchange
of culture more quickly and intelligently than unofficial persons like myself can do it here.

                         with cordial recollections of our meeting
                              I remain yours very sincerely
                                   Ezra Pound

Ezra Pound to Yosuke Matsuoka, Japanese Ambassador to Rome
TLS-1   29 March 1941

To His Excellency YOSUKE MATSUOKA

Ernest Fenollosa's literary executor begs leave to present his respects and
to hope that after the present tension has passed Fenollosa's work may
be better continued.

It has been my experience that no occidental decently aware of the
qualities of your Noh drama can be infected with anti-japanese propaganda, especially of the beastly sort I found two years ago in the U.S.,
the theme being "yah / we can starve you out," and this meanly expressed cinematographicly.

Men like myself would cheerfully give you Guam for a few sound
films such as that of *Awoi no Uye,* which was shown for me in Washington. I regret deeply that there are not more of us.

But in any case the least, and alas probably the most that I can do is
to assure you that the seeds of respect and affection sown by Fenollosa
have not been wholly unfruitful. I mean in a few American minds for
the qualities of Japanese spirit.

> I beg your Excellency to accept this
> assurance of my respect.
> *Ezra Pound*

Tami Koumé (photograph by Arnold Genthe)

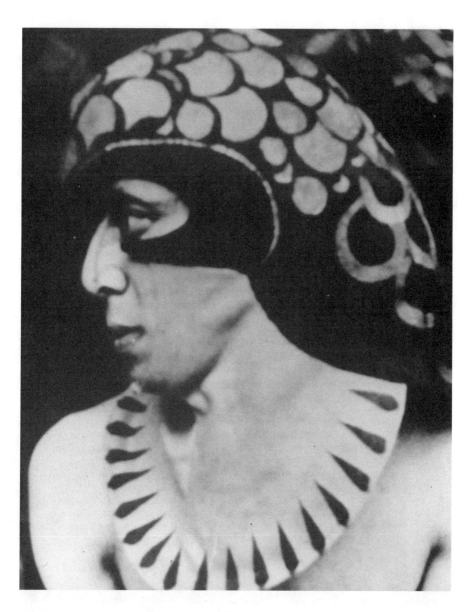

Michio Ito in Yeats' At the Hawk's Well *(1916)*
(Photograph by Alvin Langdon Coburn)

Katue Kitasono

Mary de Rachewiltz at La Quiete (1937)

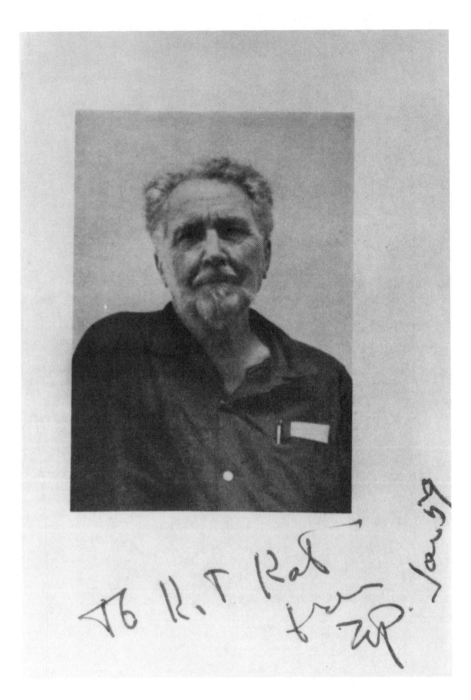

Photograph of Ezra Pound inscribed "To Kit Kat" (1959)

Ryozo Iwasaki

Ezra Pound and the editor in Italy (1968)

Mary de Rachewiltz with the editor in Japan (1986)